IRIS MURDOCH
AS I KNEW HER

Also by A.N. Wilson

IRIS MURDOCH
AS I KNEW HER

A.N. WILSON

HUTCHINSON
LONDON

First published in 2003 by Hutchinson

1 3 5 7 9 10 8 6 4 2

Copyright © A.N. Wilson 2003

A.N. Wilson has asserted his right under the Copyright, Designs and Patents Act, 1988, to be identified as the author of this work

Hutchinson
The Random House Group Limited
20 Vauxhall Bridge Road, London SW1V 2SA

Random House Australia (Pty) Limited
20 Alfred Street, Milsons Point, Sydney
New South Wales 2061, Australia

Random House New Zealand Limited
18 Poland Road, Glenfield
Auckland 10, New Zealand

Random House (Pty) Limited
Endulini, 5a Jubilee Road
Parktown 2193, South Africa

The Random House Group Limited Reg. No. 954009

www.randomhouse.co.uk

A CIP catalogue record for this book is available
from the British Library

Papers used by Random House are natural, recyclable products made from wood grown in sustainable forests. The manufacturing processes conform to the environmental regulations of the country of origin

Typeset in Goudy Old Style by Palimpsest Book Production Limited,
Polmont, Stirlingshire
Printed and bound in Great Britain by
Mackays of Chatham plc, Chatham, Kent

ISBN 0 09 174246 3

Contents

Acknowledgements

I have had generous help with the illustrations, from John and Jean Jones, from Lucy Neville-Rolfe (Lady Packer), from Dr David Starkey, James Brown and Barbara Dorf, from Dr Julia Trevelyan Oman, Dr Ruth Guilding and Dame Beryl Bainbridge. Douglas Matthews made the index while James Nightingale and Sue Freestone were kind midwives.

I would also like to thank the following authors and publishers for their permission to reproduce copyright material: John Bayley, *Iris* and *Iris and the Friends* (Gerald Duckworth & Company Ltd); Alan Bennett, *Writing Home* (Faber and Faber Ltd) and 'What I did in 1999' (*London Review of Books*); Malcolm Bradbury, *Who Do You Think You Are?* (Secker & Warburg); Vincent Brome, *J.B. Priestley* (Hamish Hamilton); A.S. Byatt, *Degrees of Freedom* (Vintage); Elias Canetti, *The Torch in My Ear* (Granta Books); Diana Collins, *Time and the Priestleys* (Sutton Publishing Ltd); John Cowper Powys, *Wolf Solent* (Pollinger Ltd); Terry Eagleton, *Against the Grain* (Verso); Michael Holroyd, *George Bernard Shaw* (A.P. Watt on behalf of Michael Holroyd); Michael Innes, *The New Sonia Wayward* (A.P. Watt on behalf of Michael Innes); Roy Jenkins, *A Life at the Centre* (Pam Macmillan); Philip Larkin, 'Dockery and Son' from *Collected Poems* (Faber and Faber Ltd); Iris Murdoch, *The Bell, The Black Prince, Henry and Cato, Nuns and Soldiers, Metaphysics as a Guide to Morals, The Red and*

The Green, Sartre, The Sea, The Sea, The Time of Angels, The Unicorn, A Word Child (Chatto & Windus); J.B. Priestley, *An English Journey* (William Heinemann); Barbara Pym, *A Very Private Eye* (Pan Macmillan); John Sutherland (*Guardian*). Every effort has been made to contact all copyright holders. The publishers will be glad to make good in future editions any errors or omissions brought to their attention.

Illustrations

Iris Murdoch aged twelve in Dublin bay
Painting by Iris Murdoch
Rene and Hughes Murdoch
Hughes Murdoch
Jean Robinson and John Jones
Iris Murdoch sewing costumes for undergraduate dramatics
John Jones and Iris Murdoch
Iris Murdoch on Dartmoor
Iris Murdoch with her god-daughter, Janet Jones and John Jones
Bowen Court (*Reproduced with permission of Curtis Brown Group Ltd, London, on behalf of the Estate of Elizabeth Bowen. Copyright © Elizabeth Bowen*)
Group photograph, Michaelmas term 1969, New College Oxford
Christopher Tolkien
A.N. Wilson outside Iris Murdoch's birthplace
Cedar Lodge, Steeple Aston (*Oman Productions Ltd*)
Iris Murdoch and John Bayley at A.N. Wilson's wedding to Katherine Duncan-Jones
John Bayley, A.N. Wilson, Iris Murdoch and Katherine Duncan-Jones at a wedding
A.N. Wilson, Katherine Duncan-Jones and their daughter Emily, with Philip Larkin
Portrait of Iris Murdoch by Barbara Dorf
John Bayley

Caroline Dawnay
John Bayley and Iris Murdoch in Israel
Ruth Guilding
Gillian Avery
Iris Murdoch and Beryl Bainbridge
Iris Murdoch (*Oman Productions Ltd*)

Jedes gesprochene Wort ist falsch. Jedes geschriebene Wort ist falsch. Jedes Wort ist falsch. Was aber gibt es ohne Worte?
Elias Canetti, *Aufzeichnungen,* 1956

As I may sometimes seem in what follows to mock the Impiatts let me make it clear once and for all that I thoroughly liked them both, as we often do those whom we mock. I thought they were decent people and I admired them because they were happily married, quite a feat in my estimation. Of course the latter quality is not always totally endearing. The assertion made by a happy marriage often alienates, and often is at least half intended to alienate, the excluded spectator.

Iris Murdoch, A *Word Child*

Could you go through Iris's files and reviews and look up the names of people who could do a major interview of [*sic*] her for Arena? Ed [Victor] has suggested A. N. Wilson to her, but Alan [Yentob?] is not keen: too alienating.

Memo from Carmen Callil, 1989,
Chatto & Windus Archive at Reading University

One

1

The film

The name which appears on the cinema-screen is *Iris* in her unmistakable handwriting. The images which follow are all familiar, either from my actual memories of her, or from her husband's books, or from the reminiscences of friends. This is a woman who has been inside my head, one way and another, for thirty-five years: as a novelist whose stories have been part of my inner life; as a friend; as the subject of a book she asked me, and I promised, to write.

There is a Charles Addams cartoon of a cinema audience, all in tears as they watch the screen. Just one member of the audience is roaring with laughter. On a number of occasions, for conversational effect, I have claimed that, when watching Richard Eyre's film *Iris*, based on John Bayley's memoirs, I was that man. This seemed the neat, or witty, thing to say. Laughter is a substitute both for feeling and for the true expression of feeling. In fact, I saw this well-made film several times, with the mixture of emotions that was inevitable when watching two well-known actresses, Kate Winslet and Dame Judi Dench, depicting a woman whom I had known, on one level, quite well and who had been, on other levels, and those perhaps the most important, completely mysterious to me in all the years, 1969–99, that I used to meet her.

The truth is, that like most audiences who saw Eyre's *Iris*, I found myself weeping at the story. The animated, intelligent, highly sexed being, depicted by Kate Winslet, riding round Oxford on a bicycle, turns into a confused old frump in a dirty cardigan, living in squalor with an adoring Jim Broadbent who, just occasionally, loses his temper with her.

Some of the critics – and they all loved this film – spoke of it as the greatest love story ever told. Newspapers and magazines printed dozens of articles by pundits, all to the effect that the film taught us the meaning of true love. Here was a man so completely devoted to a woman that he cared for her to the end; their love story went on being a love story, even, or especially, when they were wading round their house ankle-deep in filth.

Why this pair, perfectly comfortably off (Dame Iris left more than £2 million in her will), did not employ a cleaner, or a nurse, and why John Bayley needed to be King of this particular castle or mud-pie was a mystery either too mundane or too difficult for a film to answer. Iris Murdoch's novels, by contrast, are a coruscating analysis of the human capacity to turn love into power-games; the most uncompromising scrutiny of what takes place in the tyrant's cage which masquerades as a happy marriage. More than any English writer of her generation, she stared with wide-awake intensity into the muddied waters of our emotional lives, exposing our confusions, our need to deceive ourselves and other people.

A film, especially a film designed for a mass audience, could not tell the story of a writer's life. Eyre's *Iris* could depict a young woman discovering the delights of sex; and it could depict, with horribly distressing realism, the misery of an old woman who felt her mental powers vanishing, the lights in her head, one by one, being extinguished by fingers not her own.

In spite of a few gallant scenes in which Dame Judi Dench sat at a desk with a pen in her hand, however, the film – any film – was bound to fail in depicting what goes on inside, what happens in a person's secret self, to make them a writer; to make them, moreover, not any writer, but that writer. To make 'them' Iris Murdoch.

A film which made a shot at explaining this would probably have ceased to be a film. A biography of a writer which came close to understanding the mystery of its subject would in all likelihood have ceased to be a biography. It would in fact have become a novel. And an accurate book about Iris Murdoch, one which conveyed her essence, would perhaps be simply that: a novel. Or several novels. The best picture of Iris Murdoch is actually to be found in the novels of Iris Murdoch. She certainly felt this. She was a more than usually secretive person.

'Do you have somewhere to stay when you go to London?' I asked her, in the early days, when John Bayley was still my tutor.

'My mother lives in Barnes, I can usually . . . when I go to see my mother . . .'

She was hesitating before telling an outright lie.

'So you don't keep a London flat?' I nosily persisted.

'No,' she said firmly.

There was no reason why a teenage student should have considered it his business where his tutor's wife lived. The lie was revealing, though. More, even, than most novelists, Iris Murdoch existed behind a self-constructed stockade. The worlds of a novelist's invention, both in their frequently odd, or affected, social demeanour, and in their art, come into being through necessary habits of concealment. Many individuals find concealment useful: adulterers, homosexuals, spies, social climbers ashamed of humble origins, or physical grotesques especially self-conscious about their appearance. It is no accident that so many novelists fall into some or all of these categories because concealment and deception are a *sine qua non* of their very existence: but it is a concealment of a highly paradoxical order. Whereas the professional deceivers in my list deceive for the simple motive of concealing, the novelist distorts and conceals with the motive of telling the truth, of discovering or actually making the truth.

The great novelists make a world which seems truer than that of the historians. Has anyone ever written a truer analysis of the climate in which a Russian revolution was made possible than Dostoevsky in *The Possessed*? Proust's history of France is truer than any political historian's; more, and more mysteriously, his 'memories' seem truer than our own.

Iris Murdoch may be seen as a lesser writer than Dostoevsky or Proust, but she aspired to be in their league. She devoted her life to becoming a great novelist. Many would say that she failed. Perhaps the reasons for that lay partly in herself, partly in the society of which she was a part. Her lover and mentor Elias Canetti once asked, 'Was there a Tolstoy in the world today? And if there was, would people know that he was?'*

Those of us who had the privilege of knowing Iris Murdoch – and it was a privilege – and the millions of men and women throughout the world who read her novels might sometimes have

---

*Elias Canetti, *The Torch in my Ear*, Andre Deutsch, 1989, p.463.

wondered whether there was not something very remarkable in their midst: certainly something more remarkable than is conveyed by John Bayley's memoirs of his wife in her decrepitude. Would it ever be possible to capture the essence of this imagination, this person, this unique soul, in the pages of a book?

The last time I saw the Eyre film, I came out blinking into the Soho afternoon, possessed by a sensation like rage. It was like rage, rather than being rage itself. I was not angry with Richard Eyre, who had made a very good film about an old woman suffering from Alzheimer's disease, and whose actors deserved the plaudits of the critics. I was not angry with John Bayley, either, though I was sickened by his repeated claims in the public prints that his wife, such an intensely private person, would have wanted 'fame' of this kind. The books that he wrote about her, which began as an exercise in tender recollection, appeared to me a Pandora's box of which he quite clearly lost control. The resentments, envy, poisonously strong misogyny and outright hatred of his wife which seemed to me to come from the books, like some ghastly truth-drug, or course of psychotherapy, brought to the surface of the page, were things of which he probably had only a hazy conscious-ness. To one old friend who expressed her dismay at the books, he admitted that he thought he had gone mad.

In Soho Square there came before my mind a picture of Iris Murdoch's face, smiling, wise, humorous, as she had been in the days of all her vigour and creativity. The film, with its well-intentioned actors and actresses, the many newspaper articles, the drivel written so ineptly and so indiscreetly since her death, did not really seem to matter any more. My all but visionary sense of her – *there* – in Soho Square coincided with my muttering to myself some lines from *Samson Agonistes*:

Nothing is here for tears, nothing to wail
Or knock the breast, no weakness, no contempt,
Dispraise, or blame, nothing but well and fair,
And what may quiet us in a death so noble.

I don't know why the lines came into my head: they are not especially appropriate, but the repetition of them on top of the 24 bus as I made my way home to Camden Town crystallised my desire to write something myself about Iris Murdoch.

'Nothing but well and fair': that was what I wished to write; not a hagiography, and not – for I rather doubt whether such a thing could be written – a wholly dispassionate view, either. I did not want to write a folksy book in which, like the heroine(s) of the film, this secret being was colonised and made falsely intimate with us by being referred to throughout as 'Iris'. Nor did I want the pomposity of an obituary which might call her 'Dame Iris', or the modern brutality which refers to her by surname alone. To refer to her throughout by initials – her as IM and her husband as JOB – would capture the sort of focus I wished to achieve, not least because this is how they might be referred to in letters or diaries. And in what follows, I have made use of my own diary-snapshots of the Bayleys over a thirty-year period.

On this side of the grave, and beneath the visiting moon, there isn't a Last Word. What follows is certainly not an attempt to write it. As the bus made its way homewards, conveying me to a room where Iris Murdoch's complete works sit on the shelf and the photograph of herself as a child, which she once gave me, looks down from the mantelpiece, I remembered some of the wiser sayings in those books – such as that if we were characters in a novel, we would all be *comic* characters.

Enoch Powell said that all political lives end in failure. Most artistic lives do – certainly the lives of most novelists, for the novel is an untidy, ramshackle form which is demanding, and *tiring*, to write. No one was more conscious than IM of her own failure to write a novel as good as the great ones she so admired. At the moment her reputation is low. It will rise. In the course of writing the short pages that follow, my estimation of her novels has grown. As I made my way home on the bus, I wanted to convey some of that gratitude for all the pleasure these books have given me. But – as Bradley Pearson exclaims in *The Black Prince* – 'Oh! The tormenting strangeness of our ignorance of other minds, the privileged comfort of the secrecy of our own.'

2

How I met them

They were parents to me in some ways. The boarding school-educated child, taught from the age of seven to cut off from his real parents, looks around, as adolescence draws to its close, for substitutes.

Unlike real parents, toy-parents cannot have the dire influences that, according to Larkin's most celebrated poem ('This Be The Verse'), the real ones impart to us. Whether my real Ma and Pa did a Larkin, as it were, on me, I'm not sure. I recall Rick Stein, another pupil of JOB's* and my exact undergraduate contemporary at New College, in my year reading English, turning a benign but troubled grin on me one day in our first term and saying, ''Ere – what happened to all yer hang-ups, then? Why 'aven't yer got any?'

Since investigating IM's life, it strikes me that she was remarkably free of 'hang-ups' too. Plenty of metaphysical angst, as I have.

---

*JOB was a Fellow and Tutor in English Literature at New College from 1955 to 1974. After he became Warton Professor of English Literature, he moved to St Catherine's College.

Plenty of staring into the abyss of life's meaninglessness and wondering, if God does not exist, whether anything is permitted. But, from day to day, a remarkable sunniness of disposition. I used to share this. (Incidentally, I share the view once expressed to me by a boyfriend of my elder daughter that Larkin's poem would be truer for most people if it read, 'They TUCK you up, your mum and dad' . . .)

IM's story, if written down on a postcard, would seem as though it could quite possibly have created a melancholic figure. She was born in shabby-genteel circumstances to parents who were aspirant enough to feel the ignominy of poverty. ('Mine were humble people and conservative/As neither the rich nor the working class know,' as Eliot wrote in some cancelled lines of *The Waste Land*.) Her parents were more tuckers than fuckers-up, and she minded intensely being sent away to school. According to some of the crueller of her contemporaries (I wouldn't meet them, when they wrote malicious letters to the publisher who commissioned my book, Richard Cohen), she was bullied at Badminton. Some of the girls said she smelt.

She was a riotously successful undergraduate, and loved the work. She was also deeply involved in drama and politics, if the two things can be separated. She joined the Communist Party, and she had many lovers.

It is here that one begins to see in her life the carapace, the thick outer coating, which those of us who live inside our heads, and who tell ourselves stories from an early age, have developed. The next five or ten years of IM's life were outwardly hellish. Frank Thompson, a great love, was shot by the Bulgarian Fascists in 1944; and when, after the war, IM returned to Oxford and was almost married to Franz Steiner, poet and anthropologist, he too

13

died. Along the way, there were many unhappy love affairs. Such griefs, for the non-novelist, might scar a person for life. Such is the mysterious inner process of a novelistic psychology that, if you are lucky enough to possess the inner mechanism of *making life into a story*, even quite terrible events in one's past can be processed. By the time they have become stories, their pain is neutered.

It is not for me, or anyone else, to say what IM did or did not feel, but all who knew her remarked upon the extraordinary serenity of her features. The journeys and the adventures and the pitfalls were all, to employ a useful demotic word from the vocabulary of estuary English, 'sorted'. If you have the novelist's temperament, it is as if painful experiences can almost automatically be compartmentalised, put away for further use. This can make novelists alarming figures to have as parents, husbands or wives, as innumerable biographies testify.

I came to JOB and IM, then, as one of their toy-children – they always had a handful of them in their lives. Their childlessness was a vital ingredient in their own relationship, and in their social dealings.

Long before the matter of writing her life cropped up, I asked her about her childlessness. She was easily prone to weeping. I am, and now that I have passed the age of fifty, I find that more and more things, a bar of familiar music, a line of poetry, the smile of a particularly sympathetic waitress, can set me off. Hitler and Stalin were both great weepers – but at sentimental films; not at the prospect of their own destructiveness, which one suspects was largely hidden from them. I bring in that aside because one can make too much of the tears of novelists as of tyrants. Nevertheless, when I mentioned her lack of children, she wept. Tears streamed over her cheeks.

'That was something which was not to be.'

Subsequently I noted the breezy way in which JOB would refer to their childlessness in positively gleeful terms. 'I'm happy to say the matter simply never cropped up!' Or 'Thank God, when we got married, Iris was past childbearing age.' (She was thirty-six.) 'We simply n-n-never wanted them.'

On another occasion, when we were lunching together at Dino's, the restaurant in Gloucester Road which she liked to patronise, IM told me in a quiet matter-of-fact tone that she would very much have liked to have children and she envied those who had done so.

Abortion crops up quite often in the novels – notably in *A Severed Head.* 'You don't take into account the *regret*, the terrible *regret* a woman might feel who had done this thing,' IM once said in my hearing, to a woman defending the right to choose to termi-nate a life in her womb.

JOB, in his books about himself and IM, has made much of his own childishness. In his autobiographical novel, *In Another Country*, he calls himself Oliver (in real life his second name) Childers.

Like a spoilt child, JOB reacts petulantly to the presence of other, real children invading his space or claiming the attention of his Protectress or Playmate. I vividly recollect an evening in the late Seventies when my daughter Bee was about four years old. Her elder sister Emily had dutifully gone to bed, although it wasn't late, probably only half-past seven or so, as her mother, JOB and IM stood around downstairs having drinks before supper in our tiny house. (Dons eat early, and several members of the English faculty remarked to me over the years on the bohemian lateness of the Bayleys' own dinner, which was at about eight in the evening; you would think, from the way this was spoken about, they went in for the Spanish custom of dining near midnight.) Here is the diary snapshot:

IM always likes to stand with her drink before a meal. Presumably like many writers she suffers from back pain. (Piles?) Her first tipple of the evening is white wine, the cheaper the better.

While we are drinking our Spanish white (£1.43 from the offie in Walton Street), there is a noise of footsteps on the stairs. Bee, a little angel with long golden hair, is coming down. We all peer through the door of the room and see her, smiling, inquisitive face looking at us through the banisters.

IM smiles with genuine benignity, and begins to compliment Bee on one of her elder sister's paintings, lying about.

'It is so like a Paul Klee – so confidently saying Here I am!' . . .

JOB is beaming, too.

'Hur-hur-hurlo, Emily Rose!'

Bee smiles back coyly.

Then, not relaxing the smile, but with unmistakable peremptoriness, JOB adds, 'Why not go upstairs and take a M-m-mogadon!'

JOB has never made any secret of his detestation of 'kids', implying, as Larkin and A. L. Rowse in their differing ways were wont to do, that begetting them was not merely boring but, for anyone aspiring to be taken seriously as an intelligence, discreditable.

'Look at them!' Rowse would trumpet, when driving me into the hinterland of St Austell or Bodmin, and waving a contemptuous hand at the rows of ugly bungalows. 'FUCK hutches, deah! For all those stupid heteros, and their bloody KIDS! Why are they too stupid to see that there are too many bloody PEOPLE in the world as it is!'

Larkin, in his poem 'Dockery & Son', is shocked, on revisiting his old college, to discover that one of his undergraduate contemporaries has had a child almost as soon as going down from university – the child is himself now a student at the college. 'How convinced he was he should be added to!' he exclaims about the elder Dockery. 'Why did he think that adding meant increase/To me it was dilution.'

I was first introduced to Larkin by JOB in 1970 but it was only later, when I knew him much better, that I asked if these lines were considered. Much as many of us might want a child, at any age, did the act of procreation imply that one had been making a cerebral equation between adding and increase? Surely one just made love, had children, without such theorising coming into the picture?

He was adamant that he had meant every word of this poem, and that he thought that Kingsley Amis, for example, was a 'bloody fool' for having kids.

'Surely in that particular case,' I said to the curmudgeon of Hull, 'you could say that the kids had been rather a credit to old Kingsley?'

'I want someone to compile a list,' he replied. 'Talentless Kids of Famous Fathers. Notice I didn't say Talented Kids of Talented Fathers.'

'Who would be on the list?'

'Auberon Waugh. Little Martin, of course.'

To 'kids' themselves, in what one might call real life, old Larks could actually be kind in his quiet way. He was very fond of the Amises. JOB, by contrast, seemed twinkly and kind, but his detestation of 'kids' – people in general? – was palpable. I only came to this conclusion about him very late in the day.

When Emily, my eldest child, her mother and I were bound for a garden party at St Hilda's College, Larkin asked if he could come too, to soak up some of the memory of the sainted Barbara Pym. (It had been her old college and she had enjoyed the gaudies and garden parties.) Emily and Larkin were both shy, but they formed a bond in the discussion of her pet rabbit, and when this beloved creature died, he sent her, aged nine, a letter of condolence. Like the poet, Francis the rabbit was large, timorous, yet in his strange way companionable.

Since mention was made in that diary entry of the off-licence and cheap wine, two footnotes should perhaps be added, for the benefit of future literary historians. The first concerns the Bayleys. When I first knew them, they drank sherry when in JOB's college rooms and, as their domestic snifter, gin and french, ready-mixed in a plastic bottle. Later, they both came off the 'hard stuff' and IM's preferred tipple, in pubs or as an aperitif, was white wine. She firmly practised her doctrine that one should never allow one's palate to grow accustomed to good wine; one should drink cheap wine and plenty of it. Only at a late stage of the evening did she move on to the whisky, and by then she would be repeating herself, and wanting, as like as not, to rehearse either the Irish question or the origins of the doctrine of the Trinity.

If it was most unusual to be served 'good' wine at their table, there was one such occasion. It occurred not long after they had moved into Oxford and had so incomprehensibly taken up residence in a tiny house which IM hated: 68 Hamilton Road.

Squeezed into the dolls'-sized 'dining area' of their new kitchen were Janet Stone, the Wilsons, the Bayleys and Paul and Penny Levy. Paul is an American-born *bon vivant*, an expert in food and drink and a man of exuberant generosity. He told us all that we were going to drink something really special, and asked JOB several times about the magnum which he had presented to the Bayleys a week or two before. Had JOB opened it to let it breathe? Should they consider decanting it? These were the questions of a man who cared about his wine. JOB, with the look of a smiling pixie – how well IM captures him with her phrase 'grossly boyish' in *The Sea, The Sea* – served us with perfectly drinkable white wine while we chomped our parma ham and melon. It was with the next course – sausages scattered with curry powder, some quite nice roast chicken, potatoes – that Paul's magnum was produced. JOB poured us all a glass and asked us what we thought.

Everyone drank, but Paul took a mouthful and held it there, as he savoured the special qualities of the – as it were – Margaux or Pomerol.

'I think it's very nice,' said Paul, but you could tell there was great puzzlement in his voice as he looked at JOB.

'We had a few glasses the other day, didn't we, darling?' said JOB to IM, who smiled her inscrutable smile.

'But you've just poured from a full magnum.'

'Ah, my dear P-Paul, I topped your lovely wine up with a bottle of V-v-valpolicella!'

Was this a cruel prank, putting Paul in his place, or just the anarchy of the nursery – as a child might have seen no difference between the finest claret and Ribena?

The other thing which mention of the Walton Street off-licence brings to mind is a memory of Larkin coming to see us for tea, before returning to All Souls for a college dinner. All Souls is awash with booze, but Larkin was going back the next morning to Hull, and he wanted to have a supply of hooch in his suitcase. I said that we were only a short walk from the off-licence, so we strolled up there.

He wanted a cheap whisky called, I think, Claymore. They did have it, but it was six or seven pence more expensive than in his own off-licence in Hull.

When we had walked out of the shop and were on the pavement, I asked him if the price was not understandable? After all, the rent and rates on a shop in Oxford were considerably higher than they were in Hull and . . .

Did I have any idea, he asked me, what proportion of the price of a bottle of whisky was taken in tax and duty? He was buggered if he was going to spend a sodding penny more than he had to on whisky.

'I drink so much of it, Andrew, and it makes me so ill . . .'

Parsimony no doubt has many psychological causes, but I think that those who drink really considerable quantities, as IM did and as Larkin did, try to reconcile it with their consciences by buying the cheapest they can. Larkin and I got in a car and drove to about five different off-licences for Claymore at a price he found acceptable. We had thereby wasted several pounds in petrol. In the event, there was no such bottle to be found, and he settled for some gut-wrenching, instant-hangover-producing blend of cheap Scotch.

My first visit to Oxford had been on a school trip. The Architectural Society from my school was to be shown the newish (finished 1964) buildings at St Catherine's College by Arne

20

Jacobsen – the scene, were I to know it, of countless future lunches and 'little walks' with JOB in the 1970s and 1980s.

The school Architectural Society was a good one to belong to. The master who ran it was an enlightened, intelligent man with a genuine interest in buildings, and in the past; but he also liked the idea of getting out of Rugby for the day. On the Oxford jaunts, which were as I recollect termly, he evidently wanted to visit old friends, saunter around Blackwell's and Thornton's bookshops, or merely enjoy those blissful Oxford solitudes (is there anywhere on earth where solitude is more to be enjoyed?) before he dutifully showed us a college or some other building.

I had not yet made up my mind about university, somewhat inclining against the whole idea, and hoping I might be good enough to get into an art school instead.

We must have arrived mid-morning on that September day in 1966. The trees in St Giles', not yet autumnal yellow, were on the turn. Bright sunlight dappled the pavement. To the left, at the top of Beaumont Street, the façade of the Ashmolean in all its classical perfection was revealed in a Grecian blaze of bright light. The Martyrs' Memorial, built by Victorians to commemorate the courage of sixteenth-century Protestants, in fact awoke medieval pieties, seeming like an old Eleanor Cross and a throwback to that very religion which had consigned the heroes, sculpted round its base, to a heretics' death by burning.

The wide street which the eye immediately took in was bounded on one side by colleges, and on the other by a library, by a Catholic priory, by Pusey House and by eighteenth-century houses. Yet it was still recognisably not merely a seat of piety and learning, but a Cotswold market-town that I was seeing. Presumably there were buses and cars driving about, but as it comes back into my mind,

I see only the buildings, and the sunlight, peopled entirely by beautiful young women in gowns, cycling to lectures, 'Kant on the handle-bars, Marx in the saddle-bag' as Betjeman put it.

I had stepped off the coach into a dream.

Presumably Mr Moore had told us when to reassemble, and how to reach St Catz. Presumably the others in the party went their separate ways. My only recollection is of a purely solipsistic fantasy into which I had plunged, and from which I have never entirely or satisfactorily set myself free.

Almost as soon as I had taken in 'the vision', known myself part of it, I turned and entered the church which fills the traffic island behind the Martyrs' Memorial. Everything about this building was promising from the outside: the blackened, crumbling medieval stone of its four aisles; the bookstall, painted bright blue and selling a variety of items, none priced more than sixpence (in today's money, two and a half pence) – *The King's Highway*, *A Manual of Anglo-Catholic Devotion*, *The End of the House of Alard* by Sheila Kaye-Smith, *The Towers of Trebizond* (Reader's Library Edition) . . .

Through the side door, down some worn old steps and in! The smell of incense was the first sensation, then the darkness. Immediately facing me was a seemingly impenitent Magdalen, dressed to the nines in a thickly brocaded cope and holding up her alabaster pot of rich ointment with some triumph, having discovered – as one suspected was the case for many who passed that door – that incense could be as exciting as debauchery.

Here were all the things which in my strange inner life at school I had fantasised about, and which were so lacking in Rugby School chapel! Holy-water stoups; votive-candle stands, spluttering with golden light before Our Lady of Joy; and, against the peeling plaster of one wall, a blackened oil painting of the Royal Martyr. This was the one aspect of the Anglo-Catholic rigmarole which, if I'm honest, I was never quite able to 'take'. Just beneath the Royal Martyr someone was muttering into a grille, telling their confessions to a priest.

Consumed with self-important 'guilt' about schoolboy homosexuality and about a weird bout of kleptomania which had possessed me for some three months about a year previously, never, I am happy to say, to return, I had made my first confession to a clerical schoolmaster at Rugby.

He was not at all the sort of man who seemed 'High Church'. A manly, married man, who had played hockey for Ireland, he taught maths. Noticing my absence from the Communion service, he told me that Anglicans were not obliged to go to confession, but that they could do so. 'It is a method thorough, painful, decisive, full of comfort. The priest is no barrier, rather does his ministry enable you to find Christ near in his own vivid forgiveness' (Michael Ramsey).

Finding Christ was the point of it all. The lure of Anglo-Catholicism, its appeal to head and to heart, was its rootedness in the Incarnation, its belief that the enfleshed God was still enfleshed; not as the child of Bethlehem, who was an unimaginable being, but as the visible church on earth, inspired by His spirit and healed by His sacraments.

Hence my deep sense of awe as I entered St Mary Mags and found that this religion, which I had read about in books, *was still going on*. Somehow or another, even in my teens, I'd discovered that most of the things one liked, from modes of transport and clothes to art and literature, had become obsolete.

I carried into St Mary Magdalen's church no particular interest in vestments or lace, or any of the camp fripperies of the thing, but an instinctual response to what a church that used these things had to offer. Here was a place where one's deepest aspiration to be Good and to know God would be allowed free range. Outside, as it were, one would have to button up; here one could 'be still, and know'.

It was here that I decided, or rather instinctively knew, that Oxford was the place for me.

When I consider the difficulty which now faces young people trying to get into colleges and universities, it strikes me that I had things quite disgustingly easy. At Rugby, we were encouraged to sit lightly to public exams. The headmaster, Walter Hamilton, rushed the cleverer little boys through O levels before the end of their first year. A couple of years later one took the minimum number of A levels required to get into university. The rest of the time was one's own, to read and study as one wished. I must have taken some A levels and done well in them, but I don't remember having done so. I know that at some stage I filled in an application form for Oxford.

The English master, the inspirational Tim Tosswill, had been a pupil of Nevil Coghill's at Exeter College before the Second World War. He discovered that one of the English tutors at New College was called Tolkien, and assumed (wrongly) that this was the same as some man with whom he had been in the army during the war. So, it was to New College that I applied.

A few weeks later, Tosswill or I (I forget which) received a letter in that handwriting which was to be so familiar to me – a hand which seems at first glance to be a wholly chaotic italic, but which, on further examination, is seen to be firm and authoritative. JOB wrote to say that at the time of the scholarship exam that winter, he was to be abroad. Would I come up to New College quite soon, in the next couple of weeks, for an interview – or, as he phrased it, 'a bit of a chat'?

I did so, and entered for the first time JOB's rooms in the front quad. The Tolkien with whom Tosswill had been in the army was the brother of the one who interviewed me. The New College medievalist was Christopher Tolkien, an in some ways agonised Roman Catholic, who had only lately separated from his wife.

It said in my reference, written by my housemaster, that I was destined to be a bishop, so Christopher asked me what I thought of the Bishop of Woolwich and his controversial book *Honest to God*. This was not what I had expected at all. I had thought there would be questions about Chaucer and Shakespeare, and whether I had any hobbies.

In a completely crass way, I said, 'I suppose you could say that the Bishop of Woolwich makes people think.'

Christopher assumed a pained expression, which was to become very familiar to me over the coming years, and lit his pipe with short intakes of breath, letting the smoke out again with violent exhalations.

'What is the point,' he asked, 'in making people think if you make them think the wrong things?'

JOB rescued me.

'D-d-dear old C of E,' he murmured.

Christopher Tolkien was so much more articulate than JOB, and so much taller, that I had at first barely taken in the man who was, notionally at least, in charge of this interview. JOB looked, in my recollection, exactly the same in 1968 as he did in all the subsequent years: bald, twinkling, smiling and always apparently on the verge both of physical collapse and laughter.

He explained that his wife and he were going on a world tour with the British Council, which was why he was not going to be present when the entrance exams took place. He asked me a few very rudimentary questions about what I enjoyed reading and I spoke, I seem to remember, about the novels of Rose Macaulay, which at that date obsessed me. The interview, such as it was, did not take long and I was soon outside in the quad, once again, as on my first visit to Oxford, staring about with astonished rapture at the beauty of it all. Before catching my train back to Rugby, I walked round the medieval cloisters, and then back into the quads and round the garden, all in their summer glory. I felt a sudden sorrow that, by taking such a cavalier attitude to the conversation with the two tutors, I had blown my chances of ever coming up to this extraordinary and beautiful place. Damn the Bishop of Woolwich!

Within a few days I received a personal letter from JOB – 'Dear Mr Wilson'. It was the first time I had ever been addressed in this way. He said that he looked forward to my coming to the college in 1969; my place was assured, but would I mind taking the scholarship exam, since he was fairly sure that I stood a strong chance of coming up as a scholar, if I were to do so.

It all seems quite unimaginably casual. It determined the subsequent course of my life. JOB's letter repeated that he was going abroad for the British Council with his wife, but who that wife was, and why the British Council should have wished her to make a tour, I did not know.

3

I want you to write my biography

4th June 1988: the Queen of the Upper Volta tells me that Richard Cohen, an editor at Hutchinson, is going to commission a biography of Iris Murdoch. Would I be interested? I ask for more details. Is he looking around on her behalf? No, apparently he wants the book, whether or not IM herself approves.

I have now known IM and JOB for what? Twenty years, nearly. At times, we have seen a lot of one another. JOB was my tutor at New College, and has been a dear friend and mentor and supporter of mine. Relations with IM have always been more distant, but very friendly; 'Codlin's the friend, not Short' more or less summing up the nature of the case. I like her and on many levels revere her. Some of her novels – or do I mean some parts of most of her novels? – are better than anything written in England in my life-time. I've certainly read and reread her novels. Whether she has been a good influence on my own work, I slightly question. For, as well as being brilliant, her novels are also, surely, pretty good tosh? Ditto the 'philosophy' which isn't really philosophy at all, just secular sermonising based on Plato, Simone Weil, etc.? Or am I being unfair? Anyhow, it would be impossible to write about her without some of this view-point, however tactfully disguised, coming out.

In any case, she surely won't want to be written about.

Even if one wholeheartedly admired the books, how would one cope with the promiscuity? In today's climate, it would have to be mentioned, but bloody difficult when the subject is still alive – not to mention most of her lovers. (Canetti still alive? I'm not sure.) But Brigid Brophy, two or three of the St Anne's dons, G*** R***'s son, half IM's age – these are certainly always spoken about as her lovers. There must be dozens of them.

When IM became engaged to JOB, Maurice Bowra is said to have remarked, 'Lovely pair, been to bed with them both.' Of course it was a joke, and of course he hadn't done so. It is one of those archetypical stories which do the rounds of High Tables and Common Rooms. In Cambridge I've heard the same story, only with Dadie (Rylands), not Bowra, making the witticism.

If one's friendship with a married couple is on a wholly pleasant, social level, one can hardly expect it to survive the investigations into sexual adventure which are the *sine qua non* of a modern biog. So, Mr Cohen, and Your Majesty of the Upper Volta, no thanks. Count me out.

7th June: I am very busy at the moment. Much against my better judgement, I said 'Yes' to the BBC, who have asked me to do a telly series called *Eminent Victorians*. It isn't based on Strachey's book. It is six programmes, fronted, or presented, or whatever the word is, by me. I chose the six Victorians. Each programme will be an hour long. I had supposed that it would not take very long to do, but over a year has passed since the project began. I have had to go round with the producer, Bill Lyons (quite a nice fellow but hardly a soulmate), doing 'recces' in Ireland, the North of England and elsewhere. We have made a dummy pilot programme about Lord Cardigan and the Crimean War, but this won't be used. There's to be a show on the Brontë sisters, another on Newman, another on Mrs Cameron, another on Gladstone, another on Josephine Butler. Oh, and Prince Albert, which gives us the excuse to go to Osborne.

If I'd known how much time the thing would take up, I'd never have undertaken it. We have not started the shooting of these programmes at all. The timetable is completely up the spout. I'm struggling, in addition, to write the biography of C. S. Lewis, and hating doing it. V. definitely want this to be the last biography I ever write. Yearn to return to fiction, and my Lampitt chronicles.

This morning, I have had a good clear two hours writing about (the by now, hateful to me) Lewis.

Interrupted by the telephone.

'Is that Andrew?'

It is a familiar voice, the upper-class 'Oxford' voice of an old-fashioned lady don, laced with a strong Irish *timbre*. One wonders how much of her work she hears inside her head or speaks aloud before committing it to paper. One suspects – a lot.

'My dear, it's Iris.'

When announcing herself on the telephone, IM always sounds rather surprised, as if she has only just discovered her own name. Hitherto, telephone conversations have been limited to social arrangements. Since these invariably involve JOB, they are more than likely to be convoluted and muddled. IM makes the dinner dates, but will then have to ring back in agitation to say the night she supposed was free was one when JOB had accepted for them to go into a college guest night, address a seminar, eat out somewhere.

IM detests the telephone. When they lived at Cedar Lodge, Steeple Aston, she and JOB, like naughty children left in charge of a house while their parents were away, used to stuff old socks or tights into the telephone bell so that they wouldn't hear it. JOB eventually bent back the hammer so that when it rang, the telephone made no more than a faint whirr.

'Look here, old thing, I want you to write my biography.'

'Iris . . . good heavens . . . I say, what an honour, what a . . .'

'There's a man in London called Cohen.'

Today the Irishness of the voice is very marked. *Wan-tud* for *wanted*. And a distinctly Ulster brogue about the vowel in *name* or *game*. (If she says IRA, syllables she can hardly utter without shaking, she sounds completely Ulster.) I only once met her mother – Irene, she was called. By then, the old lady had gone gaga, some version of Alzheimer's, I suppose. She spoke with a lilting Dublin accent, saying *turd* for *third*, and so on. I remember how anxious Iris was about getting her on to the train, but also how solicitous and gentle this only child was to her old mother. Mrs Murdoch's mental confusions were not something Iris could easily cope with. IM's childishness is an essential ingredient in her make-up. She has never made – JOB even less so – the transition from being someone's child to being someone's parent, responsible for someone else. In Irene Murdoch's presence, IM was still a child, needing the reassurance which a parent can bring. In the absence of this reassurance, the child was near to panic. I remember, I helped with bags and sat with the two women on their way back to, I think, Putney, or was it Barnes, seeing them on to the next leg of the journey which, most unwontedly for IM, was by taxi.

In spite of being a bestselling author and presumably as rich as Croesus, she trudges everywhere on the Tube and by foot.

But now IM is on the telephone with this horrendous suggestion. As she speaks to me, I wonder how it would be possible to evoke her childhood, or that imaginative inner life which has been turned to such productive effect in the novels. How would one write her emotional and spiritual *career*? This, after all, is what is of interest in a writer's life.

'This fellow Cohen' – she sounds incandescent with rage – 'I think he's a bounder, an absolute bounder . . . for going round London offering up my life for *sale.*' *Sair-ull?*

Again, the Paisleyite vowel. Her dad, whom I never met, must have been an Ulsterman. It's odd that the mini-biogs on her paperbacks always state that she was born of 'Anglo-Irish parents'. The word 'Anglo-Irish' in normal parlance means figures such as Elizabeth Bowen, gentry whose ancestors were English but who were granted lands in Ireland. I'm sure IM's background was much more modest than this.

31

'But Iris,' I say, 'it would be easy enough to stop Cohen. All you have to do is refuse permission to any biographer; say he can't quote from your work; alert all your friends and ask them not to co-operate . . .'

'Oh, but this is hopeless! Someone is going to write this book. That's clear. And I've decided, my dear, that it should be you – if, if . . .' This most eloquent and mellifluous of speakers always has a way of almost stammering on the telephone. Not proper stammering, like poor JOB's all but incapacitating stutter, but a hesitant girlish gabble. 'If you were . . . John says you are the man to do the job. And I hope it wouldn't take up too much of your time, in the midst of your other books, which we both so much admire.'

'But do you want a biography written?'

'Well – I don't think I'm being given much choice.'

She harrumphs with mirthless laughter.

'But we should be so grateful, both of us, my dear.'

She makes it sound as if she is simply asking me to step in at the last minute as the guest at a dinner table, rather than to spend years researching her past.

'I feel there must be many people so much better qualified . . .'

'John says you'd be ideal!'

It is in what is not said during this conversation that the difficulty consists. IM wants a tame friend to write the book – who better than her husband's old pupil? – in order to prevent anyone else doing so. In fact she would want to call all the shots and censor what went in. She does not say so, and nor do I, but that is what the conversation unmistakably conveys.

'Iris, we're both going to have to think about this a little bit.'

'Anyway, my dear,' she surfaces from the matter in hand to go on to the automatic pilot of her usual daily chit-chat, 'how are you?'

I'm not very well, feel overwrought about the telly programme and jittery about life in general. I've been unhappy for months, perhaps years. Wonder whether I'm on the edge of nervous collapse.

'Fine – never better.'

'And God? How's God, old thing?'

I say He's fine too, though I'm not so sure.

My first sight of her occurred when I was just about to be nineteen and she was fifty. It must have been in the second or third week of my first term at Oxford, when JOB had one of those frequent little sherry parties which were his way of 'getting to know' – or perhaps, same thing, holding at bay – his pupils. It is strange to think how much sherry was drunk in those days. I wonder if anyone drinks sherry at Oxford nowadays, or whether the tutors, when entertaining their young protégés, find themselves giving voice to the question which, for Kingsley Amis, was the question that he dreaded most when entering a party: 'Red or white?'

IM was leaning against the white-painted bookshelves which lined, to waist-level, the walls of that panelled room. Behind her were the prints of American birds, higgledy-piggledy in frames, which, as I later learned, had been her gift to JOB. In the corner was the roll-top desk which had belonged to Professor Tolkien, who was still very much extant and was living partly in Headington, the Oxford suburb, partly in a Bournemouth hotel. It was his son Christopher who taught me medieval literature.

Barbara Dorf's painting of IM, done at the time I met her, and reproduced on page six of the illustrated section, captures the mingling of spirituality and sensuality which was so marked in her features. IM's brown hair was cropped quite short. Her round face, while not being sweaty, shone, and was innocent of make-up or powder. She had a way, retained almost to the end of her life, of half looking down, like a nun keeping 'custody of the eye', while darting glances sideways and upwards, taking in her company. Cardinal Newman's phrase about the gentleman – 'He has his eye on all his company' – came to mind, only in her case one felt that, kindly disposed as she was, there was in these upward, followed by downward, glances some of the furtive inquisitiveness of the spy, or of the only child, taking in more of the parents' conversation than perhaps they realised.

She asked me, quite shortly after we had been introduced, whether I was left-wing or right-wing in my political views. This was a question which has never been satisfactorily resolved in my mind. As a schoolboy, I had joined the Labour Party and sold *The Tribune* on the streets of Rugby. On the other hand, the notion of state monopolies and political solutions to human problems always repelled me, and I much preferred the radicalism of G. K. Chesterton to that of the People's Party. When I read the Christian anarchist writings of Tolstoy, I found them to be even more congenial guides to life – and still do. At the same time, I am deeply conservative by temperament. So the truthful answer to her question was that I did not, and do not, know.

'How about you?' I asked, feeling, as perhaps one does at that age, that when grown-ups ask you a question, there either lurks a trick behind it or there must be a right or wrong answer.

'Oh, I've always been broadly in sympathy with the Left,' she said, tugging at her short fringe. Her voice was deep, musical, and that mixture of old Oxford and Northern Ireland which I have already noted. Playing tapes of her voice to myself in the years since she died, I've come to the conclusion that a very large part of IM's hypnotic grace lay in this voice. It sounds like the voice of Wisdom itself: it is playful, but serious. It is musical and sad, but interrupted by much laughter. It is in more than one sense a seductive voice.

'They seem to have been on the side of the dispossessed, the underprivileged, persons of all sorts whom the System and the Market sought to . . .'

'H-how's your g-glass, darling?' JOB said, coming round with the bottle.

My father, getting a little squiffy by eleven each morning on Harvey's Luncheon Dry, had often complained at the meanness of hosts who served South African sherry, and speculated on the likely identity of those even further beyond the reach of human imagination, who might buy bottles labelled British Sherry. He had supposed that it was bought by 'Blakies – for their birthday treats, or to stir into puddings'. Blakie was my Peggotty.

'N-no-not bad, this stuff,' said JOB, brandishing the British Sherry.

His wife held out her small glass for a refill.

'Are you both Labour then?' I asked gauchely.

'The d-d-dear old P-p-people's Party!' said JOB gnomically and then, answering for her, 'Iris rather fell out with them, didn't you, darling, over education?'

'Well, this is true,' she said.

A look came into her face which was to become very familiar to me in the coming years. It was what I privately came to term her Manning the Barricades face. Her jaw was set, and yet her eyes shone with the pleasurable anticipation of (at least verbal) fisticuffs.

'The Labour Party began in order to help poor people. What was the most efficient way of doing this? To improve housing, no doubt, to get rid of the slums, to give health care to everyone, of course. But the fundamental and obvious way in which to eliminate inequality was to provide good education for everyone regardless of whether they could afford to pay for it. And now the . . .'

A particular tone of voice. She had it when she discussed Ireland, but also politics, and sometimes philosophical schools of which she disapproved.

'The Labour Party . . . the party of the Left . . . introduces a system of education which is bad. Bad,' she repeated, going rather red.

'I suppose,' I said weakly, 'the idea is that it was unfair to make eleven-year-old children take an exam which would determine their schooling for the rest of their days, and which would ensure that only a small proportion of . . .'

'Okay,' she said, 'so the eleven-plus exam is unfair. But why introduce "mixed-ability classes"? We want schooling to be demanding. We want children to be introduced to what is difficult, to mathematical concepts, to grammar, to language. This is so vitally important. And this is what the Labour Party has taken away from everyone. That is an act of great wickedness.'

'So did you vote Conservative at the last election?' I asked.

She laughed lightly and said she did not think she would ever go quite as far as that.

'But a mixed-ability Latin class! Damn it, they wouldn't choose a mixed-ability football team.'

That was my first glimpse of the great novelist; and great I certainly believed her to be. I write these words some thirty-three years later, and some fourteen years after she asked me to write her biography.

I can only say that in her presence you felt that you were with a person who was not like other people. She was highly intelligent, obviously – but one has met other highly intelligent individuals. It was a quality of depth that you felt. It was an observant depth. And you also felt that, as well as surveying and noticing, IM was looking at that part of her friends' beings or souls of which perhaps they were not quite aware themselves. It was the part which could choose to be a good or a bad person. You felt in IM's presence a spiritual power. It was a little like meeting a mage, or a guru, and this feeling persisted even if the words proceeding from her mouth were, however beautifully articulated, commonplace or disputable. I still believe in her greatness, or near-greatness, or sort-of-greatness; though I'd be hard put to define what I mean.

This quality of sort-of-greatness has certainly been obscured by the film *Iris*, and by JOB's books about her, and by some of the subsequent journalism, which devoted more space to her love affairs than to her intellectual journey or her life as a writer. I'm sure it was not the intention of JOB to diminish her in this way. I wish that, instead of taking occasional notes of things that she said to me, I had been a Boswell – or, if not I, that another had performed this task, since there was often in her speech, and her presence, a quality which deserved to be recorded. John Jones, Professor of Poetry, polymath and friend of IM's for half a century, recalls how she would sit in pubs and deliver, quite unselfconsciously, a finished and well-modulated account of the merits of

Dostoevsky which, if written down, would have formed a perfect essay.

I think I was hampered in the task which she asked me to undertake by a number of impediments. First, at the time I was myself undergoing a personal crisis – losing my religious faith, having a marital bust-up and possibly having a minor nervous breakdown. These things were not entirely clear to her; certainly they were unclear to me at the time. I was probably being more like one of the more chaotic 'accidental men' in her own fictions than I was an authoritative Boswell in that period of 1988–90.

Second, I was handicapped by knowing JOB and IM too well on one level and not well enough on another. I was part of the loose circle of people (in no sense a set) who saw a great deal of them, but on the whole, for that very reason, we indulged in superficial and merry social talk, rather than knowing one another as family or lovers know one another. We avoided the depths. Added to this was a curious phenomenon regarding both the Bayleys, namely that they were very effectively cocooned and protected from the slightest vestige of criticism. Friends might smile indulgently, but never unkindly, behind their backs about the untidiness of the Bayley ménage and the eccentricity of the food. Anything approaching malice towards them, or attacks on their work or their way of life, would somehow have been heresy. I well recall the sense of shock caused in Oxford by Terry Eagleton's really quite mild attack on JOB as a critic and a scholar.*

Eagleton committed the solecism of noting that behind the apparently ramshackle nature of JOB's critical stance there *is*, if

---

*Published in *Against the Grain*, Verso, 1986.

not an ideology at work, then a position to be defended. 'His position is almost painful in its theoretical paucity, but . . . it is legitimated by the sheer force of his personal sensitivity and perceptiveness as a standpoint to be respected and adopted. In this sense, part of Bayley's task is to ratify English criticism's inability to confront its own intellectual nullity.' Unusually, in a work of supposedly academic analysis, Eagleton devotes a large part of his introductory remarks on JOB the critic to a biographical sketch:

What distinguishes Bayley from most prominent English critics is the impeccable ruling-class orthodoxy of his social upbringing and career. Born in 1925, he was educated at Eton and New College, Oxford, became an officer in the Grenadier Guards and served in Special Intelligence during the war; he was then elected a Fellow of three Oxford colleges in succession, and has remained at Oxford ever since as the occupant of a university chair. He is married to the novelist Iris Murdoch, herself of *haute-bourgeois* Anglo-Irish provenance, who became an Oxford academic after a high-ranking career in the Civil Service. It is . . . particularly intriguing that Bayley continues to exercise such ideological power, in a literary world where others of his sensibility and 'social tone' are undoubtedly marginal.

I quote at length to convey the nature of the broadside. Several of the Bayleys' friends – nearly all of whom were by this date ardent admirers of Mrs Thatcher, though fearing that she would not go 'far enough' – were furious that JOB had been 'outed' as a right-winger. Others were shocked that this pair, somehow vulnerable and much cherished by all who knew them at all well, should have come in for the same order of criticism that might be levelled at anyone else who went into print on frequent occasions.

Certainly, I was myself shocked by Eagleton's attack – both the mockery of JOB and the implied distaste for IM. Here was a third handicap to writing her biography: she was in some way a heroine to me. She was – I see this now – a rôle model. I had read her obsessively as a teenager, and I now think, as I look back, that she embodied many of the things which I should like to have been myself: a prolific novelist who was also taken seriously on some level or another as a 'thinker'. Behind this fact is a supplementary or fourth point, namely that I viewed her religious ideas and obsessions with a mixture of awe and fear – supposing she was right, and there was no God? Where did that leave my own hopes and aspirations? At the stage when I met her I hoped in some sense to be a writer, and also to be a priest, though I had great doubts about both ambitions . . . At certain times of my life, over a twenty-year period, the doubts and the thoughts had all focused on her.

It now seems to me that these, far from being handicaps, were all reasons why I should have made an attempt to write something about this phenomenon of our times, Iris Murdoch. Whether that 'something' should have been a formal biography, however, I somewhat doubt. There was another factor in play, concerning the project which she had for us both. It was that, in the course of 1988, I had completed a biography of C. S. Lewis, the great defender of what he called Mere Christianity. Writing the book had persuaded me, much against my dearest hopes and wishes, that I did not, very definitely did not, believe in 'Mere Christianity'; but as well as losing faith in religion, I had also lost faith in the possibility of writing biography. Wasn't it all a bit too neat, the notion that you could 'explain' a human life simply by telling the story of it in chronological order, plundering the diaries and letters of the individual concerned (if any were left behind), or interviewing the survivors who had known him or her? Did not a reading of the best fiction, psychology or, come to that, the modern philosophy of mind suggest that the human personality was altogether more protean, complex and strange than the simple exercise of biography would usually suggest? If one wanted to build up a portrait of IM, for example, would writing a biography, which began with her birth in Dublin and ended with her pathetic death, a demented old woman in a 'home' in Oxford, bulked out with stories of her erotic indiscretions, come anywhere near plucking out her mystery or capturing what made her so brilliant a writer, so charming and unusual a companion and friend? I thought, and think, not.

4

In Another Country

June 1988: K[atherine Duncan-Jones, my then wife] says I shouldn't touch the IM biography with a barge-pole. This, like so much that K says, is obvious common sense.

She thinks that, apart from anything else, it would be terribly boring to write IM's life. Also, embarrassing, because how could one ever convey the truth about IM and JOB – e.g. the filth in which they live, and the peculiar food they serve to their friends, etc., etc.? Never mind the love affairs or the, ahem, books. How could you look her in the eye again when you'd described the smell in their house?

I think more highly than K does of the books. Well, I blow hot and cold about them. Sometimes, I think IM is supremely brilliant, and sometimes, she just seems to be writing automatically, the same merry-go-round of emotional entanglements, the same old repetitious meta-physical speculations, the same mage-figure, as it were Canetti or Professor Fraenkel, dominating an increasingly ageing group of friends . . .

I certainly know what K means, too, about the boringness of much of the life which IM has led – boring to me at any rate. Wasn't she engaged once to Frank Thompson, brother of the Marxist historian EP? One would have to go into all that Communist stuff, and the not exactly enthralling lefty student contemporaries such as Denis Healey. And then one would have to work out when she had stopped being CP and become just a lefty (which she still was when I first met her). Since those days, she has absorbed John's Right-of-Genghis Khan views on most subjects, though I don't believe she shares his whooping enthusiasm for capital punishment.

Then, think again of having to write about her friends and lovers! Mervyn James, who knew her in London during the war when she was working as a Civil Servant at the Treasury, remarks on her *tendresse* for 'tearful love affairs with paunchy refugees'.

Then again, I think of all I owe in my life to this strange pair, and realise that the gifts of an older pair to a younger protégé or friend can, like qualities inherited from blood-parents, be good or bad. For the good things, one will always be grateful. As for the bad things, well, it will take me a long time to unlearn some of the lessons. In the case of JOB, the slapdash brilliance, the seldom bothering to verify a source, to look anything up, to provide any evidence of 'work' when dashing off his books . . . This surely had a poor effect on IM herself, especially in her philosophical books? It's been bad for a number of his students, I think. She needed rigour. We all do.

She has been an influence on me, both as a novelist and in her whole vision of things. But has it been a good influence?

I suppose if one wrote the book, one might discover how such influences work?

Last year, the publishers reissued IM's book on Sartre, which she gave me. It has a new introduction by her. This introduction has the quality of her talk: highly intelligent, but only periodically focused. One of the moments of focus is when she is discussing Sartre's move from writing his own fiction and philosophy to writing huge biographical works, on Flaubert and Genet:

> Sartre said in the book on Baudelaire that he was not offering literary criticism. At the same time, most explicitly in the Flaubert book, he wishes to discover how just *this* man (so like many others in general respects) becomes *this* artist.

That expresses with lapidary elegance the kind of book I would write about IM, if I could. Damn it, what am I saying? That puts very well the kind of book which one would want to *read* about IM – not the kind I would want to write! But how an individual becomes a writer, and what of their life goes into the fashioning of the books, this is interesting. It is what one looks for and seldom ever gets from a literary biography. I hope, think, that I have managed to provide such a book about C. S. Lewis, but was he worth it? IM is a much more interesting figure than Lewis, not least because she has engaged with many of the intellectual and political currents of her day . . . Hang on. Does that make her interesting? Anyway, why am I writing this down? I'm not writing her biog, and that's that.

* * *

44

June: telephone goes. JOB rings wondering if I'm free for one of our 'little lunches'. I go to St Catz. These occasions are always the same, always agreeable. The tiny little snifter in the Common Room. Then into the dining room where far-better-than-most-colleges food is on offer: good beer, a range of nice vegetarian foods. We eat some cannelloni with tomato sauce and I drink lager. John has a doll's portion of food.

St Catz is a modernist paradise, if you like that kind of architecture, which I increasingly do if it's 'good' modernism. Important conditional. Arne Jacobsen has made it a series of pure vistas: long water-gardens, expanses of plate glass, beautiful in grey light like today, though uncomfortable in bright sunshine. The Fellows dine in one such plate-glassed goldfish tank, overlooking water-gardens. The long teak (?) table is surrounded by pale wood, perhaps elm (?), chairs with high backs of a vaguely serpentine design. They look as if created for orthopaedic purposes. The cutlery is in keeping – space-age style. Amusing company. Here is John Simopoulos, an old friend of IM, dedicatee of one of her best novels, *The Bell*; toothy, tall Michael Gearin-Tosh flutters around us laughing in his high-pitched tones; he is an English don at the college but also something of a theatrical impresario. During a college Christmas play, a dramatic version of *David Copperfield*, he was inspired to cast JOB as Mr Dick; and here too is the former Master, Alan Bullock, who converses in his gravelly northern voice.

It was in this room that, during a pause in the conversation, he once remarked, 'I hear copulating ducks.' (Northern vowels – dooks. Cup-you-lairtin dooks.)

'How,' ventured someone, 'do you know, Master, that the ducks are copulating?'

'Because that's the noise I make when I copulate.' ('That's the noise that ah mairk wun ah cup-you-lairt.')

I also associate this room with a very JOB moment. Some years ago, we were all asked out to Steeple Aston to help entertain some of their swankier friends from London. A dinner party had been got up; Kingsley Amis, an exact under-graduate contemporary of IM's, was staying, with his wife Elizabeth Jane Howard. JOB, as always, was in charge of the food. Everyone complimented him on the dish, which was way above his usual level. It was a chicken casserole in a rich sauce, followed by a splendid meringue concoction with strawberries. JOB cheerfully received all the glowing compli-ments to his culinary genius, and IM too basked in the reflected glory of being married to such a cook; even suggested, by her smiles and bows, that she had perhaps had some hand in the preparation of the feast.

The next day, Jane Howard and Kingsley came into Oxford, and JOB asked them for lunch. For some reason I too was of the party. We sat in this Arne Jacobsen room, and the waiters brought in a lunch which was identical to the food that we had eaten the night before at Cedar Lodge.

'Looks like you've been rumbled, old man,' said Kingsley to JOB, who replied, accurately, 'I thought it would give you more pleasure to be told I'd cooked it myself.'

Anyway, here we are again, in St Catz, chit-chatting as we so often do. John Simop has finished his lunch and reflected, staring at his empty plate, '*Consummatum est.*' Michael has come up behind me and begun to talk about Rachel Trickett, an old friend of mine and JOB's.

JOB and Rachel were both pet pupils of David Cecil's, in post-war Oxford, and she was a confidante of his when he met, and fell in love with, IM. Unabashed by the use of anecdote as a substitute for conversation, Rachel likes to remember JOB at a party of hers, leaving the room and standing on the landing. 'John, whatever's the matter?' 'If you don't mind, Rachel, I'll go home. I'm so – *unhappy* – I don't know what to do.' It related to the time when IM had told JOB that she could not give up her love-slavery to Canetti.

For some years now Michael Gearin-Tosh and Rachel have shared a ménage – another slightly Miss Trotwood and Mr Dick arrangement, I should have guessed. Certainly they both tell their friends that it is no more than a domestic companionship. As often happens when one has treated another as a confidante, there is now something of a coolness between JOB and Rachel. She is jealous of IM's literary triumphs. I am devoted to Rachel. She is one of the great originals. Her parents, who ran a small shop in Wigan, were both enthusiastic lay preachers at their local Wesleyan chapel. She, as Principal of St Hugh's College, enjoys taking chapel services and is an accomplished preacher. George Eliot herself would have admired Rachel's sermon on the text 'Turn our captivity, O Lord, as the rivers in the south'.

A convert to the Established Church, Rachel shows none of the stereotypical Methodist austerities. She likes to drink very strong admixtures of gin and vermouth while smoking menthol cigarettes. The eighteenth is 'her' century. She wrote a fine book on Augustan poetry, *The Honest Muse*, and her robust common sense and absence of emotional folly make her a wise friend. (She has had affairs, including one of long standing with a married man, but she has never, she once told me, been in love. Friendship is her passion.)

One of the heroic mysteries of her character is her manner of coping with almost complete baldness, the result of alopecia. Why does she not wear a turban or a wig? There might be practical answers to this. Her poor old scalp is scabby and to cover it might be itchy. But I think the true, the meta-physical, explanation lies in her detestation of artifice. The ill-favoured John Wilkes said that in half an hour in any company he could *talk away* his face, and Rachel likewise could talk away her bald old pate.

Michael and I fall into chat about her and I say that she has been asking me about possible publishers; she dreams of getting her novels back into print.

In the 1950s, at about the time that IM shot across the sky like a comet, Rachel Trickett published a series of beau-tifully written but slightly dull novels, some set in her native t'North, others in Oxford. Reading them is a little like eating food of the period where everything – brown windsor soup, the coating of sauce on the over-boiled carrots and cauli-flower, the custard which comes with the pud – seems to be of uniformly flavourless quality. Yet all wholesome and in its way sustaining.

JOB laughingly recalls the occasion when his old tutor (and Rachel's) David Cecil, who was always kindly anxious for Rachel's literary career to take off, arranged a dinner for four. The table consisted of JOB, himself at the time an aspi-rant novelist, Rachel Trickett, David Cecil and his great friend Elizabeth Bowen. The two women disliked one another on sight. Lord David, who was the gentlest of men and full of politesse, hated anything approaching the nature of a 'scene' and did his best to pour oil on what were clearly going to be stormy waters. All Rachel's flow of mildly malicious, gossipy talk was received in silence by the great Irish novelist, as were her reflections on literature. Elizabeth Bowen was fiercely jealous by temperament and was possessive of her male friends. She and Lord David were never lovers, but they were very close, and Mrs Cameron (as Elizabeth Bowen was) preferred to see him *à deux*, or in the company of his wife and family, rather than with a female protégée.

At length, even Lord David's diplomatic skills could not prevent actual hostilities breaking out between the two women. While Rachel Trickett was in the middle of an anecdote about the eccentric behaviour of Miss Proctor, the head of the college where she taught, Elizabeth Bowen leaned across the table with a fork and struck the young woman very hard on the knuckles.

'I don't think,' she said, with her paralysing stammer, 'you should speak of your P-p-' – agonizing silence – 'principal in that manner!'

'Elizabeth was a great admirer of yours, John,' I say now.

JOB makes his usual purring noises, mutteringly calling me darling and denying any such thing. But she had been. When I was an undergraduate at New College, and JOB was my tutor, he gave classes on Jane Austen, which Elizabeth Bowen, wintering at the Bear Hotel in Woodstock, used to attend.

She was a formidable character, tall, powdery white, chain-smoking, decidedly upper-class. I came across her a few times.

49

Only now, with the knowledge that being grown-up does not preclude a writer's need for reassurance, do I wish – passionately wish – that I had told her how consumedly and utterly I admired her work, considering her novels easily the most distinguished of her generation, better even than Evelyn Waugh or Anthony Powell, much as I revere them both. Though under the spell of Henry James and Virginia Woolf, she manages to be quite assuredly herself. And, unlike IM, she seems like a writer who both early, perhaps immediately, found her own voice *and* had something very distinctive to write about. *The Death of the Heart, The Heat of the Day* and *Eva Trout* remain for me toweringly distinguished achievements.

I first met her at a dinner given by my Warden, Sir William Hayter, in, oh, 1970, I suppose. Because of my Rose Macaulay obsession, I asked, with what seems like total crassness to me now, about Rose, rather than first saying how much I admired Elizabeth Bowen's own books. We spoke of the *Letters to a Friend*. Mrs Cameron – which was how I was introduced to her, and how I always addressed her on the half-dozen times we were to meet, said, 'You'll forgive me. You are very young. You can read Rose's *Letters* as simply something in a book. For me, she was a friend, and a real person. I think I'm a sort of C-c-c—'

She paused to ignite her umpteenth untipped Senior Service, fumbling with a flat silver cigarette case.

'C-c—'

She remained silent for a while, sitting, tall and still, lighting her cigarette, waiting for the word to come. It was quite unlike JOB's stammer, which has always been playful, engaging, almost flirtatious. Mrs Cameron's stammer was totally incapacitating. She froze like a giant iceberg until she was released to say, 'Christian. But to think of Rose, just because she had had a love affair, feeling that she had to apologise to that' – many a puff of a cig, and still the awful silence – 'rat-faced little priest . . . It's simply too awful.'

A year or so later, William and Iris Hayter asked Katherine and me to dinner in the Lodgings. It was just five – us, the Hayters and Mrs Cameron. We by then had Emily, a child a few weeks old, in tow and because she was still being fed by her mother, we had to take her to the dinner. She slept like a little doll, while we ate the meal prepared by Iris Hayter, a gentle, beautiful and wonderful woman. At some point, Katherine slipped discreetly out to feed the child, and it was in all other respects a grown-up dinner.

Only as we left, and picked up the Moses basket containing Emily, did the great novelist ask if she could see her.

She leaned, this vast horse-face, thick with white powder, over the basket and peered for a full two minutes of silence at Emily.

'I n-n-n . . .'

Katherine, who also has a stammer, tried to do what you aren't supposed to do for stammerers, finish Mrs Cameron's sentence.

'I never.'

The silence was arctic. The ship had run into the ice and might be locked there all winter.

At length the words came.

'I never had a . . .' She leaned forward, and a look of great gentleness came into this terrifying old face. 'A baby,' she said gently.

On this occasion, and on the first, when I had so blunderingly refrained from a mention of her own books, Elizabeth Bowen had talked to me about the Bayleys.

She asked me which of IM's books I admired the most.

I replied, *The Bell* and *A Severed Head*.

'Not the very early ones?'

'They seem as if influenced by a quite different *type* of writer.'

'Yet from the first,' said EB, 'you feel yourself in a *world* when you open one of Iris's books. There is no writer *like* her. That is an extremely rare quality in a novelist. Have you read John's novel?'

I did not know he had written one.

'It's called *In Another Country*. I admire it enormously. Quite enormously. He is the cleverest critic we have. Cleverer than Cyril – more broad-ranging. He has the most extraordinary sense of the way a book *works*, of what a novelist or a poet was up to. His essay on Keats – do you know it? – shows he knew Keats better than Keats did himself. Try *In Another Country*.'

I remembered this conversation of 1974 when, after this lunch in June 1988, I find myself on our 'little walk', JOB and I. We stand behind the New Building at Magdalen, its crumbled black sandstone like a truckle cheese rising from the deer park. JOB says it reminds him of Ireland – of the old Ireland of Yeats and Lady Gregory.

Suddenly he says, quite authoritatively and in a different tone of voice – 'Iris is really upset by this Cohen man and the idea of a biography. She's an intensely private person and she couldn't bear the idea of her life – *our* life, as it were –

being *publicised*. But we both *trust* you, and I've told her how good you are – I've read her bits of your *Tolstoy*.'

'You wouldn't end up like the two ladies in *The Aspern Papers*, thinking . . .'

JOB theatrically points, leans forward, his tweed cap falling over his fishy-face, like the old lady's eye-shade in James's tale, and gesticulates with mock indignation.

'You publishing scoundrel!'

We both laugh, and JOB reflects, as he often does, on the strange way that Henry James, in preparing the stories for their New York edition, altered them for the worse.

'The ending of *The Aspern Papers* was perfect: "when I look at it, my chagrin at the loss of the letters becomes almost intolerable". There was all James's ambiguity there – the loss was intolerable, but so was the narrator. But in the New York edition he altered it to: "I can scarcely bear my loss – I mean of the precious papers!"'

When he says *I mean*, JOB's eyes seem to pop out of his head, and his mirth is a shared joke in which one is enfolded. Such moments are refinements of one's taste, and it is in this way that he has been a good teacher, certainly not in the sense of imparting knowledge directly, or of being conscientious about a syllabus of study.

The walk is over. We've crossed the bridge, opened the little gate back to St Catz and JOB is returning to his room where, amid a chaos of typescripts and books, and the old volumes of *Scrutiny*, and the prints of American birds now moved from the eighteenth-century panelling of New College to the spare whiteness of Jacobsen, he will chat to a few graduate students about their PhD theses.

'So I'll tell Iris that's settled,' he says, with something of the authority of an officer in the Grenadiers.

'Settled?'

He melts. Coos. Woos.

'Between ourselves, d-dear Andrew, you can just write more or less anything. She won't *read* it, you know.'

'But, you . . .'

'I'll tell her you've said *Yes*.'

5

Iris and the cakes

In 1989 I left Oxford and occupied, full-time, the London flat which I had purchased some time before. The year was dominated by the nightmare of divorce. Janet Stone, at IM's seventieth birthday party that summer, told me how much IM minded this development in my life, how bitterly she hated her friends splitting up. 'But Iris is being "absolutely marvellous" about it.'

I thought this was a strange way of viewing things. There were plenty of people who were in a position to take a censorious view of my behaviour during that year. Those most closely concerned were indeed amazingly, and heart-wrenchingly, uncensorious. I did not think at the time that it was for IM to behave 'marvellously' or otherwise. But it showed how, for some of her friends, she was seen as their 'Guide to Morals'.

Over the years I had noticed a paradox in the Bayleys' attitudes to the marital upsets of their friends. They took the same excited interest that anyone else would do if one of their friends fell in love, eloped with a lover, made an idiot of themselves. How well I remember their over-excitement when one of IM's fellow-

55

philosophers in Oxford (and brother of one of her own lovers), believed to have a stable and happy marriage, suddenly discovered himself cuckolded by a friend. I can recall the flaming rows which resulted; the separation of the pair and, after about a year, their reconciliation. *I never met these people.* Blow-by-blow details of this matter would be regaled by *both* Bayleys to us, even though we were *much* younger, and indeed did not even know the couple concerned.

Perhaps in this case IM had a storyteller's inner knowledge of how things would resolve themselves? Perhaps she could see they would get together again. Clearly it had been part of the deal between IM and JOB that, however unfaithful she was, they would never, ever separate. The seriousness of an early lesbian affair with a fellow of St Anne's was that it had, very nearly, broken up the marriage after only a year or so. Thereafter, JOB and IM were as firmly married as anyone in England. Divorce was unthinkable, and they always spoke of it as the ultimate folly.

'Just when he'd got used to all the marital shorthand, the little domestic routines . . . He wanted to smash it all up and start again from scratch!' JOB once said to me scornfully, uncomprehendingly, of a Lothario in the English faculty.

IM certainly took a great deal of interest in my own failed marriage, writing long consolatory letters and frequently meeting me for lunch during that year.

'What?' asked Rachel Trickett when I made some allusion to having had lunch with IM in a restaurant not far from my flat in Paddington. 'You mean you met IM alone – without John?'

'Yes – we quite often do this.'

'When did this start?' Rachel asked sharply.

'I don't know, really. I think when the idea of this biography cropped up.'

'But you were always *John*'s friend. He was the one you saw alone.'

'Can't one do both?'

'You wait.'

I thought a little. Then I realised that, although I had seen JOB with IM since the biography plan was mooted, our 'little lunches' had mysteriously ceased. Because of the business of the divorce, and the move to London, and the general turmoil of life I had failed to notice this huge change.

Indeed, completely credulous as I was, and accepting of the myth of the Bayleys as a model married couple, I was heedless of the signs of how passionately and unreasonably jealous JOB could appear.

When IM began to teach philosophy at the Royal College of Art, she had a routine. After her last lecture she would catch a train from London and meet John Jones in a pub in central Oxford, usually the Roebuck. They almost invariably discussed philosophy. John Jones is an inspired lecturer who speaks without notes. IM feared to speak unless she had written down every word, and over their drinks she would discuss with Jones the philosopher whom she had been teaching that week. He realised in retrospect that her lectures at the Royal College must have constituted a substantial history of Western philosophy.

It was the Joneses who had first introduced JOB to IM one Sunday lunch in the early 1950s. One evening, years later, when the Joneses and the Bayleys were supping *à quatre*, Jean Jones innocently remarked upon how much her husband enjoyed these pub meetings with IM. Clearly, it was the first JOB had heard of them. Thereafter there were no more meetings *à deux* between IM and John Jones.

JOB hated going to London. IM went regularly, still maintaining, until the early Nineties, her habit of spending a few nights each week in the flat in Cornwall Gardens. We sometimes travelled up to London together by train, often in time for lunch at an Italian restaurant in Craven Road, which was of the kind she liked – that is, a perfectly ordinary one, not a gastronome's restaurant: just a place which served her favourite dish, osso bucco, with plenty of house red. Sometimes she was hungry and would wolf down her food. More often, she would order more and more things to accompany the dish – vegetables, even sautéd potatoes – but leave most messed with, unconsumed. She hardly ever left a clean plate: the mark of a spoiled only child.

One of the things which sustained her writing life was a regular intake of sweet food, milky drinks, farinaceous snacks. When she was working, she would break mid-morning for a foaming cup of Horlicks, often accompanied either by Mr Kipling cakes or by sweets such as Mars Bars or Crunchies; and this explained, I think, the fact that while she continued to put on weight, she seldom displayed much interest in food at the table.

After one Italian lunch, she came to sit in my flat for the afternoon, and was excited when I produced from a shopping bag not one, but two cakes. Knowing her fondness for cake, I had intended to offer her one of these treats to take back to Cornwall Gardens. Which would she prefer to take – the walnut sponge or the Jamaica ginger?

She had been her usual friendly, smiling self all afternoon, but it was at the prospect of being given a cake that she really brightened. Her face became quite flushed, like an excited schoolgirl, and she said, with not entirely mock-pomposity, 'I think I shall have to consider this important proposition very seriously.'

Her bright eyes passed from the walnut sponge to the Jamaican ginger – and back again. Her great mind might have been weighing up the rival merits of Wittgenstein's and Heidegger's Theory of the Will.

'This is difficult' – a chess master playing for time. Then the solution came to her: 'I think I'm going to take BOTH, my dear.' Which she did. Since, in those early days of solitude, I had rather peculiar eating habits, hardly ever bothering to cook for myself or to go out in the evenings, I had been rather relying on *one*, at least, of the cakes to see me through until breakfast. On parting, perhaps in gratitude for her booty, she placed both forearms on my shoulders and stared dreamily, almost amorously, into my eyes. She quite often did this at the end of an evening, but as a gesture in the afternoon, it somehow carried a suggestion in it which was lacking when the words 'goodbye' had already been said. The flickering moment was the only one when I felt I had glimpsed what her life of a hundred emotional intimacies had been like. Settling, later, to an evening of silence, of the lamplight and the book, I thought of her with very great affection. Through the wistful features of a youthful almost-seventy-year-old I had seen the face of a playful, sexy girl. I can remember putting down my whisky glass and my Agatha Christie novel late that night and thinking how much, much more I should prefer having an affair with IM to writing her biography. *Dammit, why not?* She had clearly been one of those delightful young women – and continued to be such a person well into middle, perhaps into old, age – who was prepared to go to bed with almost anyone. For a moment or two, the whisky guided my hand towards the telephone, but of course cowardice triumphed and I turned to the solitary routine of tooth-cleaning, pyjamas and bed.

6

Hull is other people

July 1989: now IM and I have made a television programme
to coincide with the publication of *The Message to the Planet*,
and her seventieth birthday. I have just watched a video of
the programme, made by a man called Kevin Hull.
Throughout all the preliminary discussions, and the filming
itself, he was extremely nervous. Nigel Williams, a genial man
who oversees the *Bookmark* programmes, explains that it is
the first programme that Kevin has made on his own.

I don't blame Hull for his nervousness. When I finished
doing the *Eminent Victorians* programme, I decided that I must
never do telly work again. The whole experience was not
merely uncongenial – it was something much worse. I hated
having to be on display. I hated hearing my voice and seeing
my tics and mannerisms on the screen afterwards. I hated
having to compress thoughts into thirty-second (or shorter)
'bites' for 'pieces to camera', and I hated having these words
mangled and rewritten by producers. At the end of a day's
filming I felt as though my guts had been ripped out. Tearful

exhaustion was my usual condition on going to bed. I had nightmares. The sense of days, weeks going by in which there was no innerness, no quietness, no time for books to grow, or books to be read, gave me the heebie-jeebies. And the lonely nights in bad provincial hotels, where the choice was forced: be a snooty, stuck-up bastard and stay in your room all evening, or sit in the bar, being a jolly good sport with the 'sparks' gaffer, grip, sound and all the rest . . .

So, when *Bookmark* approached me asking me to 'front' a programme about IM, I said no. Then she came back and asked me to do it, saying that she would only consent to be interviewed for telly if I were the one who did it.

I now think that the experience of doing this television programme is going to be a paradigmatic projection of what lies in store for me as IM's biographer. On the one hand, she clearly wants some publicity. Her popularity as a novelist has slumped since she began to write these interminably long books. The title of the new one (*The Message to the Planet*) is ominous in so far as she clearly does believe with one part of her brain that she has such a message herself . . . She insisted that I came with her when she had her preliminary meeting with Mr Hull. She was shirty with him, as was I. He, quite understandably, poor man, wants to make a programme which explains who she *is*, and, given the way the world wags, this process is bound to have biographical shape. She bitterly resented the idea that it should be biographical, and says that it must concentrate entirely on her 'ideas'.

I had breakfast with Beryl Bainbridge one day while these early discussions were in progress. (A friend of mine for years, she is now a neighbour since I moved flats.) I told her the difficulties I was having with IM.

'Just say,' said Beryl, '"Look, pet. No one cares when you changed your mind about the philosophy of Wittgenstein. All we want to know is who you've been to bed with."'

I suppose that IM is aware that such a view is a widely held approach to the challenges of literary biography, not just in her own case. It makes her cagey. On the other hand, she reacted to Mr Hull's questions about where she was born, or went to school, or who her undergraduate friends had been as if he had no right to be asking them. This did not stop her grilling *him* with endless questions about himself, beginning with the basic enquiry how he comes to be called Hull. Upon hearing that Hull was the port where some Jewish forebears – grandparents or great-grandparents – arrived from the Baltic, she melted. Tears filled her eyes at the thought of those exiles. When we had parted from Kevin on the first day, she asked me eagerly if I thought he was homosexual. I'm terribly bad at knowing this, and said I guessed not. She seemed crestfallen, but hugged to herself the thought of all his relations talking Yiddish and German and Russian and Latvian to one another, no doubt in reality discussing the cheapest way of getting a roof over their heads in Hull, but probably in her fantasy agonising about the Death of God. I irrelevantly recalled that when our friend Jonathan Cecil, actor son of Lord David, was in rep in the town he had sent me a postcard reading: 'Hull is other people'. She paused silently on hearing this. I thought it was a joke which would appeal to a woman who had written a book on Sartre, but she merely nodded seriously as if this were a proposition that would need further consideration.

Kevin Hull was far, far better than I at getting information out of IM. There were two reasons for this. One was that he *was* just better at it: at grilling, asking. The second was that, as I realised quite early on in our researches for this programme, I did not really want to know. I want my friendship with IM and JOB, which has been such a bright light in my life, to go on as before. Unlike the readers imagined by Beryl Bainbridge, I have no desire whatever to know who, or how many people, IM has slept with.

I had assumed that such information would be strictly classified. But Kevin Hull astonished me by giving me, before we began the interviews, an article from the *Mail on Sunday* which appeared last year. The article, by Sue Summers, in *You* magazine for 5th June 1988, is a superb piece of research entitled 'The Lost Loves of Iris Murdoch'. Given how extremely secretive, and deliberately misleading, IM tends to be about her life, it seems little short of miraculous that so much has come to light. It is obvious, and I mean this with no hint of irony, that Sue Summers should be writing 'my' book on IM. Summers writes that 'IM's private life has, in fact, been as rich, complex and romantic as that of any of her novels – and as marked by sadness. Before her marriage, 36 years ago to the critic John Bayley, she was in love with two remarkable men. Both of them died young in tragic circumstances.'

I realise already, after only a few months of 'working on' IM as a subject, how unfair my initial response was to the nature of the task. The figures of Frank Thompson and Franz

Steiner were highly distinguished, interesting men. The one as a war hero, the other as a poet and anthropologist. IM's demeanour with me has suggested an absolute unwillingness that her emotional history was to be discussed in print – by me, or anyone else. In fact, she has given this interview to the *Mail*. IM has spoken comparatively freely, JOB with absolute abandon: he tells Sue Summers that he was 'shaken', when he got to know IM, to discover that she had had many affairs. 'I never felt shy of her, physically or in any other way . . . I had assumed she was completely virginal and fancy-free.'

Reading the Sue Summers article now, in August 2002, I see JOB's contribution as a harbinger of what was to come – a great outpouring from his own pen about IM's 'private life' and, eventually, its dramatisation, in the form of a film, with Dame Judi Dench playing IM and Jim Broadbent JOB. I came to the conclusion that much of the information about IM's 'private life' must have been fed to Summers by JOB himself. IM would not have performed an act of such blatant self-revelation. Presumably her *extreme* caginess with Mr Hull, and with me, results from feeling worried about this article by Summers?

When the filming was over, I wrote to IM asking whether she really wanted me to continue with the book, and if I did, how were we to deal with such matters as her love affairs with Frank Thompson, Franz Steiner and Elias Canetti? I said that it embarrassed me to write about them, and I had no wish – no wish *at all* – to pry into them. A biography which failed to mention these things might seem odd . . . Should we give up the project, or devise some way to signal to the reader that emotional involvement, with a figure named within the pages of the biography, was of greater or less intensity? Had she read, for example, Rupert Hart-Davis's excellent life of Hugh Walpole, which conveys a fully rounded portrait without explicit reference to the fact that Walpole was homosexual?

In my letter I cringed and squirmed, though not as much as I do now, to recollect the writing and the posting of it. I ended with a whimsical little note that I knew that the truly important men in her life were Plato, Shakespeare and JOB.

She wrote back promptly:

It was jolly good to see you. Yes, Plato, Shakespeare and JB! I must also add my father. No sentimental [illegible] *please*. Mention of the illustrious people, yes. (Nothing happened in the case mentioned.)

We'd been talking of Raymond Queneau.

I'm afraid I'm not up to the standard of Tom Driberg! (I met him once in a High Anglican context.) I am looking at diaries. How quickly the past vanishes. I am very grateful to you, Andrew, for taking the (you know) job on. I wouldn't have wanted anyone else. I'll try to buck up (as my famous head mistress used constantly to tell us to) – she should figure a little. Much love, my dear, ever, I.

Will communicate.

7

Iris Murdoch: a Brief Life

ANW Have you ever felt inclined to write a big book about everything?

IM Yes. *Yes*.

BBC Bookmark: 'A Certain Lady'

If I were to write a 'Brief Life' of IM, it might read something like this. Iris Murdoch was born in Dublin on 15th July 1919 of a nineteen-year-old woman called Rene Richardson, who had, seven months previously, married a twenty-eight-year-old Ulsterman named Hughes Murdoch. The Richardsons were of shabby-genteel impoverishment. Rene's father, described on her birth certificate as a solicitor, was in fact a lawyer's clerk. As in the case of Newman Noggs, who followed the same avocation in *Nicholas Nickleby*, there was some memory of gentility. IM carried this around with her throughout her life.

Her father was comparably the son of a family in decline, if not disarray. His own father was said to have drunk away what profits there were from their small farm at Hill Hall, eight miles outside

Belfast. Hughes Murdoch, always described by IM as 'a bookish, quiet man', joined the Civil Service at a very junior level in boyhood. After serving in the army during the First World War, he returned to the Civil Service and worked in London, first as a second-class clerk in the Ministry of Health. When a few weeks old, IM was brought to live in Acton, west London, in the tiny rented flat which her father had found. Soon thereafter her parents moved to Caithness Road, Brook Green, perhaps half thinking of its proximity to St Paul's School for Girls.

Mr Murdoch remained in the Ministry of Health until 1942, when he was transferred to Somerset House to work on the Census. This he did until his retirement in 1950. IM was herself, after taking her degree, a Civil Servant, working for the Treasury. The aspirant writer-philosopher Bradley Pearson, narrator of *The Black Prince*, worked, rather similarly, as a Civil Servant in the office of the Inland Revenue. He was reluctant to call himself a taxman. 'For some reason which I cannot fully understand the profession of "taxman", like the profession of "dentist", seems to excite laughter.' A number of IM's relations in Northern Ireland were, or are, dentists. The life of the patient, anonymous Civil Servant was one that IM always claimed she had enjoyed. It was a profession, she claimed, which she would have been happy to pursue. Certainly the novels are full of Civil Servants. They are also peopled by the exceptionally gifted children of modest homes. Bradley Pearson still dreams of the small shop run by his mother and father; Hilary Burde, the 'Word Child', is similarly haunted by a family background which is quite at variance with the sophisticated metropolitan circles in which he now moves. Dozens more examples from the IM corpus could be adduced.

During a quarrel in grown-up life between IM and a female

lover, the writer Brigid Brophy, harsh words were exchanged. Brophy accused IM of being 'a poor girl who made it into a rich girls' school', and therefore of being fundamentally a coward socially, and a conformist. As so often in the case of lovers' tiffs between highly intelligent people, there was a deep element of truth in the unfairness. IM treasured her status and her success in later life. After she had been made DBE, she attended a Royal Academy dinner and loudly corrected the toast-master who announced her as 'Miss Iris Murdoch'. 'It's DAME Iris Murdoch,' she said angrily.

Behind such outbursts were the uncharted and unrecorded years of her childhood. Her parents did not entertain. Her father had no friends. When he retired from the Civil Service there was no gathering of friends or colleagues in the office. A chain-smoking addict of the Irish cigarettes Sweet Afton (made by Carroll and Sons, who were to endow a chair of Irish History at Oxford with their profits), he died not long after retirement.

His whole adult life, after the birth of IM, seems to have been directed towards giving her the domestic stability in childhood, and the educational qualifications in maturity, of which he and his wife in their different ways had both been deprived. IM was indeed 'a poor girl who made it into a rich girls' school'; and it was school and university which made her what she so uniquely was.

Once, when I carelessly spoke of her lurch, or drift, away from youthful left-wing ideology, she retorted firmly, 'I don't like the images of lurching or drifting. I have *thought* about these matters.'

There is nothing, therefore, especially surprising about the change in her political opinions. Like so many in her generation, she moved from a young adulthood of enthusiastic Communism to a maturity of no less keenly felt admiration for Karl Popper's free society and the economic liberalism that was believed to underpin it. The consistent thread linking her young and old selves was a commitment to education and a belief that formal education, if offered to children, could save individuals from chaos and civilisations from barbarism. She owed her own life to school and believed the same would be true of everyone.

'Iris, aren't you confusing Virtue with Intelligence?' Lord David Cecil once pertinently asked in my presence. She paused – always before answering a question, however trivial, she paused – and one could see that she was flummoxed.

'I don't think I *am*,' she insisted. But Intelligence and Virtue were for her in many respects not so much confused as synonymous. When the Left, in Britain, forced through a new educational system – the comprehensive schools – which in her eyes removed the very concept of excellence from the horizons of many young lives, she could no longer call herself a leftist.

The high-minded left-wingery of IM's youth was inextricably connected with intellectual goals. After the Demonstration School in Colet Gardens, Brook Green, where the high intelligence of 'the Irish girl' was immediately noted, she went, aged thirteen, to Badminton School near Bristol. It was a 'progressive' establishment with 163 pupils. The headmistress, Beatrice Mary Baker (known as BMB) was a Socialist-Quaker who taught the girls, who included Indira Gandhi, not merely intellectual rigour, but a sympathy with all the world's liberal causes. IM's first visit abroad was a school trip with BMB to the League of Nations, whose optimistic and ineffectual view of the world situation appealed to many kindly minded people at the time.

Even after her change to Conservatism, IM retained the belief, once expressed to me in conversation, that the Soviet Union was 'a good State and not a bad State'. Wittgenstein entertained this view, at a date when perhaps rather less was known in the West about the millions who died from enforced starvation in the Ukraine, about the Stalinist purges, the show-trials, the Gulag exposed to the world by Alexander Solzhenitsyn, Nadezhda Mandelstam and countless other witnesses.

An aesthetic and temperamental taste for the austere prepared puritan minds to receive the fallacy that the spread of austerity would make human society more equal or more just. The fact that the rich had been sent away empty must, to such minds, untrained in economics, suggest that there would be a larger share of material goods to be offered to the unfortunate. One suspects that what appealed, to IM (as to Wittgenstein), about the Soviet Union, what made her see it as 'a good State', was its resemblance to a high-minded English boarding school, with its strict rules, unnourishing diet and relentlessly authoritarian regimen. There was a 'Quaker' greyness, a general notion that rice pudding was more 'virtuous' than haute cuisine, in both the life views of Miss Baker and of the Politburo. There was also a sense, picked up by IM, that while being religious in temperament, BMB was perhaps – like Hughes Murdoch – a free thinker.

IM wrote a poem about her old headmistress which was printed in a booklet, *At Badminton with BMB by* THOSE WHO WERE THERE. She evidently considered it a document worth not just showing to me, but actually copying out for me in her own hand:

> Restlessly you proclaimed the upward way,
> Seeing with clarity the awful stairs,
> While we laddered our lisle stockings on the splintery
>   parquet

Kneeling to worship something at morning prayers.
But did you really believe in God,
Quakerish lady? The question is absurd.

Writers know they are writers. IM knew that this was her destiny at least from the age of nine. After the strictures of Badminton School, she came to Somerville College, Oxford, in the Michaelmas Term of 1938. For many people, the experience of university is transitory. They pass the three or four years with their books and their friends and then move on to 'grown-up' life. IM was to be rooted, emotionally and intellectually, in Oxford for the rest of her life. True, she went away, to work as a Civil Servant and as a volunteer helping displaced persons in Austria. She also had a year in Cambridge. And she never lost touch with her London origins, maintaining for most of her grown-up life some form of London residence. But Oxford and she were deeply bonded from the very first, and it was here that she blossomed.

Originally she came up to study English literature. She switched immediately, however, to Classics – five terms of studying Latin and Greek literature (Honour Moderations, or Mods) followed by a further two years studying ancient history and philosophy. Since she was destined to become a professional philosopher before she was a published novelist, the change of subject was momentous, possibly prompted by her natural interest in ideas; partly perhaps by an antipathy to Mary Lascelles, the English tutor at Somerville, who could be especially belittling to girls she considered either bumptious or lowly born.

'Some speak of their "relations" and others of their "relatives". It is important to get it right – er, which do you say, Miss So-and-so?' Miss Lascelles asked a terrified pupil. Later in life, when she received a letter from a lonely and unfortunate graduate student from the United States, saying that she had arrived in Oxford and would 'contact her supervisor as soon as may be', Miss Lascelles replied with a curt postcard – 'You may have arrived in Oxford. The verb "to contact" has not.' (IM uses the verb 'to contact' both in letters and later novels.)

IM's Irish brogue and enthusiasm for socialist dialectic is unlikely to have appealed to this brittle cousin of Lord Harewood and childhood playmate of Queen Elizabeth the Queen Mother.

IM threw herself at once into the excitement of undergraduate life. She showed no shyness or nervousness, as some of the other girls did. At Somerville she was the contemporary or near-contemporary of some remarkable budding philosophers, including Philippa Bosanquet (Foot) and Mary Midgeley, both lifelong friends. A little older, but a Somerville contemporary, was Elizabeth Anscombe, destined to become one of the closest disciples of the later Wittgenstein and translator of, among other key texts, *Philosophical Investigations*. IM, the head girl of Badminton, was now rubbing shoulders with considerable intellects who would stretch her horizons.

The first of the great refugees whom she met was Eduard Fraenkel, who had come to England in 1935 and was elected at the beginning of the war to the Corpus Christi Chair of Latin. 'Oxford, lucky Oxford, received so many of these Jewish intellectuals. We were very privileged in Oxford to receive so many great Jewish thinkers,' IM said. It was unusual for undergraduates to be given tutorials by professors, but the heart has its reasons and Fraenkel, one of the greatest Latin scholars of twentieth-century Europe, liked his regular supply of female pupils. IM's Somerville tutor, Isobel Henderson, warned her that

Fraenkel would probably 'paw her about a bit', which was indeed the case. IM evidently found nothing too objectionable in this, sharing with Fraenkel a robust and apparently guilt-free attitude to sex. Though a bisexual who was largely lesbian in approach, IM had a rather simple idea of 'what men wanted' and was happy to share it with them so long as the man in question was able to provide friendship and/or intellectual stimulus. Of her huge and distinguished acquaintance – Michael Oakeshott, M. R. D. Foot, Tommy Balogh, Asa Briggs, Geoffrey de Ste Croix, Stuart Hampshire, David Hicks, Wallace Robson, Tino de Marchi, Arnoldo Momigliano – most, if not all, were lovers at one time or another.

Fraenkel introduced her to the notion of real intellectual rigour. Year by year in Oxford, right down to my own day, his classes were legendary. Sometimes the whole hour would be spent discussing the meaning of a single phrase. In a poem IM wrote about Fraenkel's *Agamemnon* she recalled:

> In that pellucid unforgiving air
> The aftermath experienced before,
> Focused by dread into a lurid flicker,
> A most uncanny composite of sun and rain,
> Did we expect the war? What did we fear,
> First love's incinerating crippling flame,
> Or that it would appear
> In public that we could not name
> The aorist of some familiar verb.

It was a remarkable generation. Her signature in the Bodleian Library register is immediately before that of Philip Larkin. Kingsley

Amis was another contemporary. Roy Jenkins, Tony Crosland, Denis Healey, Robert Conquest were all to be met at the Labour Club at which, Communist as she was, IM was a constant presence.

The Labour Club split, in a manner that was to foreshadow the future of the British Labour Party; 400 members broke away from the increasingly Marxist Labour Club. Tony Crosland was their leader, Roy Jenkins the Treasurer, a future Chancellor of the Exchequer and Chancellor of the University. In his memoirs, *A Life at the Centre*, Jenkins recollected:

> The main duty that I remember going with this office was that of engaging in a long and unrewarding correspondence with Iris Murdoch, my opposite number in the old club, about the sharing of its assets and/or liabilities. Both our different ideological positions and the arm's-length nature of our negotiations were indicated by our respective salutations. 'Dear Comrade Jenkins,' she began. 'Dear Miss Murdoch,' I replied. Forty-seven years later I compensated by giving her an Oxford honorary degree.[*]

She was caught up from a distant student perspective with the coming war; but this distant perspective would soon be brought into sharp relief when the men went away to fight. Several men who had been her lovers were killed in the war, but of these the most important in her life was Frank Thompson, a passionate soulmate who was in love with IM, but with whom she had a platonic relationship.

---

[*]Roy Jenkins, *A Life at the Centre*, Pan in association with Macmillan, 1992, pp. 36–7.

The Book and the Brotherhood, with its story of a closely knit group of Oxford friends who had all been taught by an old classical scholar called Levquist, was manifestly based upon her own 'set'. It was rare for her to admit that characters in her books were based on life, but IM admitted that Levquist was a (highly flattering) portrait of Fraenkel.

From the purely educational perspective, however, the departure of the Oxford men had its advantages. In the late Thirties the Oxford philosophy school had undergone a great change. A. J. Ayer had published *Language, Truth and Logic* in 1936 when he was twenty-six years old. Almost overnight, the Idealism which had been taught in Oxford since the days of T. H. Green and F. H. Bradley became painfully old-hat. The fashion for Logical Positivism and, when this was modified, for purely analytical or linguistic approaches to philosophy would last for most of IM's philosophical career. But when war broke out, the young Logical Positivists put on their uniforms, leaving the Oxford lecture halls empty save for 'a few ordinands, a few conscientious objectors, a few people with bad health'. For the first time in the history of the university, there were more women than men studying philosophy.

While the cats were away, the mice could play. As Mary Midgeley recalled, 'This gave us the chance to do what indeed we'd chosen philosophy to do. We'd come up to Oxford because we were really interested in Plato, in what Plato was trying to do.'

IM was sent to be taught by Donald MacKinnon of Keble College, an old-fashioned metaphysician with a particular interest in Kant. MacKinnon was a large man in all senses; and a big figure in IM's history (In later life, he would be a major influence on Rowan Williams, future Archbishop of Canterbury). He was a devout Christian, often to be seen, from undergraduate days, at early mass in Pusey House, groaning in ecstatic worship before the Blessed Sacrament. Shambolic and badly co-ordinated, he acted up his eccentricities. 'Why,' asked one of the priests at Pusey House, 'are you wearing one brown shoe and one black?' 'Peculiar, isn't it?' agreed MacKinnon. 'And the strange thing is, I have another pair just like it in my rooms.' Educated at Winchester, MacKinnon had learned the schoolmasterish trick of buffoonery as a teaching aid, and would give tutorials while lying in the bath, or while playing dangerous games with razor blades, which he would suck, or hold between his lips, or twirl on his fingers while he spoke of Kant's *Critique of Pure Reason*.

Philosophy, more than most subjects, is taught before it is learned. Some of the very greatest philosophers, such as Hegel or Wittgenstein, were more or less self-taught in the discipline. But most learned the rudiments of their skill at the foot of another philosopher. They might well have reacted against it, as Aristotle reacted against Plato, or Russell against the Hegelianism of McTaggart, and in so doing been 'awoken from their dogmatic slumbers' – as Kant said he had been after reading Hume. But nearly all philosophers have learned philosophy by doing the subject with someone else. And the stamp of the tutor remains on the pupil. Everyone recognised, when IM published *The Philosopher's Pupil* in 1983, that Rozanov was a sinister portrait of MacKinnon. The Philosopher's Pupil she remained. When she was asked to give the Gifford Lectures in Edinburgh in 1982, she chose a title and a theme – 'Metaphysics as a Guide to Morals' – which echoed directly the preoccupations of MacKinnon's own Gifford Lectures eight years previously – 'The Problem of Metaphysics'. Kant, as much as Plato, would always be 'her' philosopher.

IM depicted her own parents as a chaste child-centred pair. The only child of such unions is perhaps seeking in all subsequent relationships the primary degree of attention bestowed upon her by doting parents. The only child does not have to wait for treats or take turns with siblings. The last cake or jam tart on the plate is always reserved for her.

The sexual attentions of Professor Fraenkel were entirely unworrying to IM. The emotional involvement of MacKinnon, seven years her senior, was even more exciting, since it involved not sex but tormented, guilty love, and a jealous, unhappy wife. IM's tutorials with MacKinnon, which turned into extended examinations of one another's souls, were an obvious seedbed not just for her later metaphysical speculations, but also for her fiction. For here was a relationship which could not be defused by a few weeks of sexual gymnastics, but rather simmered into a grand passion before turning to actual hatred – at least on his side. Against the background of the guilty involvement, there was taking place in the younger woman an eager philosophical learning-process, a confrontation with the great questions of European philosophy. One of MacKinnon's obsessions was the old debate between Idealism and Realism – is there a world outside our minds? If so, how can we be said to know it, and by what processes can we give to our fleeting consciousness the status of a truth-arbiter? As a neo-Kantian he wished to maintain the distinction between truths which could be established through the means of experience or sense-perception, and those which could only be known *a priori*, as things-in-themselves. Such a thing was The Good, as conceived by Plato. Many ideas and forces were at work to undermine a 'realist' belief in The Good as a thing-in-itself, many determinisms, disguised as Freudianism, or Darwinianism, or watered-down

Hegel. The Good, and our responsibility to it, was not dependent upon our own whim, or our own capacity to choose: it was an Absolute, demanding our submission and, MacKinnon would say as a troubled but devout believer in the Creeds, our worship.

These intellectual considerations would remain with IM for the rest of her life, and the flood of opposing thoughts, together with the crowds of morally confused persons who filled her imagination in life and in fiction, did nothing to alter the inward convictions she learned in MacKinnon's tutorials.

But IM was never, at any time, a monist. She never had a single set of beliefs, or a fixed sexual preference, or, until the very end, a solitary partner, forsaking all other. She was a pluralist. While enjoying tormenting MacKinnon with her love, she had many other sexual partners. And while struggling with Kant and Plato in the tutorial, she absorbed another mode of thought altogether during her evenings with the Marxists.

Historical hindsight is blinding. From the distance of half a century we see Stalin and his Gulag Archipelago of prisons; his extended empire more repressive than anything devised by the cruellest of the Tsars; a world in which no one trusted another, in which children betrayed parents, and siblings, neighbours and friends were taught to denounce one another in the Party's name. We see the statistics of those killed, tens of millions starved, tortured, shot. And we see the effects of the Soviet Empire extending its tentacles over the entire area of the Warsaw Pact countries, with catastrophic effects upon countless lives. It is hard in these circumstances to see how an intelligent and compassionate individual, particularly one such as IM with a passionate interest in moral philosophy, should have espoused such a creed at such a moment in history.

To capture the spirit of the times, let us go to Bulgaria in May 1944. Major Frank Thompson, a few months short of his twenty-fourth birthday, is facing a show-trial at Litakovo. Like other British army officers in Balkan countries, he had sided with the Communist partisans against the forces of Fascism. (Fitzroy Maclean comes to mind; he was a Conservative, and a friend of Churchill, who was largely responsible for the victory of the Communist Tito in taking over the united Yugoslavia at the end of the war.)

Frank Thompson and his men, Bulgarian and British, had fought with extraordinary bravery against the pro-German *gendarmerie* and Fascist army. He was caught, and put on trial. The village hall was packed with spectators.

'By what right do you, an Englishman, enter our country and wage war on us?' he was asked.

He answered, 'I came because this war is something very much deeper than a struggle of nation against nation. The greatest thing in the world now is the struggle of anti-Fascism against Fascism.'

The crowd was deeply stirred, and when he was asked if he knew that such words could result in his being shot, he replied, 'I am ready to die for freedom. And I am proud to die with Bulgarian patriots as companions.' Just before he was shot, he raised a clenched fist and called out to the people, 'I give you the Salute of Freedom.'

We now know what a horrible world was brought into being, in Bulgaria and elsewhere, by Frank Thompson's Communist comrades. At the time, they were fighting the Gestapo.

IM and Thompson were never lovers, but they were thinking about marriage. During the Spanish Civil War, these idealistic schoolchildren and students had imagined that the Republican government, with its willingness to shoot whole convents full of nuns, was advancing the cause of freedom; just as the French revolutionaries had imagined liberty and fraternity to be the consequence of hanging the last aristocrat with the guts of the last priest.

Frank Thompson, a brilliant boy who had been educated at the Dragon School, Oxford, and Winchester, was one of the most remarkable of his generation in intellectual brilliance and courage, but in his political views he was archetypical. These were the bright stars of IM's Oxford generation, and she shared their ideology with passionate intensity.

After Oxford, she was drafted into the Civil Service, working for the Treasury under the formidable Evelyn (later Dame Evelyn) Sharp. It is hard to know how many, at this period, of IM's friends, or indeed relations, were actual members of the Communist Party. Her father, from all I have heard of him, always sounds like a classic CP member, an apparent loner, a diligent Civil Servant who might well – as IM did from Day One in her Treasury job – have fed all secret information from the in-tray to the local branch of the Party.

How well I recollect an early morning in the 1980s when Jennifer Hart, the history don at St Anne's College when IM taught philosophy there, was 'exposed' in a newspaper as a former Soviet agent. I happened to be catching an early train to London. In the misty chill of 7 a.m., I saw the two of them on a bench, deep in talk, Hart in her habitual white ankle-socks, IM in her duffel coat and ski-pants, eyes down, talk, talk, talk.

IM had always been open about her Communist allegiance. This led in later life to many an altercation at the American Embassy, since her scrupulous honesty compelled her, when filling in the routine visa applications to enter the United States, to answer affirmatively when asked if she had belonged to the CP. Most of the old lefties who had done so, to save themselves and the embassy staff trouble, simply lied: why not? Lying was a virtue to the loyal Communist.

When I saw the two old women on the bench, I felt certain that they were discussing the possibility of IM being the next 'spy' to be exposed. Although she had freely admitted an ideological enthusiasm for the Communist cause, she was much more cagey, for obvious reasons, about having betrayed her position of trust in the Civil Service. Because she was in a junior job, she never had much information to pass on, but what she had was loyally posted into a hollow tree in Hyde Park and collected by a 'postman' – as one of her friends was quick to tell me, the moment it became known that I was writing her biography.

My purpose in this book is not to 'expose' every detail of IM's private life, as a Communist, a lover, a wife or a friend. It is, rather, to see whether it is possible to discover from the life those elements of her revealed personality that gave birth to the works.

As soon as I began to compare things which she had told me about herself with the facts as they unfolded, I became aware of a disparity between appearance and reality.

Almost the first thing she announced about herself, when we were filming for the TV documentary, was, 'Yes, my mother's family were sort of plantation squires' – a strange picture of a pregnant teenager living in a Dublin rooming-house, which would later (if it didn't at the time) contain a betting shop on the ground floor. Over the years – her assertion that she did not have an agent of any kind, that she did not have a London flat, that religious principle forbade her to be anyone's godmother – I discovered that, slightly more than most people, she protected herself by shame-less and habitual social lying.

All novelists create make-believe worlds which are homes for their imagination. IM was happy in Murdochland, and not always at home in the world of the real. Her membership of the Communist Party, like her varied and energetic emotional life, compelled an elaborate network of deceit. She thrived, in fact, on acts of betrayal, once telling her journal that she lied to all and sundry.

If her Treasury career, laced with many a love-tangle in wartime London, reflects some of the darker sides of Communist treachery (one cannot doubt that had she worked for the Air Ministry, for example, she would have handed over secrets just as cheerfully as she did from the Treasury), then her next move – to work abroad with refugees in Austria – showed the benevolence and idealism of the young Communist. Her father, revealingly, was cross with her for spending so little time at Innsbruck, working in the camps for displaced persons established by UNRRA (United Nations Relief and Rehabilitation Administration).

She freely admitted that her motives for volunteering for this hard and in many ways distressing work were mixed. 'I wanted to get out of England – well, everybody did. They were cooped up in England, four years, five years.'

She once showed me the journals she had kept in those camps. Subsequently she claimed to have destroyed them because they were 'making my life into a story', something her Platonist soul deemed impure. Later, when I alluded to the journals, she denied their existence.

I recollect two things very vividly from the diaries of these years. One was the extraordinary clarity of her narrative gift – describing the administration of the camps, the individuals she met from differing lands, the conversations she had in her pretty fluent French and her 'bad German spoken fluently'. There could be no doubt, if one read these pages, in their clear, confident and absolutely unmistakable hand, that here was a *writer*; the twenty-five-year-old wrote with all the confidence of the mature novelist.

Second, in the midst of all the confusion and human chaos that surrounded her, one was aware of her singleness of purpose. The journals record her resolution to be a writer. The important friendship she formed in the camps was with Raymond Queneau, whose brilliantly original picaresque *Pierrot mon ami* IM knew well. She was working in the French-occupied zone of Innsbruck and he came to address a literary conference. As well as providing refugees with soup and blankets, the French army was attempting to rebuild the broken bridges of European culture.

I have no reason to doubt IM's assertion that she and Queneau had never actually been lovers. 'First one of us was keen, and the other held back . . . then a little later the positions were reversed.' 'Which? When?' She shook her head and smiled. They certainly enjoyed an *amitié amoureuse* and talked about contemporary literature, above all about Sartre, whose *L'être et le néant* IM was also reading. Their friendship/love would fizzle, but Queneau was a major influence. Her first novel, *Under the Net*, was a spirited pastiche of *Pierrot mon ami* and was dedicated to Queneau. She always resented the fact that he was not more appreciative of this gesture, and that he dropped her as a friend. She failed to see perhaps that men do not always want to keep up with women who have in some senses made a fool of them. Nor is it true in literature that imitation is the sincerest form of flattery; it can be simply annoying.

After the war, she looked about for opportunities to continue with her academic studies and to enter academic life. There were various dead-ends, including suggestions by MacKinnon that she apply for teaching posts at Welsh universities (Cardiff, Bangor) and a Commonwealth Scholarship to study at Vassar, which came adrift when her membership of the Communist Party was declared.

Instead, she entered Newnham College, Cambridge, for one year, 1947–8, where she studied philosophy at graduate level. The idea of her teaching philosophy at Bangor, or studying it in earnest in America, for example as a PhD student, was in fact unthinkable. 'I intended to make my mark,' she admitted later, and she always wanted to be based either in a metropolitan world or in the orbit of the brighter stars in the firmament. On her way back to England, she had gone to see Sartre in a Brussels bookshop. In 1950 she signed a contract with Bowes & Bowes to write a book entitled *The French Existentialists*.* (The contract was witnessed by Wallace Robson.) The work never got written, though her reading of Sartre's prolix metaphysical lucubrations would result in a short book, her first, and the first serious study of the existentialist genius in English: *Sartre: Romantic Rationalist* (1953).

At Cambridge, she encountered the circle of young disciples gathered at the feet of Ludwig Wittgenstein. She herself met Wittgenstein only occasionally, but she met a group of Wittgenstein enthusiasts who were to be her friends for life – Wasfi Hijab, a Palestinian from Nablus, Kanti Shah from southern India, and Georg Kreisel, whose mathematical logic was much admired by Wittgenstein. Here too began her combative and in many ways

---

*Chatto & Windus Archive, Reading University.

unhappy friendship with Elizabeth Anscombe, who was in every way a much more substantial philosopher than IM, and who allowed her, at frequent intervals, to know it.

The group of 'disciples' around a great man, a mage or wizard-figure of dubious moral goodness, is a repeated theme in IM's fictions. Other friendships formed at Cambridge included that with Jean Robinson, of Girton College, who would marry John Jones, polymath Fellow of Merton and future Professor of Poetry. The Joneses were among IM's closest and most constant friends and she deeply admired them both – John as a talker of Coleridgean brilliance, and as a mind whose books ranged on subjects as various as Aristotle and Dostoevsky, Keats and Shakespeare; and Jean, whose expressionist paintings would, IM believed, one day be spoken of in the same breath as those of Van Gogh. She often said this to me.

Jean Robinson introduced IM to her friend Pierre Riches, then a pleasure-loving Jewish agnostic, who was soon to be converted to Roman Catholicism and to become a priest. He was seen by many of their friends as a model for the many priest-figures in IM's books, though his short and powerful work of apologetics suggests a less tormented approach to the Christian faith than that of many of her unbelieving clerics.

It was in 1948 that she met Franz Steiner. 'He was a delightful, funny, clever, charming creature in the Anthropology Department. He was an expert on tribes . . . he used to go and visit various tribes . . . He must have been, I should think, eight to ten years older than me, but he died suddenly of a heart attack in 1952.'

Steiner had been part of the large German-speaking Jewish community in Prague before the war. He had originally intended to be a biologist, but his poor eyesight precluded microscope work.

He moved into the sphere of anthropology and had studied in England since 1936. His parents were killed in Treblinka in 1942 and many of his relations perished in Hitler's camps. When he himself reached Oxford, the suitcase containing his thesis on the sociology of slavery had been stolen and years of original research lost. The loss was devastating to him and, though he finished a doctorate in 1949, he never really recovered.

He and IM were much in love. She showed him her first novel, *Under the Net*, and he was seen by other friends as the midwife of her genius. As well as being a scholar, Steiner was a poet, who wrote many lyrics to and about IM. 'He was one of Hitler's victims, but one of the wittiest, merriest, sweetest people I ever met.'

Steiner always felt ashamed of his physical weakness in IM's company. It was a bitter source of shame to him, for instance, that she had to carry his luggage up a steep staircase to his flat because of his weak heart. His death, when it came at the age of forty-three – in all probability when she was in his arms – was a devastating shock to her. She ran in tears to Holywell Cottage in Manor Road. When her friend Jean Jones opened the door, IM ran past her to see John. She was closeted with him for many tearful hours.

Jewish funerals happen within twenty-four hours of death. At Steiner's funeral the next day, 28th November 1952, she encountered a man to whom Franz had introduced her some months before: Elias Canetti.

If Steiner was in some senses the love of her life, Canetti was of immense importance not merely in emotional terms, but as a representative of what she wanted to do with her life: her intellectual and literary career.

Both Steiner and Canetti despised England, identifying it with all that was second-rate and philistine. Canetti's memoirs are his best work, sometimes comic *sans le savoir*, sometimes magnificent. He thinks continually of those who are truly great. The lists of the great ones he has known – Bertolt Brecht, Thomas Mann, Alban Berg, Stefan Zweig, Robert Musil, Hermann Broch – found no counterpart in British culture. His novel *Auto da Fé* is a flawed masterpiece: the misanthropic bookman who lives in and by his library, and who hates the human race, is an obvious self-projection. The extent to which the story, brilliant as its first 200 pages are, can carry the ideological weight of its conclusion, and the degree to which the incinerated apartment, like the lost library of Alexandria, can stand as an appropriate symbol for a besieged European civilisation, are rather more doubtful. The debts owed by the plot to Thomas Mann and Dostoevsky are clumsy.

Canetti, however, had the highest possible view of himself and it was a view that he expected his many acolytes to share. IM happily complied. The Nobel Prize which was awarded to Canetti in 1981 had been awarded by the author to himself, inside his own psyche, a good half-century earlier. Like Fraenkel, Canetti convinced IM to consider herself his intellectual inferior. Unlike Fraenkel, who was one of the very greatest scholars of modern times, Canetti's postures could easily upon examination appear more like impostures. The generalisations of his long book *Crowds and Power*, accepted by IM as evidence of his polymathic genius, sound to a later generation like an over-confident, clever man who has not read quite enough.

Canetti was a Sephardic Jew, born in Ruschuk, Bulgaria, in 1905. His first language was Ladino. His polyglot merchant father moved to Manchester in 1911, where Elias learned English. In 1919, the year of IM's birth, the fourteen-year-old Canetti moved with his mother to Vienna where he learned German – the language he spoke, and in which he wrote, in grown-up life. It was in Paris that he met and married his long-suffering wife, but it was always understood between them that a genius required a gaggle of mistresses and adorers.

Canetti was a cruel man. Not only did he behave with physical violence to IM during the acts of love – incidents which often took place with his wife in the next room (Veza was required to bring in trays of coffee afterwards); but he was mentally sadistic. He openly mocked IM to their mutual friends, and quoted her copious letters to him. He held court in various Hampstead cafés and she was often to be found at his side, usually snubbed or ignored. It was no surprise, after a few years of the exhaustion of this, that IM should have sought the consolations of domesticity. Even when she told Canetti of the arrival in her life of John Bayley, however, the mage forbade intimacy between the affianced pair. On one visit to Paris, IM obediently insisted that JOB stay in a separate hotel.

In some senses, IM never broke free from the spell of Canetti, though their affair ended in the 1950s. Her novels, which now began to flow from her pen, are often haunted by the spectre of a Magician, a Lord of Power who exercises spiritual or erotic dominion over the weaker characters in the book.

In other ways it could be said that when she married, and moved to a large village house some fourteen miles to the north of Oxford – Cedar Lodge, Steeple Aston – IM had achieved some of the liberation felt at the end of *The Wind in the Willows*, when the weasels and the stoats had been seen off and Toad Hall repossessed; Ithaca had been regained, the suitors banished, and IM's wild, earlier selves could be transformed into the figures of fiction.

There was no doubt, among her large circle of Oxford friends, that marriage brought with it phases of very great happiness and calm. It was 1956 when she married. This was a time in England when even in bohemian households the principles of feminism had not very often taken hold. In Oxford, the male dons would bicycle down to dine in their colleges at seven o'clock most evenings, leaving their wives to eat baked beans on toast with the children. These wives were very often academics themselves, balancing the demands of domesticity with their tutorials and research.

Such balancing-feats would in IM's mind have been a waste of time. Instinct or luck led her to a man who would not expect her to cook or sew or keep house. Her own father, she once told me, did most of the housework and cooking, and was even responsible for buying her school uniform; so she was, like so many of us, looking about, however subconsciously, for a replication of home when she married. But as a writer she must have known that the ideal partner would be one who did not expect her to be a wife in conventional terms. As someone who was not by nature monogamous, she would also instinctively have sought a partner who could be left alone for days on end, safely buried in books and country. 'We were separate but never separated,' JOB once said to me, describing their relationship.

Cedar Lodge would today be considered a large house for two people. IM loved it passionately, and it was the last piece in the jigsaw puzzle which enabled her, after the mid-1950s, to have those long stretches of quiet concentration without which fiction cannot grow. The first two hectic novels, *Under the Net* (1954) and *Flight from the Enchanter* (1955), had been bestsellers, and had precipitated her to instant fame. A third, *The Sandcastle* (1957), was an oddly conventional *roman-à-clef* about her relationship with MacKinnon, by way of also being a somewhat malicious portrait of another pair of Oxford friends. All this could be regarded as apprentice-work: spirited, humorous and magnificently stylish work, but nevertheless beginners' stuff. It was with *The Bell* (1958) and *A Severed Head* (1961) that IM's mature voice was found. These are among her most successful works, both commercially and artistically, the latter being adapted as a highly popular stage play in the West End.

Her popularity stemmed partly from the instant readability of her stories, and from the fact that she was writing about the inner lives of men and women with a frankness which, to a somewhat pinched post-war generation, was marvellously liberating. Here were unhappily married couples who longed for, and usually had, affairs; here were homosexuals, agonised and otherwise. Above all, she analysed the ways in which men and women, in their erotic dealings and feelings, exercise power.

She needed the stability of Cedar Lodge and the happy companionship of JOB, perhaps, to be able to write these fables of erotic mayhem and misery. But she also needed a heart which was continually open to new experiences of love, hope, disappointment, lust. These are not distillations of emotion recollected in tranquillity. They are the outpourings of a woman who was 'all over the place', and subject, at any moment, to the whims and diktats of Eros.

As a young student she had written a fan letter to Samuel Beckett. 'Beckett's novel called *Murphy* became a sort of sacred text. There was only one copy which belonged to Denis Healey and he lent it to various people including me. I became enchanted by Beckett and I wrote saying that there was a copy of *Murphy* in the Buckingham Palace Road public library, and should I steal it? He wrote back saying, "Yes, I think you should steal it."' It was at first as an imaginative writer, rather than as a philosopher, that she aspired to make her name, and it was in some great European tradition of modern writing – Beckett, Queneau, Sartre and Canetti – that IM aspired to place herself.

When she did begin to publish novels and was placed by imperceptive critics beneath the umbrella of Angry Young Men, this was wide of the mark. It is hard to see much resemblance between IM's imaginative canvas and the blokeish, essentially narrow comedies of John Wain, John Braine and Kingsley Amis, all of whose first essays in fiction, funny as they undoubtedly are, are steeped in autobiography. From the very first, IM's use of her own experiences and life-sensations is altogether much more oblique. All novelists pretend to deplore the philistinism of readers who identify characters in the books with those in 'real life'. This is not necessarily simple dishonesty on their part, however, it being extremely difficult even for the writers themselves (in some cases especially for themselves) to see what uses the imagination has made of experience. That IM's novels reflect her experience is unquestionably true; but much of her 'experience' is lacking from the books altogether. There are, for example, no Dickensian or Proustian evocations of her childhood, which she described so frequently as 'a perfect Trinity of love', but which had no place in the fictive part of her brain. Nor do her novels depict that important, and perhaps most important, element of her emotional life, namely lesbian love.

Upon her marriage one formidable friend, Audrey Beecham, had remarked that 'Iris was one of us until that horrid little man took her away.' Audrey, niece of Sir Thomas Beecham, had been a heroine in the French Resistance, where her capacity for mimicry allowed her to impersonate various French types, from Burgundian peasant to Parisian intellectual; she claimed to have rabbit-punched Gestapo officers to death. A keen Anglo-Catholic, her pastimes included wrestling. Yet she herself had once been engaged to a man: Maurice Bowra. It was hard for their friends to know whether there was much affection on either side or whether he had formed the alliance simply so as to be able to mouth the one-liner, 'Buggers can't be choosers.'

IM was pursued by many men, had many lovers and was engaged, first to Franz Steiner, at the same time as having a 'semi-formal' engagement to the Catholic literary scholar and Fellow of Lincoln College, Wallace Robson, who clearly found it difficult to keep up with her emotional adventures. He described her as being 'quite ludicrously unfaithful' to him. JOB would seem to have been a more tolerant partner, but not so tolerant as to put up with a very public affair in Oxford. When, after only a year or so of marriage, IM was causing a scandal in her college, St Anne's, by having a tearful and much talked-about affair with one of her (female) fellow-dons, a crisis point had been reached. The Principal of the college felt that the situation could not continue without some resolution, and perhaps the resignation of one or both women. JOB, who had started the marriage having to contend with IM's continued attachment to Canetti, insisted by 1963 that his wife resign from St Anne's and take a job in London. She became a lecturer in philosophy not at a philosophical faculty, but at the Royal College of Art.

It was a liberating moment for her in many ways. She no longer needed to pretend to 'do philosophy' in the way that the Oxford syllabus required, or as the largely male, largely analytical philo-sophical school at Oxford practised the subject. She could, for the benefit of her non-philosophical pupils, talk about subjects such as Love, Art, God and The Good, which were of small interest to such figures as A. J. Ayer.

London in the 1960s was IM's golden time. She loved the music of the Beatles and knew all their songs by heart. Many would say that her most distinctive and successful novels belonged to this period: *A Severed Head,* whose formidable and demanding heroine Honor Klein was seen by many of their friends to resemble IM's friend Margaret Hubbard; *An Unofficial Rose, The Time of the Angels, The Nice and the Good, Bruno's Dream.* The last book, incidentally, with its happy, *homme moyen sensuel* hero Danby, grew out of the experience of an enjoyable association with the architectural writer Stephen Gardiner.

Canetti railed at her vulgar success, which riled him on many levels. She had, it is true, mysteriously failed to be the great writer that she wanted to become, but she had become a mirror to the age. As Auden said of Freud:

> To us he is no more a person
> Now but a whole climate of opinion.

For some years this really was a true description of the relationship between IM and her largely middle- or upper-class, largely metropolitan, largely well-educated readership.

By the time she was entering her sixth decade, her fluency was perhaps both a blessing and a curse. Her plots became repetitive, and her novels ran the dangers of self-parody. No one was more acutely aware than she of what had and had not happened to the career which had begun with such promise in the early 1950s.

In a remarkable novel, *The Black Prince,* IM confronted her own muse, and the nature of the fictive imagination. A central passage – central both in place and in importance – is occupied by a conversation about *Hamlet.* The Prince of Denmark, incidentally, is the Black Prince of the title, and when a history don at Oxford told IM that the phrase usually refers to the eldest son of Edward III, she was astonished. The conversation, or tutorial, about *Hamlet* takes place between Bradley Pearson, the narrator of the story, and his young protégée, with whom he is about to fall in love, Julian Baffin. Shakespeare was, Bradley maintains, at his most cryptic when talking about himself in the sonnets. Yet *Hamlet* is the most famous and accessible of his plays:

> because Shakespeare, by the sheer intensity of his own medi-tation upon the problem of his identity, has produced a new language, a special rhetoric of consciousness . . . He has performed a supreme creative feat, a work endlessly reflecting upon itself, not discursively but in its very substance . . . Hamlet is the tormented empty sinful consciousness of man seared by the bright light of art, the god's flayed victim dancing the dance of creation.

Myths, or great works of literature, were often used by Iris Murdoch as what another critic called scaffolding, around which she constructed her own tales. She used the myth of Vulcan, Mars and Venus in her first book *Under the Net*. Proust's *La Prisonnière* underpins *The Sea, The Sea*. *The Black Prince* is obviously enough a novel which concerns itself precisely with the nature of a writer's consciousness and identity and how this can be transmuted or transposed into Art.

More than most writers perhaps, IM played games with the notion of her own personality and consciousness. When ques-tioned, she dismissed Bradley Pearson's notions about Shakespeare's personality as 'one of those daft theories'. She claimed to have very little sense of herself, but it is obvious that this novel, as well as being a meditation in general on the nature of Art, is also a specific examination of her own daimon, of those aspects of her nature which fed into the novels.

The book is about two men, both of whose first names are those of well-known Shakespearean critics – Arnold Baffin and Bradley Pearson. The first's surname is a combination of Bayley and Boffin, Dickens's Golden Dustman. The second, apart from being a reference to a private joke (IM's typist once rendered her word Reason as Pearson throughout a philosophical essay), is a partial anagram of Shakespeare himself. The tale is 'edited' by Bradley's prison companion Mr Loxias – that is, the god Apollo – who is 'a notorious rapist and murderer, a well-known musical virtuoso, whose murder, by a peculiarly horrible method, of a successful fellow-musician made the headlines some considerable time ago'. In other words, the tale is filtered through the god who flayed Marsyas.

Arnold and Bradley are both writers. Arnold Baffin appears to have written the works of Iris Murdoch – 'He lives in a sort of rosy haze with Jesus and Mary and Buddha and Shiva and the Fisher King, all chasing round dressed up as people in Chelsea.'

Bradley, who is a much more reticent writer, despises Baffin for his fluency, though for one who prides himself on reticence and exactitude and whose manuscript is being edited by a god, he writes with surprising sloppiness. The phrase 'sort of' is repeated sometimes as often as six times in one paragraph: 'It was a sort of moment of illumination . . . He broke two sort of cups . . . The globe [a kite] seemed to glow with a sort of milky alabaster radiance.' 'The whole book,' says one of the 'postscripts', 'seems to me to be sort of off key'.

Yet once started, the novel is hard to put down and its readability must partly be explained by the fact that it is all coming from IM herself. The frivolity and almost absurd facility of Arnold is something of which she is acutely aware. Likewise, the self-deception of the would-be philosopher Bradley is something the god Apollo, in flaying her, lays bare. And the central emotional event of the book, an obsessive love for an androgyne girl called Julian, is described with an intensity and vividness which few readers of the story will ever forget – the evening at *Der Rosenkavalier* at which Bradley is so in love that he is sick outside the opera house will live in the memory. So too will his domestic arrangements, eating tinned curry, cold, direct from its tin, or filling a hot-water bottle direct from the tap – 'its soiled woolly cover smelt of sweat and sleep':

Feeding my hangover, I had consumed a lunch which consisted of three aspirins, followed by a glass of creamy milk, followed by milk chocolate, followed by shepherd's pie, followed by Turkish delight, followed by milky coffee. I felt physically better and clearer in the head.

The emotional texture of the book is what stays in the reader's mind so freshly. Bradley shaves and has a hairy chest, but one feels these to be thin disguises for the central intelligence of the book, which is lesbian sadist. All the women in the book are described in violently disparaging terms and even the object of his passion, Julian, is exposed as silly and badly educated. (She doesn't even know Latin!)

As for marriage, the book is a compendium of anti-marital sayings. 'All married people are unhappy.' 'I hate you, I hate you, I hate you. All spouses are murmuring that to each other all the time. It is the fundamental litany of marriage . . . People who boast of happy marriages are, I submit, usually self-deceivers, if not actually liars.'

No one was writing quite like this in the quarter-century of IM's literary career. Her novels are hit-and-miss affairs, but they have an unforgettable pungency. The novels that are misses are those when Arnold Baffin is on automatic pilot and IM has not hooked those deep places of her unconscious soul, which were the beds of her imaginative development. The hits are when she is, as in *The Black Prince*, quite shamelessly writing about herself.

In another novel, *The Sea, The Sea*, which won the Booker Prize in 1978, IM's imagination appeared to be wondering whether the blissfully happily married Bayleys of legend were in fact not prisoners of something rather hellish. She depicted herself as Hartley, an overweight, lower-class woman married to a peppery domestic tyrant in a neat little bungalow miles from anywhere. Not long afterwards, while IM was away on some conference or lecture tour, her husband bought a tiny suburban house in Oxford overlooking a noisy children's crèche.

In his memoirs of their marriage, JOB says that the house – in fact 68 Hamilton Road – was in Hartley Road, a clear reference to her as La Prisonnière of the suburbs. 'In almost every marriage,' wrote the narrator of *A Severed Head*, 'there is a selfish and an unselfish partner. A pattern is set up and soon becomes inflexible, of one person always making the demands and one person always giving way.'

IM was not happy in Hamilton Road. The normally sunny woman became in fact desperately miserable, tottering on the edges of despair and incurable depression. Asthma, always a problem, threatened to overcome her altogether. She became a little mad.

Reflecting in 1987 upon Sartre's book of Flaubert, IM said, 'I cannot help wishing that Sartre had devoted all that tremendous time-consuming energy to the writing of a 4000-page novel about everybody and everything.' She freely admitted, when asked, that she would like to write such a novel. Her books became longer, and her reputation began to wobble.

She and her husband continued, as if nothing were amiss, to entertain friends and to be entertained in return. Their Oxford circle was wide. Indeed, to avoid having to cook, JOB would accept invitations from anyone, and IM – as he once, and for once, truthfully observed – never found anyone boring. She went to London less often, and became increasingly preoccupied with philosophical work – *Metaphysics as a Guide to Morals*, which was a much-expanded version of her Gifford Lectures in 1982.

They moved house again to a larger, but still depressing, suburban villa, this time near the Oxford High School for Girls and next door to the writer Gillian Avery, who cooked for them and tried to help cleanse the increasing domestic squalor.

IM's writings and conversation on the subject of 'religionless Christianity' became repetitive as the alcohol intake increased. Her vision of a revived Christianity which admitted the non-existence of a personal God, but which worshipped a mystic Christ, was shared with almost every dining companion she met.

Her views, as well as becoming more mystic and quasi-religious, had almost become more simply conservative in party terms. She sided with the Democratic Unionists in Northern Ireland. When the young editor of the *TLS*, Jeremy Treglown, met her on the London train at the time of the miners' strike in 1981, he expressed some sympathy with the strikers. Fixing him with a stare which Treglown found faintly reminiscent of Kingsley Amis, she slowly said, 'I think they should be put up against a wall and shot.'

Her favourite modern philosopher became Roger Scruton, though she was troubled by his enthusiasm for hunting.

Some time during the 1990s her general 'dottiness' changed, and became something different. By 1996 it was clear that she was suffering from dementia, and in the following year this was formally diagnosed as Alzheimer's disease.

When she died, the obituaries and appreciations were adulatory. She was praised not only for her books, but for her qualities of goodness.

It was my dear friend Sarah Sands, by then deputy editor of the *Daily Telegraph*, who telephoned me to tell me the news of IM's death. I burst spontaneously into tears. I have never sobbed aloud, as I did on that afternoon, since childhood. It was in such a condition, I suspect, that many of the articles about her were written, for the next morning's newspaper. This was partly because of the wretchedness of her latter years, partly because we sensed, without being able to articulate the feeling very well, that a uniquely lovable being had been removed from us.

It was inevitable that those who only knew IM as an acquaintance should respond quizzically to some of the outpourings of grief and adulation.

In his 1999 diary, first published in the *London Review of Books* on 20th January 2000, under the headline 'What I did in 1999', Alan Bennett noted:

Dame Iris Murdoch dies and gets excellent reviews, all saying how (morally) good she was, though hers was not goodness which seemed to require much effort, just a grace she had been given; so she was plump and she was also good, both attributes she had been born with and didn't trouble herself over. I wonder if it's easier to be good if you don't care whether you're wearing knickers or mind, as Wittgenstein didn't, living on porridge; goodness more accessible if you're what my mother used to call 'a sluppers'.

Nobody explains (or seems to think an explanation required) how this unworldly woman managed to be made a dame by Margaret Thatcher and was laden with honorary degrees. Sheer inadvertence perhaps. In a later obituary it's said she approved of the Falklands War and one begins to see that for all her goodness and mild appeal she may have trod the same path as her contemporaries Amis and Larkin. Masked though she was in kindliness and general benevolence she may have ended up as far from her radical beginnings.

There are many questions begged here. Is support for Mr Major, however unpalatable to a gentle old Labour supporter, really less benevolent than support for Stalin, which is what was involved in the days of Amis and IM's 'radicalism'? Do you have to be 'radical', in Alan Bennett's definition of the term, to qualify as benevolent or morally good? Perhaps, in many eyes, you do.

As one who saw a lot of IM in the years before her descent into the abyss of Alzheimer's, I should say that these objections are not hitting a target. They are not describing the woman we knew. It is true that when she came to express 'views' about the state of the world, they were often 'right-wing'; but in an extra-ordinarily detached way. The truth is that she took almost no day-to-day interest in politics, and if a newspaper was in her hands, it would as like as not be the *Evening Standard*, which she read for the cartoon strip, Modesty Blaise.

We do not know how much 'effort' it costs anyone to be 'good'. It seems unfair to hold her to account for such an unknowable assertion. The more one knew her, the more one was aware of:

> that best portion of a good man's life
> [Her] little, nameless, unremembered, acts
> Of kindness and of love.

She was a generous friend to those who were down on their luck, and a reckless giver of money, both to individuals and to charities. 'Please could I have the £2000 *R[ed] & G[reen]* money now?' she scribbled in a characteristic note to her publisher in 1965. 'I want to lend some dough to a relation!' But 'goodness' is not to be measured solely in deeds. It would be absurd to say that one person was better than another because she had been more assiduous in visiting the sick, or the imprisoned, or the destitute. IM was more of a contemplative than an active sister, as befitted a writer. You did have the sense in her presence that life was a serious business, and that she was engaged in a struggle which was not necessarily either easy or complete. Those who read her novels, with their many exposures of marital unhappiness, might often have wondered whether her smiling and patient insistence that she enjoyed unblemished domestic felicity was not sometimes in itself a form of martyrdom. 'Every persisting marriage is based on fear' – *The Sea, The Sea*. Whatever we decide about that, we might think that the repeated public 'revelations' by her husband in recent years, which began before her death and which

101

have done so much to demean her in dignity, were not something that any domestic partner deserves from another.

Whether she qualified for the epithet 'good' is ultimately perhaps a pointlessly censorious question. She was certainly something rather different, a life-enhancing person. Though her acute mind ranged over the deepest questions of which thought is capable, she was by nature joyous. She had said a universal yes to life, and that was perhaps one reason why so many people felt joy in her company. There was also the palpable fact, which could not be analysed, that she was deeply lovable.

8

Life framed

A standard question, posed by most of those who interviewed IM about her work, concerned the relationship between her fiction and her philosophy. She resisted the notion that she wrote philosophical novels, or 'novels of ideas', even though, in almost all her books, at least one of the characters is interested in ideas. In many of the later books there is a character, such as Crimond in *The Book and the Brotherhood*, who is engaged in writing a philosophical work.

IM's philosophical writing is actually as distinctive as her fiction: that is, she did not attempt to write about philosophy in a manner or a language which even remotely resembled the essays in the field by her male contemporaries. Fascinated as she sometimes was by their lucubrations and cogitations, and much as she had enjoyed her philosophy tutorials with Donald MacKinnon, she was never interested in 'doing philosophy' in the dry and rigorous manner of other academics.

In a novel that IM much admired, *Wolf Solent*, by John Cowper Powys, the hero forms a passionate but, unhappily for her, platonic relationship with Christie Malakite, daughter of a bookseller in the West Country where he has taken up residence.

'I see you read Leibnitz, Miss Malakite,' he said. 'Don't you find those "monads" of his hard to understand?'

There follows a conversation about the philosophers which is apposite, highly, to the Murdochian 'philosophical novel'.

'I don't understand half of what I read,' Christie begins, speaking with extreme precision. 'All I know is that every one of those old books has its own atmosphere for me.' She says that the non-human abstractions of the thinkers she enjoys reading 'seem to melt . . . I don't think I regard philosophy in the light of "truth" at all . . . I regard each philosophy, not as the "truth", but just as a particular country, in which I can go about – countries with their own peculiar light, their Gothic buildings, their pointed roofs, their avenues of trees.'

She endeavours to explain to Solent that 'you get a sudden feeling of life going on outside' when you read certain philosophers. He responds eagerly with 'I know perfectly well what you mean. Philosophy to you and to me, too, isn't science at all! It's life mirrored and heightened. It's the essence of life caught on the wing. It's life framed . . .'

As they continue the conversation, her profile 'reminded him of a portrait of the philosopher Descartes'.

IM would not, with her conversational or purely reasonable self, have agreed with Christie Malakite. IM was, more and more, a Platonic 'realist' in philosophy, who thought more than mere 'atmosphere' could be derived from philosophical texts. She shared Kant's certainty in the reality of The Good, as something we have not made up for ourselves. On a deeper, imaginative level, however, she was wholly at one with Christie. It is on this level that philosophy works in IM's novels. One thinks, for example, of Pattie conceiving how horrible life would be if one viewed it through the lens of Martin Heidegger. Much more than that, however, IM's characters and fictions palpably come to reflect the felt life – 'the essence of life caught on the wing' of the thinkers who had captured her imagination.

I first became aware of this some twenty years before she died. I found myself near her at a dinner table, and she had lately come back from Italy where she'd given (I think, in Turin) a lecture.

'Was it in Italian, your lecture?'

'Yes. I got an Italian friend – Tino de Marchi – you've met him – to read it and correct it for me before I delivered it.'

'Was it a literary – a philosophical lecture?'

'Both.'

'I *wish* I'd kept up my Italian.'

'Oh?'

'Yes, I learned it, and went to Italy to do that course at the British Institute in Florence. Then I simply let it *go*.'

'But it is a reasonably easy language to get back, as it were, to pick up. One does it simply by reading.'

The conversation turned to other things. I forgot having uttered my wish that I'd kept up Italian.

About a week later my front-door bell rang. It was IM standing there.

'I won't come in, old thing, but I've brought you some books to be getting on with.'

They were: A *Practical Italian Grammar*, and her own copies of *Il Gattopardo* by Lampedusa and *La coscienza di Zeno* by Italo Svevo. Both books were dear to her and, since she gave them to me and talked, subsequently, of her love for them, I have seen echoes of them both in her novels – particularly of the Svevo.

Now, I'm sure that IM's impulse to give me the books and her natural pedagogic desire to help a friend brush up a language were quite spontaneous and needed no explanation. I thought at the time, however, of an anecdote she had told me some years earlier, about Simone Weil.

Someone said to Simone Weil, in a social, chatty way, not really meaning it – 'Oh, I wish I knew Greek!' The next day he heard the clink of a bicycle being leaned against his railings. The earnest, bespectacled figure of Mlle Weil stood on his doorstep clutching sharpened pencils, two Greek grammars, two *Iliads*, two exercise books.

To describe Simone Weil as an influence, either on IM's books or her life, would encourage a painstakingly careful trawl through the non-fiction and the novels to identify scenes, passages, to identify moments when we sense the French thinker's hand. This exercise has been done, triumphantly well, by Gabriele Griffin, in *The Influence of the Writings of Simone Weil on the Fiction of Iris Murdoch.** It persuasively reveals the extent to which IM was haunted by Simone Weil.

To be touched by Simone Weil at all, however, is not to be won over to this or that specific idea so much as to be scorched by something like love.

I know, from many conversations with IM, that she was as haunted as I am by the figure of Simone Weil herself. In order to convey something of Weil's importance to IM, it is probably necessary to sketch a picture of her short life and career. The letters Weil wrote from London in her thirty-fifth, and last, year

---

*Mellen Research University Press, San Francisco, 1993.

of life, in 1943, reveal an appreciation of English humour, English pluck during air-raids and, most improbably in some ways, the jolly atmosphere in the pubs. It is a strange thought that the thirty-three- or thirty-four-year-old Simone might have gazed through the smoky atmosphere of some crowded bar and seen the twenty-three- or twenty-four-year-old IM flirting with colleagues at the Treasury or crying into her pint over the end of an affair. (Both women worked quite close to one another, during the brief interlude when Weil was working for the Free French at their headquarters in Carlton House Gardens and IM at the Treasury in Whitehall.)

Born into a prosperous, agnostic, bourgeois family in 1909 (her father was a much-respected doctor), Weil had brilliant school-days. She attended the Lycée Henri IV, a few hundred yards from her parents' home in the Boulevard St-Michel, and was taught philosophy by the legendary Alain (whose actual name was Emile Chartier), the most celebrated philosophy teacher of the Third Republic. He was a radical in politics (he had been a Dreyfusard) and, though a pacifist, he had served as a foot-soldier in the First World War to show solidarity. He was an agnostic with a deep reverence for Christianity, a rationalist in the mould of Plato and Descartes. He saw it as a political duty to weaken strong govern-ment. Thus, he sided with the proletariat in their struggles, but deplored Socialism. All these ideas, and above all his intellectual vigour, had their effect on his most brilliant pupil.

After the École Normale, Simone Weil taught in various provin-cial lycées, at Le Puy, Saint-Étienne and Auxerre. It had always been part of Alain's teaching that practical work should accom-pany intellectual. From the first, at Le Puy, Weil would fall foul of her headmistress, by taking manual work in her spare time and by her involvement as a revolutionary anarchist in the struggles of her fellow-workers. She was always close to the Communists but could not join them, not least because of what had happened in Soviet Russia. 'In Russia the employer is gone, but the factory is still there. It makes no difference.'* She took a year out from teaching to work in various factories near Paris and experienced for herself the dehumanising drudgery of life on the production-line. She took part in protests and factory sit-ins, but at Trade Union Congresses she warned the Syndicalistes of the murderous nature of Stalin's regime, and she was unimpressed by Trotsky on the one occasion when they met. She went, as a pacifist witness, to the Spanish Civil War in the uniform of the anar-chist militia and, obviously, yearned for the victory of the Republic, while seeing the inevitability of its defeat. Even from the beginning, however, Weil's response to the sheer degrada-tion and tragedy of most human lives was one that transcended politics.

In one of her finest essays, 'The Iliad, Poem of Might' ('L'Iliade le Poème de la Force'), she quotes the scene when Andromache orders hot baths to be prepared for the returning Hector, her beloved and heroic husband, from the battlefields in the plains of Troy, unaware of the fact that Hector is dead, his corpse dragged round the Achaean camp by the horses of Achilles:

Foolish one!
        exclaims Homer,
She knew not how far from hot baths

---

*Simone Weil, *Lectures on Philosophy*, Cambridge University Press, 1978, p.148.

The arm of Achilles had felled him because of green-eyed
    Athena.

Weil adds, 'indeed he was far from hot baths, this sufferer. He
was not the only one. Nearly all the *Iliad* takes place far from
hot baths. Nearly all of human life has always passed far from hot
baths.'

Weil's magisterial reading of the first great work of European
literature went unpublished in her lifetime, as did nearly everything else she wrote. She had intended it for publication in 1940.

By then, France had been defeated by Germany, and the great
theme of her essay, and of the *Iliad* itself, how individual human
freedoms, human lives, are reduced by Force to the status of things
– as corpses or as slaves – was coming to pass on the European
land-mass from the east of the Soviet Union to the English
Channel.

Her love affair with Greece, and with Homer and Plato in particular, was interrupted, and changed, by a spiritual encounter of a
different kind, the mystical certainty that she had known Christ.

In IM's novel *Nuns and Soldiers*, Anne Cavidge's vision of Christ
is powerfully derivative of Weil. Anne's spiritual journey is not a
copy of Weil's, but it is flavoured by Weil's ardour, intensity. As
a young student, 'she took to a fervent belief in a personal God,
a personal Saviour, with an ease which took her friends' breath
away'. There are innumerable differences between Anne and Weil;
Anne becomes a nun, Weil refused to be baptised; Anne loses her
faith, Weil's mysticism deepened as she approached death, tuber-
cular and starving, aged thirty-four; Anne is of English Christian,
Weil of agnostic French Jewish, background. But you *feel Weil* in
the book.

If we knew how novels came into being, it is possible that we should not need to read them. Clearly, they are an example of the primitive storytelling instinct of the human race, that instinct which recognised, primally, that myth, epic, religion were responses to the universe nourished more fully by story than by ratiocination. Plato, who banished the poets from his imaginary Republic, was himself a storyteller, a mythopoeist, but he wasn't a novelist. Novels came into being at the same point in the history of literature as modern biographies. They derive not as myth does, from archetypes common to all (though they can draw upon myth): they derive from the personal. Anyone could tell you the story of Orpheus and Eurydice. Different poets and storytellers would give it a special twist, but its mythopoeic power would haunt you even if it were conveyed artlessly. Richardson's *Pamela* can only come alive because of Richardson. *Pickwick* retold by another storyteller would not be *Pickwick*.

This this-ness, the special quality of every novel, derives from, and is entwined with, the personality of the novelist. IM did not, in inventing the figure of Anne Cavidge, draw a portrait of Simone Weil. It would be closer to the truth to see Anne Cavidge as the figure IM would have become had she been through Simone Weil's range of experiences.

Happiness sought anywhere but in God tends to corruption. That sentence is pure Weil. But as the Anne Cavidge meditation at the end of the novel progresses, it becomes more characteristically Murdochian:

This, which had once been doctrine for her, she held to now simply as a personal showing. She had been right after all, and the events of the last year had confirmed it, to think that she had been irrevocably spoilt for the world by God. And spoilt, and rightly spoilt, even though she no longer believed in Him . . .

There was no God, but Christ lived, at any rate her Christ lived, her nomadic cosmic Christ, uniquely hers, focused upon her alone by all the rays of being.

The philosopher or the seeker *tout court* might ask when confronted by the writings of Simone Weil: how much of this is true? Such a reader would – when confronted by her assertions that there are no Latin epics, or that the Lord's Prayer was originally delivered in Greek – very likely feel the force of her difficult personality and be irritated or enraptured, or both. The novelist when reading Weil absorbs her, imagines what it would be like to be her, *pretends to be her*. Much of IM's reading of philosophy takes form in the setting of fiction. She is in this respect very like Christie Malakite and Wolf Solent: philosophy isn't a science at all. It's the essence of life caught on the wing. It's life framed.

Two

1

Considers herself Irish

It is time we did something about Iris in Ireland. She was born in Dublin and considers herself Irish. Our Irish sales are appalling for her books.

Memo from Carmen Callil, Managing Director,
Chatto & Windus, 25th October 1988

Like a Grand Master who could move to checkmate in three or four swift moves, she could weave the talk back to Ireland very quickly when the whisky wanted her to do so. Here's an exchange I recorded in a notebook in 1978. I said that I should like to be able to speak Welsh. It was the language spoken in this island before the arrival of the Germanic tribes. I'd like to be able to read the legends in the Mabinogion and *The Black Book of Carmarthen*.

IM	I think it is a wickedness to teach a child Welsh.
ANW	At all – or as a first language?
IM	(Pausing quite a long time): At all. Think of the

time it takes to learn a language. Consider how isolating it would be to think in Welsh when you might know German or French, languages in which great literature and philosophy have been written. Only a few hundred thousand – at most a few million people – know Welsh.

ANW Wouldn't that argument preclude learning Norwegian – or conversational Hebrew – or Dutch?

IM If you are Dutch you have to learn *another* language.

ANW Exactly – it improves your language skills. The more languages you learn, the greater your facility. If a child grows up with Welsh . . .

IM It will have no language skills whatever. You might as well teach it Irish – a language which *no one* speaks, but which they pretend is a spoken language. Ah, my benighted country! Bloody Ireland!

And we were off.

J. R. R. Tolkien once wrote an essay about his friend C. S. Lewis entitled 'The Ulsterior Motive'. It examined the psychological phenomenon of Lewis the sensitive literary critic, the man who could read the great Catholic poets of the Middle Ages with as much pleasure as he read those of the English Renaissance, suddenly being replaced, with a jutting of the jaw and a new harshness of tone, by a Member of the Orange Lodge.

The Ulsterior Motive was noticeable in IM too, the more so as the years went by. One grew to dread the subject of Ireland arising at dinner, because once she was on to the Emerald Isle, two uncongenial forces appeared to take possession of her troubled, hot face:

a need to claim an inheritance with Oirish literary chic (Beckett and all) brawling with sheer Paisleyite prejudices. My copy of *The Red and the Green* says, 'Iris Murdoch was born in Dublin and, although most of her life has been spent in England, she still calls herself an Irish writer.'

In 1990, IM told me that this novel is the only published novel of which she felt ashamed. When I asked her to expand, she said that it appeared to glorify Irish nationalism and, by extension, to give a romance to the present-day Republican terrorists.

A few years before she made this judgement, she was invited to Maynooth, the large Catholic seminary just south of Dublin, to address the young aspirant-priests on the subject of Plato and the Sovereignty of Good.

I have known several academics, Protestant and Catholic, who have opted to mark Irish exam papers because of the final examiners' meeting, held at Maynooth, which is followed by the celebrated Maynooth dinner. Even hardened drinkers such as Professor Richard Cobb have been impressed by the amount of whiskey offered to the guests and by the subsequent duration of the hangover. One can imagine that when IM was entertained by the priests, they were generous hosts, and though she liked to drink white wine as an aperitif, followed by lashings of red, she would never turn down the offer of a glass or two of whiskey as an evening grew late. I only have her account of this dinner. She said, 'When I looked up and saw these rows of young faces – *priests* – I said, "Look here! You've asked me here to talk about the Good, and I have a very simple question for you – Do you support the IRA?"'

It would seem as if the mayhem which ensued was of a highly satisfactory level, with some raised voices, and flushed faces, though no actual smashing of the furniture. IM liked to remind anyone who would listen that the Roman Catholic Church actively supported the IRA, gave shelter to terrorists in its monasteries and condoned murder.

JOB, never more like Mr Dick than when Miss Trotwood was roused to what he deemed righteous anger, cheered her on. Literally. 'Bravo! Iris, let them have it!'

I recall someone saying in her presence that he could not see why the Protestants in the North so much objected to the notion of a United Ireland.

'Do you know,' IM asked belligerently in reply, 'that every single school – EVERY school – in the Irish Republic is a Roman Catholic school? These good people,' her voice was now shaking with emotion, 'these God-fearing good Protestants, you are asking them to have their children taught by NUNS.'

'Would that really be so terrible?'

'Okay!' she said with a sudden splurge of anger. 'Let your children be sent to a Nazi school, and then I'll ask you if you think *that* is so terrible.'

She identified entirely with the Protestants of the North, and regarded the Reverend Ian Paisley with indulgent affection.

It could be said that there was nothing inconsistent about all this, nor about the desire to be considered an 'Irish' writer. Nevertheless, there seems something a little *voulu* about the description of herself as Irish, technically accurate as it may have been. To say, in the book-blurb, that 'most of her life was spent in England' implies that at least some of it was spent elsewhere. She left Dublin as a tiny babe in arms and only returned to Dublin Bay for two-week summer holidays with cousins.

* * *

Elizabeth Bowen saw herself as one of IM's early champions, as she made clear on each of the occasions that she and I met. She also, without needing to be overtly snobbish about this, felt that as an Ascendancy *grande dame*, a Bowen of Bowen's Court, she had exercised a very proper patronage towards a fellow-Irish Protestant of much more modest origins.

In Victoria Glendinning's biography of Bowen there is a photograph of IM having dinner at a small round table at Bowen's Court, with Mrs Cameron, Lady Ursula Vernon and suchlike grandees. IM can, and I'm sure always could, hold her own in any company, but it looks a frosty little scene. Alan Cameron, Elizabeth Bowen's husband, was assumed by many of the novelist's friends to be a figure in her past, if not actually dead. Peter Quennell told me of a dinner he had attended at their house on the edge of Regent's Park. Stumbling towards the loo in the middle of the meal, Quennell opened a door and found he had mistakenly opened the cupboard under the stairs. Mr Cameron was sitting there with a tray on his knees, mournfully eating a solitary supper among the mops and vacuum cleaners. In fact, the Camerons were a devoted pair, and she relied upon him, but he was not so socially voracious as his wife.

IM never put her husband under the stairs, but for the first quarter-century of her married life she was to behave, when it suited her, as if he had a comparably shadowy existence.

What of this Irish business?

IM and I were once having a conversation about prison. She was a law-abiding child who did not get into trouble at school, slavishly obeying the rules. I appeared to be law-abiding, but would suddenly find myself getting into real trouble. This happened at both of my schools. At my prep school, expulsion was threatened when I suddenly erupted with rage and threw a plate of hot porridge at the headmaster's wife. At Rugby, similar instances of rebellion suddenly showed themselves, of total and anarchic refusal to accept the system. Knowing this streak in my outwardly conformist nature, I'd therefore always had at the back of my mind the fantasy, or half-belief, that I would find myself on the wrong side of the law in grown-up life and go to prison for it. How would one cope with the other prisoners? How would one manage to disguise the irritating voice? I could do a plausible North Country accent, and estuary English, but . . .

IM immediately began to speak in stage Irish.

'Sure, and I'd be all right, they'd be thinking here was the broth of an Irish girl . . .'

She spoke in this accent for the next twenty minutes, copiously refilling and draining her glass as she did so.

In *The Philosopher's Pupil*, someone says, 'You're just pretend Irish,' only to receive the reply, 'All Irish are pretend Irish.'

This isn't true. We all know that most Irish are real Irish. There are, however, strange beings who pretend to be Irish for one reason or another. Micheál Mac Liammóir is the most famous case, an actor who was most celebrated for his impersonations of Oscar Wilde, but who was also a professional Irishman. He claimed to have been born in Blackrock, a suburb of Cork. In reality he was born at no. 150 Purves Road, Kensal Green, London NW10 and during his childhood years his name was Alfred Wilmore.* There was no ancestral connection with Ireland whatever and the name Mac Liammóir does not appear in the lexicon of Irish clans and families.

---

*See Christopher Fitz-Simon, *The Boys*, Nick Hern Books, 1994, pp.21–2.

I was told this by Honor Tracy, a friend of IM's, who was herself a phoney Irishwoman, having been born in England of, I think, English parents, certainly of one English parent. Her original name was Honor Lilbush Wingfield. She converted to Catholicism, adopted an Irish brogue and made her literary reputation out of comic tales exposing the mild corruption, the superstitions and absurdities of rural Irish life. Honor Tracy was destitute at the end of her days, and in great pain with her eyes and her gut. If she took a drug to alleviate the pain in her eyes, it exacerbated her stomach ulcers, and if she took analgesics for the ulcers, it increased the pain in her eyes. IM got her into an Abbeyfield home in Oxford, and, believing me to be a quasi-vicar character, organised me into being Honor's visitor and companion. This I did for most weeks in the last year or so of her life.

Milton was 'cheerful, even in his gout-fits and would sing'. Honor, blind like Milton, was also capable of cheerfulness more or less to the end, though the cheer was often laced with appalling malice. IM had helped her for years with money, and with practical kindness towards the end, finding her nursing and care, and paying for her to have talking books from the RNIB. Given this fact, one might have thought that Honor could have repaid this by always having kind words for her old friend. Not a bit of it. She saw IM and JOB as ridiculous figures. This, to me, was a heresy! Until hearing Honor's malice, it had never occurred to me that IM was anything but a great and serious philosopher and, for all her unevenness, the best novelist of her generation, while the Bayleys were a loving married couple who were the envy of all their friends.

Honor, I'm afraid, rather punctured this vision for me. Of course I exaggerate, and my reverence for JOB and IM was not quite as unrealistic as I have suggested. But I did place them on a pedestal, and Honor's refusal to do so was certainly a revelation.

She said that it was easy to be a 'perfect couple' if you weren't really a couple. IM, she insisted, was basically lesbian, though she had affairs with men when it suited her to inject yet more drama into her life. JOB did not even know what sex was, Honor would aver, with gales of laughter. 'Iris has made a fool of him all her married life.'

There was much more such talk.

I have come to the view that no one is able to tell 'the truth' about a marriage. There are many truths, and most of them are invisible to the closest friends and family of the marital pair. Some of the 'truths' are hidden even from the man and woman themselves. I don't particularly want to know 'the truth' about the Bayley marriage, though in so far as JOB has made it public knowledge, and a film has been made about it, the matter is clearly rather more than just prurient private curiosity on my part.

Honor Tracy did not admit to being a bogus Irishwoman. On the contrary, she spoke as if she were as Irish as shamrock and Guinness. She had one very characteristic set-piece anecdote about herself spending a few months in Belfast when she was working for the *Irish Times*, in order to write a series of articles about the way of life in 'The North'.

Every Sunday, she would slip into the Martyrs' Memorial Church and join the huge throngs of people who had assembled to hear the Reverend Ian Paisley. She loved every second of the great booming sermons, the references to the blood of the Saviour, the denunciations of the sons and daughters of perdition who had worshipped the Whore of Babylon on the Seven Hills of ROME!

After about four weeks, Dr Paisley paused in the middle of his homily and looked at the congregation of several thousand people.

'And we shud alwusss like to extend a warm welcome to our Vuzutuss!' he said. 'It might inturusst yer tae know that we have a VUZUTTA this morning frum DUBLIN! And she uz a RUPARDA un the *Airish Tayums* und, thuss uz also vurry unterusstun, she uz a MUMBA UV THUH ROMAN' – his huge banana finger began to gesticulate and to point in the direction of Honor, who then felt very small – 'CATHULUK CHORCH!'

Honor was naturally amused that IM always described herself, in the mini-biographies that adorned her paperbacks, as 'born in Dublin of Anglo-Irish parents'.

When I came to attempt my biography of IM, it was over the Irish question that we began to come unstuck. Word got about in late 1988 that I had been nominated the 'official' biographer. It was then that I began to hear from Arthur Green, a retired Civil Servant living in Portadown, whose remarkable pastime, during the last how many years, had been to study the surnames in the novels of Iris Murdoch. He had written a learned monograph on the subject, demonstrating beyond question that very many of the names in her fiction are drawn from IM's own family.

It was Arthur Green who first pointed out to me how many family names IM used in her fiction. In *The Unicorn*, for example, there is a character called Effingham Cooper. IM's mother was the daughter of Effingham Lynch Richardson, and grew up in the house of her grandfather Robert Cooper Richardson.

IM's conviction that her mother's family were 'squires' must have come from somewhere and the likeliest source is Rene herself. There is a form of intellectual or inverted snobbery which despises snobs. But snobbery has produced some of the greatest literature. As well as Proust and Evelyn Waugh, one thinks of Shakespeare who, if Katherine Duncan-Jones is to be believed, was obsessed by his own lack of gentility.[*]

I began to correspond with Arthur Green. It was clear that he was very interested in IM's family, and had met most, perhaps all, of her extant relatives in Belfast and its environs. By now, IM and I had begun the task of writing her life.

She was remarkably good at fielding questions which had the smallest bearing on matters of fact. Our interviews, some of which were recorded, some of which I transcribed, were not unlike Cardinal Newman's *Apologia pro Vita Sua*. That is to say, it was an autobiography of opinions. She spoke at great length about what had drawn her to the Left in politics. It sounded like good stuff while she was saying it, because she was an eloquent woman, who spoke in good vigorous prose and with decided tones. When one came to examine what she had said, however, and tried to sieve it for anything that could conceivably be of interest in a 'biography', there was nothing there about *her*. The wickedness of the Fascist dictators; the incredible bravery of those, such as Frank Thompson, who gave their lives to resisting them; the wreckage of human lives caused by the events leading up to the war, and by the persecution and slaughter of Jews in particular . . . All this was unexceptionable stuff in its way, but it did not tell me very much about IM herself. When one asked her about Frank Thompson, for example, or Franz Steiner, she could only speak of them in hyperboles. There was no suggestion that she would describe their friendships and loves, or produce anything

---

[*]See *Ungentle Shakespeare*, Arden Shakespeare, 2001.

like letters with which one could enflesh the bones of the book.

Fair enough – I did not want to pry. But there was a growing sense, even after a few months, that IM, in asking me to be her biographer, was really asking me to make bricks without any straw.

Arthur Green came, in these circumstances, like an angel from the skies. Here was a man who was giving me a huge amount of factual information, and urging me to come over to Ireland to meet the Murdoch relations. In particular, he urged me to come while Iris's Aunt Ella was still alive, a woman who had devoted her life to the attempted conversion of Egypt to evangelical Christianity. On her return to Belfast at the age of about sixty, she had married a man who, said Arthur Green, he would tell me more about when we met. He had laughed good-humouredly down the telephone and said that Ella's husband had been 'more or less a gun-runner for the Loyalists'.

IM had by now filled several tapes with accounts of her family holidays in Ireland, her serenely happy relationship with both her parents and the very great distinction of her mother's pedigree.

'What about your family in Ireland today?'

'There is none,' said IM.

'What – no one? No cousins, for example?'

'No, my father came to London at the time of the Irish Free State being set up, and we never really went back – except for holidays, of course.'

'But, you mentioned lots of cousins in those tapes.'

'Did I?'

'And your father had two sisters.'

'Ah! Ella and Sarah.' A beneficent smile.

'Still alive?'

'No, alas! They both died a long time ago.'

'So there'd be no point in going to Ireland to try and meet your family?'

'No, none.'

'I thought I might go and look up the house, and then perhaps go to Dublin and look at 59 Blessington Street.'

'Well' – very cautiously – 'you could do that, but I don't think you'd find out much.'

I should have come clean with IM and admitted that Arthur Green had already arranged for me to meet her Aunt Ella, her cousins Miss Muriel Chapman and Mrs Sybil Livingston, and her other cousin Max Wright, a philosopher, during a tour of 'Murdoch's Ireland', north and south of the border.

When she found out that I had done this, she was furious.

'Mr Arthur Green,' she managed to make the syllables of the man's name sound unclean, 'is a very BAD man.'

She was red, shaking; her jaw jutted out.

'I believe,' said George Bernard Shaw, 'that while we are alive we lie to protect ourselves from the truth itself. The lies we tell are part of the life we live and therefore part of the truth.'*

On my return from Belfast I gave her some photographs which her Aunt Ella had given to me, and her father's medals. She said she forgave me and I think this was half true.

Her Aunt Ella, who died shortly after I met her, was in a nursing home at the time and was all but blind. She bore the most disconcerting resemblance to her niece, sharing with IM a seemingly ageless quality. She had no dark secrets to reveal, any more than

---

*Michael Holroyd, *Bernard Shaw: The Search for Love*, Chatto and Windus, 1988 p. 276.

did IM's charming cousins Muriel and Sybil, one a dentist, the other a teacher, respectable intelligent women living in Belfast and with, on the whole, affectionate memories of IM.

They qualified their affection only in two areas. During the late 1940s, one or both of them, firm Prots as they were, went to stay with IM's parents in Chiswick. IM was there, and surprised them by saying that she would like to take them to church on Sunday morning. They had always understood that church was not especially IM's type of thing, though her parents, said Sybil and Muriel, were occasional church-goers. Rather than catering for her cousin's Protestant tastes and views, IM took them to an extreme Anglo-Catholic church, full of incense and mystery. They were both very much shocked, not so much by the Romish ceremonials as by the expression on IM's face. They felt there was something unseemly about using church-going as an occasion for a malicious trick.

Their other complaint was that IM had not kept up with them as much as she could. As children they had been friends, and until her middle age, if she did come to Northern Ireland, which wasn't often, she would go and see them.

'But when she came to get her honorary degree at the Queen's University, she didn't even write to tell us about it. We read that she'd been here in the local papers, and that she'd been to stay afterwards with the Marquess of Dufferin and Ava.'

I did not ask them, since there was no need, for their views on Iris's desire, in book after book, to describe herself as being of 'Anglo-Irish' parentage. The phrase, which suggests the rich man's flowering lawns of Yeats's poetry, is a good deal more chic than the respectable suburbs of poor old Belfast.

* * *

Ireland had been the subject where IM and I came closest to a quarrel. Some raw nerve had been touched. If we are prodding about with our scalpel, trying to find the part of a writer's soul which produces their best work, then we start looking near the raw nerves.

The Unicorn is not merely IM's best bit of Irish fiction: it contains, in its first half, some of the best work in her entire oeuvre. Freely borrowing from Daphne du Maurier's *Rebecca* and from *Lady Chatterley's Lover*, IM concocted, in this fantasy about a creepy household on the west coast of Ireland, a highly distinctive and completely Murdochian creation.

There is another pair of writers who helped the book into being, and they are Elizabeth Bowen and her own master, Henry James.

'What are we going to do, you and I, about Mrs Crean-Smith?' Effingham had not expected this. Or had he? Had he not, ever since he had set eyes on the clever long-nosed girl, expected to be thus brought to the point?

Shown this passage 'blind', would not most literate people guess that the sentences were Bowen at her most Jamesian? The story of a governess arriving in a strange household, a middle-class girl of lower-class origin feeling awkward in an Irish country house, obviously began with IM's own feelings of excitement and fear at staying in the unknown world of the real Irish ascendancy, Bowen's Court.

Marian, with her intense curiosity, and her combination of eagerness to make friends and social fear, is an obvious vessel for the author's own feelings. The setting of the scene, and the *mélange* of beautiful description, suspense and spiritual symbolism, are for the first half of the book handled with consummate brio. Mrs Crean-Smith, kept a prisoner in her own house, is surrounded by adorers who are also her prison-guards. Long ago, she had an affair with a neighbour. Her brutal husband found out, there was a scuffle, he fell down a cliff, but mysteriously survived. Henceforward the husband arranges for her to be kept at Gaze as a virtual prisoner – a fact Marian first recognises when she admires Hannah Crean-Smith's beautiful new shoes (their soles unworn), only to be told that they are seven years old.

The story descends into melodrama of the most ridiculous kind when Peter Crean-Smith returns home. He, his wife and her lover end up dead.

The weight which this melodrama is expected to bear – the theological, metaphysical weight – is too heavy. Yet the book contains insights which are as interesting as any modern disquisition on ethical theory by a professional philosopher. 'Freedom may be a value in politics, but it's not a value in morals,' says the Platonist Max Lejour, and it signals a very significant shift in IM's own thinking, away from the existentialism of Sartre towards the moral absolutism of Simone Weil, whom IM had started to read in the 1950s, and back towards the Plato whom she had found so uncongenial as an undergraduate.

'Good is a matter of choosing, acting,' says Effingham. The Platonist replies, 'That is a vulgar doctrine, my dear Effingham. What we can *see* determines what we choose. Good is the distant source of light, it is the unimaginable object of our desire.' This was to be IM's theme for the next thirty years. The two Irish houses in *The Unicorn* contain the bustling tweedy gardener Alice Lejour and the imprisoned Hannah. The Lejour house is called Riders, it is a place of action; the other house is Gaze, it is a place of contemplation. Good is not something we choose to do, it is something we see, we gaze upon it. God/Good is someone/thing which we wait upon. *L'attente* is at the basis of Weil's thinking; just as the later Heidegger said that his whole thinking was a kind of waiting.

It is easy enough to say how the novel falls apart. One explanation for its fracture, its descent into unintended farce, could well be simple impatience. IM wrote fast, but less fast than the workings of her imagination. By the time she had plotted *The Unicorn*, worked out the story and written 40,000 or 50,000 words, she was in all likelihood thinking of the next book – which was her other Irish tale, *The Red and the Green.**

Impatience is not, however, an explanation for why she created such a flawed work of art in *The Unicorn*. The truth is surely that this pluralist imagination was attempting to make a monist book. The lonely woman in her tower is all but a figure of allegory. 'Only the spiritual life has no story and is not tragic. Hannah [Crean-Smith] had been for them an image of God; and if she was a false God they had certainly worked hard to make her so.'

Hannah herself says, 'I lived in your gaze like a false God. But it is the punishment of a false God to become unreal. I have become unreal.'

The trouble, from an artistic point of view, was that Hannah Crean-Smith always was unreal. If there were a Platonist novel, it might be rather like the worse parts of *The Unicorn*.

IM did not abandon philosophy, but she was not at her best when writing purely philosophical novels. Like the great nineteenth-century novelists whom she read and reread so often, she would

---

The Italian Girl, the next novel after *The Unicorn* to be published, was written earlier.

increasingly attempt to write books in which ideas were depicted as living movements in the minds of living people, rather than books in which characters were merely symbols of ideas. Had she ever resolved her own philosophical questions, she would perhaps not have needed to write fiction. Dostoevsky the journalist was an ardent Orthodox Russophile and denouncer of atheists. Dostoevsky the novelist was both believer and unbeliever, the two wildly at war. IM could animate mutually contradictory notions in the pages of her fiction.

Ideas date as rapidly as clothes. The metaphysical preoccupations of the nineteenth century – and even those of the early and middle years of our own twentieth century – have an extraordinary deadness when we encounter them in the works of the great sages, on whatever side of the argument they happened to be. Newman's obsession with the origin of the Christian Church touches us as little as Nietzsche's fantasies about the *Übermensch*. Shaw's beliefs in a Life-force as God-substitute, or H. G. Wells's vision of an ever-increasing enlightenment as the human race discarded religion, are as peripheral today as the theories of their contemporaries Madame Blavatsky or Mary Baker Eddy.

And yet this is not because metaphysics do not matter. Whether there exists a world of value outside ourselves, whether it makes sense to speak of or to pursue The Good, these are matters of continuing importance whether we live in the time of the Gods or the time of the angels. I am sure that I am not alone in finding these subjects much more interestingly treated by novelists than by theologians or philosophers. Strauss's *Leben Jesu* – which changed George Eliot's life – is virtually unreadable today; likewise the sugary French equivalent, Renan's *Vie de Jésus*. Tolstoy's treatment of the same general ideas in the minds of Levin or

131

Nekhlyudov remains interesting. The assertion of old orthodoxy against all logical odds in the writings of Pusey or Lacordaire could not be more dull. Precisely the same attitudes, when struck in the pages of Dostoevsky, become as exciting as murder or sex.

I suspect that when the intellectual map of our own times comes to be sketched out, IM will occupy a position analogous to Tolstoy and Dostoevsky in this regard. Already, the 'ideas' which have gone the rounds in her lifetime, and with which she has been more than half in love, have started to curl round the edges. Thirties pro-Stalin Marxism is as out of date as the French existentialist Fifties equivalent; ditto all the French preoccupations of that era with self, nothingness and moral imperatives. The Death of God debate in the American universities now has, for those who can remember it, the same kind of retro charm as beads or flowers in your hair. If the full-blooded foreign versions of these fads seem dead, how much more the English watercolour reproductions, Colin Wilson's *The Outsider* or John Robinson's *Honest to God*. But in IM's novels, they are alive. When Don Cupitt is only a footnote in the intellectual history of our times, the priest's loss of faith in *Henry and Cato* will still seem real, as real as love, to the readers of IM, just as readers with no interest at all in nineteenth-century religious controversy burn the midnight oil reading *The Brothers Karamazov*.

This is because IM was one of those very rare novelists who could incorporate metaphysical speculation into the true stuff of fiction itself. She had some of the Dostoevskian gift of showing the way that these matters affect the inner lives of human beings. And for as long as

> someone will forever be surprising
> A hunger in himself to be more serious

132

the novel that treats of these matters will have more power to move than the naked messages, *tout court*, of self-appointed prophets and evangelists.

2

Philosopher – a girl among chaps

'If you can't be a man,' Mr Wye's expression said, 'the best thing for you to do is to read Plato.'

John Cowper Powys, *Maiden Castle*

This book is an attempt to get hold of IM, to prise out her secret, as one might use a pin to take a winkle from its shell. In some of the chapters I have been trying to match my own encounters with her, and the things which she said to me over the years, with the successes and failures in her fictions.

When she explained to me her embarrassment at reading her early journals, she said, 'Ah, but it was making my life into a story – and there's something so impure in that!'

One immediately thought of the first page of her study of Sartre, in which she is giving a résumé of *La Nausée*. The hero, Roquentin, is standing on the seashore, holding a pebble in his hand. Rather than throwing it into the sea as he had intended, he drops it in disgust. A fear of physical objects begins to oppress him. Then – here let IM continue in her own words: 'he looks at his own face

134

(*Left*) IM aged twelve in Dublin Bay, taken on holiday with her cousins. 'His various cousins, all of whom lived in Ireland, had served him in those long hated and yet loved holidays of childhood as sibling-substitutes...' *The Red and the Green*. IM gave me this photograph of herself.

(*Above right*) Another holiday, this time in North Devon, produced this oil painting, done in her early teens. IM was always a keen amateur painter. 'Anyone could do a Matisse, it would take slightly more skill to do a Vuillard,' she would say. (*Below left*) IM's parents at the time of their marriage. Like Andrew Chase-White, in *The Red and the Green*, her father was 'recently commissioned in the distinguished regiment of King Edward's horse'. (*Below right*) Hughes Murdoch in the back garden of Eastbourne Road, Chiswick, with their dog. IM often formed attachments to other people's dogs and they sometimes feature in her books, but she did not have one of her own in adult life. 'Too much of a tie' - JOB.

(*Above*) IM sewing costumes for undergraduate dramat

(*Above left*) IM met the painter Jean Robinson in Cambridge. With Jean and John Jones, a fellow of Merton College and later Professor of Poetry, she had a close, happy friendship.

(*Below*) John Jones and IM on a motorbike.

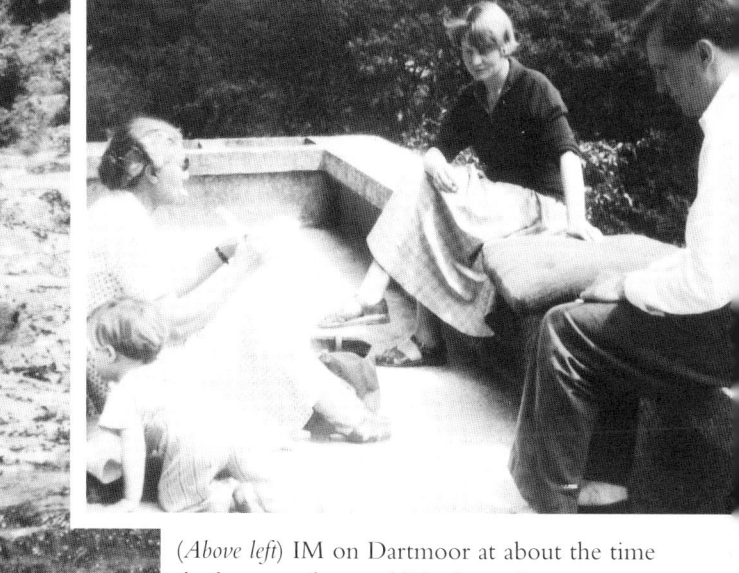

(*Above left*) IM on Dartmoor at about the time she began to be a published novelist.

(*Above*) IM with her god-daughter, Janet Jones and John Jones. She once told me how much she would have liked children herself.

(*Below*) 'Ireland's real past is the ascendancy.' *The Red and the Green*. IM liked to describe herself as being of Anglo-Irish descent, though the actual circumstances in which she grew up in England were considerably less grand than those of Bowen Court, where her friend the novelist Elizabeth Bowen resided. *Left to right*: Lady Ursula Vernon (the model for Mrs Crean Smith in *The Unicorn*), Major Jim Egan, Mary Lady Delamere, Elizabeth Bowen, Major Stephen Vernon, IM

(*Above*) Group photograph, Michaelmas Term 1969, New College Oxford. I am in the middle of the front row, on the right (facing) of the naval officer (Bim Kerr). Rick Stein, destined for fame as a TV chef, is in the back row, four along from the left.

(*Below left*) Christopher Tolkien, John Bayley's colleague at New College, who taught medieval English. 'What's the point of making people think if you make them think the wrong things?' (*Below right*) Me outside IM's birthplace – 59 Blessington Street, Dublin.

(*Left*) In 1966 the designer Julia Trevelyan Oman was looking for a film location in which to shoot Jonathan Miller's TV adaptation of *Alice in Wonderland*. At three pm on a warm afternoon in summer, she took these pictures of Cedar Lodge, Steeple Aston, IM's marital home and captured its meadowy wildness. JOB is seen, in braces, standing next to the Rector, the Reverend Michael Hayter.

(*Left*) IM and JOB at my wedding to Katherine Duncan-Jones, seen here talking to my father. He had often speculated, before I went to Oxford, on the identity of those who could possibly buy or drink 'British sherry'.

(*Below left*) *Left to right*: JOB, me, IM and Katherine at Mark Blackett-Ord's wedding to Lucy Neville-Rolfe. It was a jolly day together, clouded only by a strange explosion of anger on JOB's part on the subject of whether Shakespeare was bisexual. Here, evidently, the row has been forgotten.

(*Below right*) Philip Larkin, an exact undergraduate contemporary of IM, became my friend through a shared enthusiasm for the novels of Barbara Pym. Katherine Duncan-Jones took us to a Garden Party at Pym's (and her) old college, St Hilda's. *Left to right*: our daughter Emily, K D-J, Philip Larkin, me.

(*Left*) An impressive oil painting of IM by her friend Barbara Dorf. It captures those qualities of repose and sensuality which I recall in her features when I first knew her.

(*Right*) JOB, for most of the time a happy little pixie, had an aspect of childish petulance, captured well in IM's *The Sea, The Sea*, where she says that Ben Fitch looked 'grossly boyish'.

(*Above left*) Caroline Dawnay, the London literary agent whom IM called 'The Queen of the Upper Volta'. She telephoned me in 1988 to say that a London publisher was looking round for someone to write IM's biography. It was in response to this that IM asked me to undertake the task. (*Above right*) IM and JOB had a voracious appetite, both for social life, and for writers' conferences, free trips abroad, and the like. Seen here on a writers' delegation to Israel with Fay Weldon and Ted Willis.

(*Right*) Ruth Guilding, my second wife, and Percy, one of the dogs IM befriended in latter days (rechristened Spot by JOB).

(*Above*) Gillian Avery, IM
and JOB's devoted neighbour,
in Charlbury Road in the
sad last days.
(*Right*) IM, now ill, at the
wedding party for my second
daughter, Bee, to David
Runciman. Beryl Bainbridge is
to her right and Tony Quinton,
philosophical colleague and old
friend, stands behind.

(*Left*) IM alone,
about to walk away from us.

in a mirror, and suddenly it seems to him inhuman, fishlike. He subsequently makes the discovery: there are no adventures. Adventures are stories and one does not *live* a story.'

She claimed to have destroyed her journals not from the primitive fear (though she had this as well) that people would go round telling stories about her. That is not the point she was trying to convey at all. She was referring to her profound, existential distrust of the possibility of life resolving itself truthfully into a 'story'; of the danger when it does.

As well as examining her life as a novelist, it is going to be necessary to describe, if possible, her life as a philosopher. In this chapter I want to talk a bit about her life as an existentialist. ('I never was an existentialist,' she characteristically used to say whenever questioned about it in later interviews.) In a later chapter, it will be necessary to think a little about her unravelling, both as a thinker and as a writer. By that, I am emphatically not talking about the last phase of her terrestrial life in which she was suffering from Alzheimer's disease, but the period – really from about 1980 onwards, a good fifteen years before the onset of dementia – in which she seemed to lose the thread, both as a philosopher and as a novelist. JOB, in the lecture on Keats which established his reputation, made the paradoxical point that Keats is at his best when he is writing 'bad' poetry, and at his worst when he is trying to write Parnassian 'great verse'. It might be the case that some of IM's best *bits* are to be found in this later phase of writing. But if her novels do mysteriously fail to work, at any rate in the second part of her career, is it not possible that there is a philosophical reason for this?

IM was a professional philosopher whose job, during the nineteen fifties, was to teach philosophy at St Anne's College, Oxford, of which she was a Fellow. She was also a novelist, who during this phase changed her mind, or appeared to change her mind, about philosophy. An early absorption in the primary texts of continental existentialism – Martin Heidegger and Jean-Paul Sartre in particular – turned to a feeling of revulsion, certainly against Sartre. With Heidegger she became increasingly obsessed, though inwardly. In her latter days, she wrote and obsessively rewrote a book about Heidegger which in the event she decided not to publish.

Outwardly, in her published non-fictional work, she moved into her version of Platonism. Heidegger saw himself as a throwback to the pre-Socratic philosophers. He considered that Plato, who attempted in his Dialogues the demolition of the pre-Socratics, had been fundamentally wrong, that western philosophy had been on the wrong tack since Plato's day and that it was his, Heidegger's task to set it right.

What examples among novelists and playwrights can demonstrate what we mean by existentialist? Dostoevsky is the most considerable existentialist novelist. In each of his great books individuals, however much they yearn to lose themselves in love, whether love of Christ or of one another, are 'swept with confused alarms of struggle and flight', like the angst-ridden Victorian poet on Dover Beach. Existentialism is, or was, a philosophic viewpoint well suited to writing fiction in the modern era, in which men and women, cut loose from old faiths and restless until their hearts find new ones, confront their own confused destinies. The existentialist situation, which offends sober Anglo-Saxon philosophers by its tendency both to solipsism and to a distrust of Reason (if not downright irrationality), is well suited to fiction. Canetti's solipsistic sinologist, lost in his library of books, in *Auto da Fe*,

Joyce's Bloom, the central figures in Beckett's plays and in the plays of Pinter, the best Beckett-imitator, are all existentialist in the broadest sense, as were Sartre and Camus whose cult-books were, during the 1950s at least, the key texts of the existentialist creed.

IM was an existentialist, and her best novels are all profoundly existentialist books. Plato's view of novels would presumably have been the same as his view of poetry. Just as he banned poets from his fantasy police-state, or Republic, so he would have considered the novel to be a deplorable development. Plato thought this world is just a shadow of the other World, the True World of the Forms. Art, which imitates Nature, is therefore imitating an imitation, and the wise individuals are those who focus their attention on that Higher Reality. Plays, poems, by extension novels which try to make sense of life here and now by presenting pretend or imitation forms would be anathema to Plato. But behind this 'spiritual' objection to poetry there is also, fairly obviously, a political one. What the *Republic* advocates is a Tyranny in which individuality is subsumed to the 'net'.* The existentialist who, like Jake in IM's first novel, finds himself under this net will do all he can to get out of it. By celebrating, in whatever dark shades, the differences of human beings, their distinctness, novels are of their essence subversive to the Republic. The existentialist believes with Margaret Thatcher that 'there is no such thing as society'. The existentialist is almost by definition anarchic.

One says 'almost' since there is the curious fact that Heidegger, for however brief a period, was an enthusiast for National

---

*The image is Wittgenstein's.

Socialism, and never recanted or apologised, and Jean-Paul Sartre was a Communist. Sartre's, though, was the disruptive, stroppy, French sort of Communism; in an actual Soviet-style dictatorship, he would have been taken to the Gulag within seconds of the revolution. In the baffling case of Heidegger, one can choose between thinking that his Nazi phase was a lapse or arguing, as I would, that for all its protestations of love for *Ein Reich, Ein Volk, Ein Führer*, the Nazi ideology was essentially what a Jewish Christian theologian defined as 'pagan madness' and 'dark ecstatic nihilism'. Any Nazi 'society', if this view is true – war or no war – would have been bound to implode since it was in fact posited upon a non-social solipsism: every man for himself. Its mythologies were not 'saving mythologies' but destructive ones; its gods, like those of Richard Wagner, were programmed, fated to self-destruct.

But though an existentialist politics is probably self-contradictory, existentialist art is not. IM the existentialist or sort-of existentialist – which is all that any existentialist ever was – could function as a novelist very well. IM the ex-existentialist, the anarchic-humanist or would-be Christian seeker could very well have expanded into a richly humane, comic and broad-hearted novelist. This is something that she perpetually seems, in her books, as if she is about to do, but never quite does.

It would be a bold person who blamed Plato for this. But has there ever been a Platonist novelist? Is not such a concept self-contradictory at a very deep level? And if this is so, is this not one of the factors – one emphasises one only – which makes IM's trajectory such an odd one in literary history?

In order to see if this theory holds water, at the risk of wearying the reader who has no interest in twentieth-century philosophy, we must try a little to place IM beside her colleagues and contemporaries.

The Oxford Movement, a phrase known to more people than have ever troubled themselves to find out what it stood for, was a phenomenon of the 1830s. A tiny number of dons, religious conservatives by temperament, wrote a number of *Tracts for the Times*, in which they discussed ways of reviving the ancient practices of Christendom within the nineteenth-century established Church. They disapproved of the Whiggery of those governments that did such things as advance grants to train Roman Catholic priests in Ireland; and they deplored, above all things, the dangerous influences of German philosophy on the study of the Scriptures. Indeed, it was said at this date that there were only two men in the whole of Oxford who knew German.

Within a few years the leader of this movement, John Henry Newman, had decided that the task of recalling the Church of England to its 'Catholic' essence was a hopeless one and he had joined the Church of Rome. Thereafter, the younger dons breathed a sigh of relief. The 'Tractarian' vision of things became the preserve of a churchy sect, and the university could, about thirty years later than any comparable learned body in Europe, begin to read the great continental philosophers, above all Hegel. The grand British Hegelian tradition, which produced such philosophers as T. H. Green and F. H. Bradley, was born, and it would continue to dominate the British philosophical scene, really until A. J. Ayer published *Language, Truth and Logic* in 1936.

As I mentioned before, this book popularised the central doctrines of Logical Positivism advanced by the Vienna Circle surrounding Moritz Schlick, and it was basically a 'scientific' view of knowledge. Propositions that could not be verified by sense data, or by physical experiment (excepting the *a priori* truths of mathematics and formal logic), were in the strict sense meaningless.

It is not true that every philosopher at Oxford immediately became a logical positivist as a result of Ayer's book. (He was only twenty-five when it was published, and he would not return to Oxford from London, where he held the Chair of Philosophy at University College, in Gower Street, until 1959.) But Ayer and his followers managed to do two things to the Oxford philosphy school. First, they persuaded the next generation that the writings of the neo-Hegelian Idealists were to be consigned to the history books. There was to be no more talk of the Absolute. And the second thing which followed from this was that, with the abandonment of a metaphysic that could embrace 'everything which is', philosophy became much more modest in its aims. Philosophers could now concentrate on particular problems. Gilbert Ryle's book *The Concept of Mind* was in its way as influential as Ayer's, with its dismissal of the notion of the human mind as a 'ghost in the machine' and its discovery that God had been no more than 'a category mistake'.

It would be a gross simplification to say that the only philosophy being done at Oxford during IM's time as an undergraduate (1938–42) and, later, as a young don (1948 onwards) was of a rigidly logical positivist character. Her undergraduate contemporary Elizabeth Anscombe, later a Fellow and tutor at Somerville, was the translator of Wittgenstein's *Philosophical Investigations*, arguably one of the two most influential philosophical books, in world terms, of the mid-twentieth century; IM's old tutor MacKinnon continued to wrestle with Kant, and the insoluble great problems which Kant raised, until the 1960s; and P. F. Strawson's important book on Kant, *The Bounds of Sense*, while reading the great German metaphysician in a very English empiricist manner, strayed way beyond any of the confines which Ayer in his youth might have considered meaningful. With such figures as Stuart Hampshire, Isaiah Berlin, R. M. Hare, Anthony Quinton (in those days always chain-smoking, and pulled along by a bull-terrier bitch on a leash), Michael Dummett and others walking its streets, it could be said that the Oxford of the 1950s and 1960s had a greater concentration of philosophical talent than at any time in its history.

Nevertheless, there was a sense in the late Forties and Fifties, when IM first got her fellowship at St Anne's College, that Oxford philosophy was dominated by analytical or linguistic philosophy. If every philosopher in Oxford was not a logical positivist, there were many – and they were nearly all male, of course – who delighted in positivism's narrowness, and if they were not positivist, they looked about for some 'other 'ole' which was equally constricted in outlook.

No one was less like a Tractarian clergyman than A. J. Ayer, but in the wholesale dismissal of the major philosophical development in Europe since the 1920s, there was a sense of Oxford history repeating itself. Just as Dr Pusey kept the young High Church enthusiasts innocent of the slightest knowledge of Hegel in the 1830s, so there was no one in the Oxford philosophy faculty, except IM, who appeared to have read, or mastered, or considered important, the central texts and tenets of continental existentialism.

If you wish to catch the flavour of the way in which these Oxford men viewed the existentialists, read A. J. Ayer's essay

'Reflections on Existentialism', reprinted in *Metaphysics and Common Sense*. Two things are at work in this devastating account of Sartre, Kierkegaard and Heidegger. The first is a perfectly proper analysis of why Ayer believes that existentialism is philosophically at fault. The second, however, is the tone which suggests that sensible people, and above all sensible chaps, would not bother their heads with all this continental guff.

Existentialism takes as its starting point the simple fact that we exist. Whereas modern philosophy began with Descartes saying, 'I think, therefore I am', for Martin Heidegger and Jean-Paul Sartre the beginning must be that I am, or I would not be in a position to think, or indeed to do anything else.

Existence is, in philosophical language, prior to essence. But, says Ayer (following an argument of W. V. Quine, 'On What There Is'), the criterion for deciding whether a thing exists or not is by a definition an analysis of its properties. The apparently obvious priority of existence over essence is in fact a fallacy.

Are we not back here with a version of the old Realist-Idealist debate which knows its densest thickets in the pages of Kant? Ayer may very well be right in his analysis, but it is in the tone of his dismissals of Heidegger that we hear the notes which survive in Hume's *Dialogues Concerning Natural Religion*, in Gibbon, in Ryle with his joke about the Category Mistake.

My own father-in-law, Austin Duncan-Jones, an analytical philosopher, was once having a conversation with our old friend Francesca Wilson, a non-philosopher – a highly intelligent and well-read schoolmistress, who had devoted her life to the rescue of refugees.

'Don't you sometimes wish,' she sighed, staring into the fire, 'that we had a key to unlock the mysteries of the universe?'

'I don't know what you mean by key,' said the philosopher, 'I don't know what you mean by mystery, I don't know what you mean by universe.' That was the end of that conversation.

IM liked this story, but I think she empathised with the woman in it. I think she would have very much liked to possess the key which unlocked the mysteries of the universe; and it is precisely such a 'key' which metaphysicians have offered their adherents, whether Plato, with his definition of the universe in terms of unfolding layers of reality, with what we see and hear and touch now being mere shadows of things to come; or Hegel, with his ultimate sense of Geist encompassing Everything that Is in his *Phenomenology of Spirit*.

Ayer, in his 'Reflections on Existentialism', has great fun with Heidegger's belief that the philosopher will sometimes go 'beyond logic'.

Ayer was once asked by one of his wives what he thought of when he heard the word 'Paris'. He replied, 'I think of the letter P, the letter A, the letter R, the letter I and the letter S.'

The existentialist who heard the word *Paris* would have thought of a place where men and women, in the midst of everyday life, confront other levels of life, and by such experiences as love, or thinking about death, are faced with humankind's appalling anxieties and solitudes. IM, who had once seen Sartre in a bookshop in Brussels at the end of the war, loved Paris and spoke much in the post-war decade of her intention of spending a lot of time there. If male white English philosophers instinctually delight in the narrowness of formal logic, linguistic analysis and Humean reductionism, IM in her fantasy life enjoyed the thought of being, if not Sartre's mistress, at least a Simone de Beauvoir-type character who sat in cafés, smoked cigarettes and wrote long philosophical novels.

IM's book about Sartre is her first, and it is the first study of the French existentialist in English. It is a very good book. Some of her coevals in the philosophy faculty have described it as 'brave'; this is an epithet applied by men to books which they would have been ashamed to have written themselves. But there is nothing shaming about IM's wish to notice what was possessing the minds of most French- or German-speaking intellectuals in her time.

One should remember the scornful attitudes of the latter-day David Humes, however, as an ingredient in IM's decision to abandon her metaphysical roots. JOB might appear in the pages of his own recollections as a gentle little fawn, a fellow-babe in the wood. He is also a Fellow of two Oxford colleges, an Etonian and a former Guards officer.

He is very much what is called in Oxford a 'good college man'. When he was still at New College, he occupied a position which is what in other places of learning would be called Head of Department, or Director of Studies in English. His in many ways much more serious colleague, Christopher Tolkien, waited for more than a decade before he was promoted from the lowly position of college lecturer to a full Fellow, with the right to sit on the Governing Body of the college.

JOB spoke with habitual jests and jokes about the tedium of college 'admin' and the chore of attending the weekly meeting of the Governing Body in term time. There would be jokes about the duller dons, and spluttering protests about any additional work imposed by these meetings – for instance, having to sit on committees to organise appeals, the library, the chapel or the garden. But, crucially, these jokes and the implied anarchy of the views were a matter of private laughter shared with initiates. Christopher Tolkien did not grasp this, and behaved during college meetings like a schoolboy, doodling on his blotter, passing notes and jokes to friends and expecting JOB to join in. He was astounded when, one Wednesday afternoon, JOB gave him a ticking off, saying that he should behave with more seriousness during meetings, and that there was a fear in the college that Christopher was not 'pulling his weight'. Tolkien looked in JOB's face for the signs that this call to order were some kind of elaborate joke, but no such signs were there.

All this carried over into the generalised area of what a chap would or would not read, say or think. Colleges are, or were, little more than male clubs. JOB, whose social and intellectual antennae are more acute than most, would have glowed with pride at the prospect of his wife being, as he often used to say during her decrepitude, the 'most intelligent woman in England', but at the same time was deeply aware of what 'real' philosophers such as Isaiah or Freddy or Tony would be saying behind IM's back about her fondness for those pseudish existentialists.

There is one thing a chap does, most definitely, not do, and that is have any truck with God. Colin Haycraft, honorary Fellow of Queen's and publisher of JOB's novels, used to say, 'Religion is for women and queers.' His lofty laughter forbade contradiction.

'That was one thing John did for me,' IM told me over a lunch in the autumn of 1989, 'he got rid of God.'

'Do you mean to say that you were an actual believer until you met John?'

'Yes – well, in a sort of a way – yes, definitely.'

This was a fascinating reflection. It suggested – how accurately, how can one tell? – that throughout her affair with Canetti she had been struggling to retain her adherence to Christianity. Her later robustly expressed atheism, and fascination with Buddhism, seem completely in tune with Canetti's world-view. But in 1989 at least, when speaking to me, she imagined that God had been dismissed, not by a fellow-philosopher, or by Canetti the polymath sage, but by her husband.

Though the existentialists were held at bay in philosophy lectures at Oxford, their voice could be heard in those of the theology faculty. Once again, one senses intellectual history repeating itself. Just as Hegelianism first percolated in anything like a popular form in England through the writings of Feuerbach and Strauss, translated by George Eliot, so the ideas of Heidegger first came to England – as far as non-German readers were concerned – in the theology of Rudolf Bultmann and his followers. For Bultmann, the New Testament material was a mythology, 'realised' when the believer, in the time-honoured Lutheran manner, made it real for himself. What made the New Testament an arresting and eternally important set of documents was not the fact that they contained the putative records of some historical prophet who might or might not have said certain words, performed certain deeds or even risen from the dead. (The possibility that these things had historical reality was, *natürlich*, dismissed by Bultmann.) What made such phrases as 'the end of the world' or 'the day of the Lord' or the 'coming near of the Kingdom' *real* was if the believer, when reading the text, was confronted by Christ, the Christ-myth or Christ-idea as an existential reality.

Most, if not all, of the conventional grounds for believing in the 'God of the Philosophers', as Pascal called him, have been unpicked and discarded since the eighteenth century. Darwin appears to have done away with the most obviously plausible of these arguments, namely that from design. It would be entirely wrong to suppose that most modern philosophers are atheists, or even that most Oxford philosophers at the period we are discussing were atheists. That is not quite what I am saying. Elizabeth Anscombe, for example, was a fervent Roman Catholic, and so is Michael Dummett. But in the clubbish atmosphere which IM married into when she decided to throw in her lot with JOB, God was not part of the picture.

Her existentialism, which made her into *l'étrangère* of the philosophy faculty, would have more than qualified her for a place at the table among the theologues. And such a place was laid for her, when she joined a group of Oxford theologians called The Metaphysicals.

Her dialogue with the theologians was continuous, but it is noticeable, in *Metaphysics as a Guide to Morals*, that the theological writers whom she cites – notably Buber, Tillich, Barth – are the ones who were being read more in the late 1940s and early 1950s than by late twentieth-century students of the subject. There is nothing wrong with that, of course, but it is an indication that in her reading she tended to reflect upon old favourites rather than to break new ground.

When she began to teach philosophy at St Anne's College, her tutorial methods owed something to those of MacKinnon. She would lie on the floor, or sometimes in bed without anything on her top except a leather jerkin, to teach the girls.

Her research interests, which were to culminate in the Sartre book (1953), continued to explore the existentialists and in particular their moral philosophy or lack of it. She came to identify the existentialist theories of the Will with the utilitarianism of such Oxford philosophers as Stuart Hampshire, R. M. Hare and A. J. Ayer. Above all, she criticised Hampshire's *Thought and Action* as an implausible account of human nature. The human being in Hampshire's vision is 'rational and totally free except in so far as, in the most ordinary law-court and commonsensical sense, his degree of self-awareness may vary. He is, morally speaking, monarch of all he surveys and totally responsible for his actions.'*

She proposed a return to G. E. Moore's idea of goodness as 'a supersensible reality . . . A mysterious quality, unrepresentable and indefinable, that it was the object of knowledge and (implicitly) that to be able to see it was in some sense to have it.'

The idea that goodness or morality were functions of the will she came to regard as 'demonic', and these thoughts led her back to a wholehearted embrace of Platonism; Plato being in her reading a completely religious thinker who did not believe in a personal God.

She revived, in other words, what modern philosophy might term moral realism – the belief that the Good has as much outer reality as matter. It is not something that we summon up by acts of will. That Plato was a moral realist can hardly be doubted; but he was also a 'realist' about other things too, such as the existence of an immortal soul. Although I asked her, over a period of many years, how she could extrapolate from the *Phaedo*, for example, the notion that Plato did not really and actually expect us to believe in God and life after death, she never answered with anything but a smile and a shake of the head, or a repetition that these were 'myths'.

It was only much later in life, after I had become IM's supposed

---

* 'Against Dryness', *Encounter*, January, 1961.

'biographer', that I was introduced, by Ruth Guilding, to the novels of John Cowper Powys.

IM was a keen admirer of Powys, and there is no doubt that in her later novels she was trying to write books which were of a comparable magnitude to his own. They are – in a phrase of George Steiner's with which I could wholeheartedly agree – 'the only novels produced by an English writer that can fairly be compared with the fictions of Tolstoy and Dostoevsky . . . with an immensity to which only Blake could provide a parallel in English literature'. *Maiden Castle*, like *The Unicorn*, has a character who is a private gentleman living in the country and writing a great book on Plato. He is Mr Wye (an obvious but good name for a philosopher), whose perpetual grin was 'hardly less sardonic than the one reproduced in Houdon's famous bust of Voltaire'. Teucer Wye always carries the *Phaedrus* in his right pocket, the *Timaeus* in his left and mutters to himself in Greek. The central figure of the novel (one can hardly call him a hero) ventures to this Platonist, 'I *have* read him a certain amount, but *I* take Plato in a way peculiar to myself. I take him as an absolute sceptic, a sceptic so uncertain about everything that he could afford to turn God and immortality into poetry, and the soul and love into fairy-tales.'

When I quoted this to IM, she looked vaguely aghast, as does Mr Wye in the novel when confronted by the idea. The truth is that, while she might once have been a good philosophy tutor, she never in the quarter-century I knew her expressed ideas clearly in the way that Anthony Quinton, say, would always do when philosophy tutor at New College and subsequently. If I ask *him*, for instance, to explain to me the philosophy of Leibnitz, he will do so lucidly and entirely plausibly, with suggestions for further reading. I am not saying that IM would have been incapable of such condensations of Western thought; merely that this was not what her conversation was like when she talked about philosophy to amateurs.

She evidently disagreed with John Cowper Powys's (or his character Dud Noman's) 'post-modern' reading of Plato – yet how did it differ from her idea that Plato was merely writing 'myths'? I for one was never told. She was sphinx-like about it. I suspect that by now, her gaze fixed on The Good, she had become a mystic. To pursue Dud Noman's line of thought would be to shatter (another Powys phrase) her Life-Illusion.

The life of the novels, however, was happening at a level much deeper than conversation or conscious thought – hence perhaps the contradiction between her anti-existentialist philosophical essays and her essentially existentialist fiction. For all her early novels are in the broadest sense existentialist: that is to say, her characters seem to be making quite arbitrary choices about their lives without any clear sense of a code outside themselves. These choices are more often made under the influence of another person than of an ethical code: so, the sinister Honor Klein in A *Severed Head* controls all the other characters like a witch. (Did IM *see* Honor Klein as sinister, though? When I myself wrote my first novel, which included an improbable scene of incest, the critics described this, correctly, as a bit of Murdochian influence. She wrote me a letter saying, 'I admire your heroine's scale of values: incest perfectly OK. Cheating in exams unthinkable.')

Of course, labels can be made to mean what we like. IM didn't share Sartre's view that 'innocent' individuals discover themselves morally by pitting themselves against the values of 'society'. Nor did she perhaps ever believe that morality was a matter of asserting the will. But in the sense that Dostoevsky was an existentialist and Kierkegaard was the father of existentialism, she was surely one herself. The moments of decision in her books – whether it is Bradley Pearson realising with blinding light that he loves Julian Baffin, or Dora deciding to leave, and then return to, her horrible husband Paul, or Anne Cavidge leaving her convent, or Cato loving and then losing Christ – these are existential moments, dependent not upon some change in outward facts or circumstances, but upon changes in their own will or perception. She is surely not merely unfair but wrong to say that existentialists have denied the existence of an inner life, though she was abundantly right to suggest that the Oxford analytical moral utilitarians – or whatever you would call Hampshire, Hare and Ayer – had a pretty wooden picture of the human heart.

The realist picture of The Good and of man – as she put it in her contribution to Lord David Cecil's Festschrift – as 'frail, godless, and yet possessed of genuine intuitions of an authoritative good' lead inevitably to religion. What you do with religion when you get there is another story, and she was perhaps never able to believe in the specific claims, the particularity of Christianity: its assertions that the truths enshrined in the religion cohere around a set of falsifiable historical events – of which the Resurrection of Christ is central.

Yet she could not entirely leave Christianity alone. When she returned to Oxford, and throughout her love affair with Canetti, she continued to put in appearances at the meetings of The Metaphysicals – they included Dennis Nineham, Eric Mascall and, perhaps the most remarkable Anglican theologian of his generation, Austin Farrer. Nineham's inspiration was Newman's *Development of Doctrine*. He looked, as IM did, for a Christianity which could have organic life without being shackled to discarded thought-processes or outmoded anti-scientific ideas of the world. He would eventually be one of the contributors to *The Myth of God Incarnate*. Mascall, a much less interesting mind, was a sort of neo-Thomist. Farrer took a more 'realist' view of the New Testament historical claims than Nineham, but was a glancing, mystical intelligence which one might have imagined being to IM's taste. These, together with MacKinnon, were all representatives of a variety of viewpoints which were more attractive to her, at some visceral level, than the prosaic assumptions of Stuart Hampshire and friends. She would always be deeply religious in temperament, though after she met JOB she drifted away from The Metaphysicals and ceased to attend their lunches or contribute to their papers.

The central epistemological question with which, say, MacKinnon wrestled all his life, with Kant, was not one that interested the existentialists. Heidegger indeed believed that most of the errors in Western thought derived from the very Cartesian division of the world into subjects and objects, observers of the world and the observed. Obviously, the most extreme Idealist is Wittgenstein – whom IM described to me as 'The Devil' on more than one occasion. Likewise Cupitt's belief that we are all imprisoned in language games, we cannot make realist statements, and human thought or language can never refer to anything beyond itself; there is no criterion for assessing either the plausibility of truth claims or the reality of things beyond our perception of them. IM seemed to believe that this was a wrong belief. Therefore, one would assume, she was working out some form of Realism, even in the sphere of ethics and aesthetics, but on what this was based

I could never begin to grasp. You would think, from her pre-occupation with Heidegger, and former preoccupation with Sartre, that this would be through existentialism – *pour-soi* makes *en-soi* 'real': which is really little more than a translation of Kant's belief that though we can never know the inner reality of things in themselves, we plunge, as it were, into an accept-ance of their reality by virtue of their appearance, and its effect upon us. Subjectivity, by paradox, leads in the Kantian frame-work to an acceptance, though not a proof, of objectivity. For the existentialist, the old problems of verification are laid to one side:

> And like a man in wrath the heart
> Stood up and answered 'I have felt!'

Yet IM fiercely denied that she was an existentialist, or that she had ever been one – a surprise to anyone who has read her book on Sartre, which, while distancing herself from the master, makes it clear that she has on some levels absorbed his way of viewing the world. And the first two novels are, as well as being written in the vein of Queneau, also written in the spirit of Sartre.

Doing philosophy means two quite distinct things at least: first advancing, and secondly understanding the subject. First, it means actually advancing or changing the nature of philosophical discourse. Most philosophers are only able to do this in their careers in some tiny area: they might point to a minuscule article or a paper in a philosophical journal in which they have corrected the misconception that philosopher A once had about a position advanced by philosopher B.

There is nothing surprising or discreditable about this fact:

'doing philosophy', as IM herself always said, is 'incredibly, incredibly difficult – and tiring'.

Those philosophers, such as Bertrand Russell or A. J. Ayer, who go beyond this and seem to advance the subject by more than an iota, or who seem to have sketched out a new or different way of approaching the whole subject, or a whole area of the subject, such as the philosophy of mathematics, very often find, after five or ten years, that they radically alter, or rewrite, or discard their original position. The most conspicuous example of such a change is the difference between the Wittgenstein of the *Tractatus* and the Wittgenstein of the *Philosophical Investigations*.

Few of those who 'do philosophy' are ever going to be 'philosophers' in this sense of the word. But there will, at any one time, be a group of men and women who know what philosophy is, learn its disciplines, acquaint themselves with some of its history and try to master the concepts of particular modes of thinking which are at any one time current in Academia.

IM obviously belonged to this second category, and was a much-prized tutor at Oxford and at the RCA. You sense how very, very good she had been at teaching, when on form – an important 'when' – by reading again those radio talks on 'The novelist as Metaphysician' and 'The existentialist hero',* or the *Spectator* review, in May 1957, of the English translation of Sartre's *Being and Nothingness* ('Hegel in modern dress'). Here she is, fully aware of the fact that this post-Hegelian stuff is of no interest to the Oxford chaps, but also aware that the Hegelian questions throw up a whole series of compelling challenges to the world of her

---

*BBC, Third Programme, March 1950.

contemporaries. It is less clear from this review whether she saw the extent to which *L'être et le néant* is indebted to Heidegger's *Sein und Zeit*; could indeed be seen as a sort of pop version of *Sein und Zeit*.

Rather than labouring the point about chaps and God, I shall conclude this chapter with a flicker of college memories which are not without existential drama.

New College was exceptionally cruel to its chaplains. Lightfoot, a brilliant New Testament scholar and a tormented 'tragic Christian' in Schweitzer's terms, was so persecuted by the dons, especially by the philosophy don Joseph, as to be sometimes shy of attending meals. His successor as Dean of Divinity was in fact an historian, the Revd G. V. Bennett, a pupil of Jack Plumb's from Cambridge and the author of a study of Atterbury, the 'mitred Rochester' of Alexander Pope's lines.

Bennett was a small, pudgy-faced man with a peevish-sounding voice. Strong traces of Southend-on-Sea, whose grammar school he had attended, remained in the vowels. He made himself hated by the younger dons by – he a bachelor and likely to remain so – talking to them of his investment decisions. If some particularly impecunious junior research Fellow, struggling to pay the rent on a two-up two-down terraced house in Botley, were placed beside him at dinner, Bennett would get out a pocketful of krugerrands and clunk them up and down, speaking with wistful sorrow of the days when the price of gold kept up with inflation.

Bennett's behaviour – above all his petulance, and his malice about all his colleagues – did not suggest any slavish desire to follow the precepts of the Gospels, but it would seem that he saw himself as an orthodox churchman, 'High' in the manner of Dean

Swift and Atterbury, rather than a modern Anglo-Catholic. He very much disapproved of me and my 'extreme' ways, and gave the assistant chaplain (now the Bishop of Gibraltar, Geoffrey Rowell) a great ticking off for coming to a 'rosary evening' which – how one cringes to recall it – I had organised in my rooms during my first year.

Yet, though as an undergraduate I found Bennett an unlikeable man, when I became a lecturer at the college I came to see him as a figure of pathos. The dons liked bullying him. They mocked the fact that every time a new deanery or bishopric became vacant, Bennett would pace anxiously about the quads, hoping for the call from Number Ten, Downing Street.

One evening, a young woman came into dinner as the guest of one of the dons. Freddy (A. J.) Ayer asked her what she was working on, and she said that she was doing a thesis on social class.

'How do you classify people?' asked Freddy.

'Obviously, economically and in terms of educational attainments. You would all be in the top class, whereas a gardener, let us say . . .'

'Stop!' called Freddy – he had at times a very carrying voice, hardened by a lifetime of chain-smoking. 'Are you telling me that you are writing a thesis on social class, and that you would say that I belonged to the same social class as the chaplain?'

Silence had fallen. The grammar-school boy from Southend-on-Sea stared bitterly across the table at the rich Etonian heir to a Citroën fortune.

'I should consider,' Freddy went on, rubbing salt into the wounds both of the young woman and of Bennett, 'that any such thesis could only confuse its readers.'

156

A year or two later I was sitting at lunch in the Founder's Library when the college doctor, a very likeable man indeed called Stewart, came in. I asked him what sort of a morning he had had, and he sighed.

'A puir laddie tried to kill himself,' he said. 'He bungled it, I'm happy to say. Pills!'

He put a large dollop of mashed potato on his plate next to the excellent suet-and-steak pudding, ladled on more gravy and sat down beside me.

'Now you'd never get a doctor doing it with pills. Have you noticed how few doctors die of cancer? The minute we hear we are beyond help . . .'

The Revd G. V. Bennett leaned forward and said quietly, 'So, what method would you recommend?'

'You go to the ironmongers, and you buy a wee bit o' rubber tubing. You aren't so selfish that you are going to be found by a scout lying on the floor, like my puir laddie this morning. You drive to the ring road and pull into a layby. Attach your tubing to the exhaust of the car, and bring it round, so that it feeds in through the side window of your car. Pull up the window – not too tight, mind, or ye'll prevent the carbon monoxide passing through the tube. Turn on your engine . . . The police will find you. It's their job.'

It was a gruesome subject for lunch-talk. Years passed. I had by now left Oxford and was in the middle of making a television programme. As I sat in the offices or cutting-rooms in BBC Manchester, a large screen displayed the lunchtime news. Bennett's face had appeared. He had been named as the author of a particularly poisonous preface to *Crockford's Clerical Directory*. In a cowardly (because anonymous) attack, he had accused his

157

old friend Robert Runcie, Archbishop of Canterbury, of lowering the standards of the Church. Runcie's true offence, though the *Crockford's* preface did not say so, was his failure to make Bennett a bishop.

When his cover was blown, Bennett disappeared. He was found by poor John Cowan, the German don at New College. He had gone into the garage of his nasty little house in New Marston and, following Dr Stewart's instructions, had attached a 'wee bit o' rubber tubing' to the exhaust pipe and switched on the ignition.

Suicide is perhaps the ultimate existential protest against the inexplicable absurdity of our Condition. It is by tradition regarded as the ultimate sin for the Christian, flinging back into the void the divinely given breath of life. It was astonishing to watch the television screen and to discover that Bennett's desperate act was seen by the 'traditionalist' wing of the Anglican Church as a 'martyrdom'. A week or so later the TV news showed the front quad of New College filled with mitred figures. The Bishops of London and Chichester were joined by a mighty throng of vested priests, chanting and swinging incense. Poor, tormented little Bennett! As it happened, though he had been the author of the anonymous attack on Archbishop Runcie, some of the more withering phrases – such as 'nailing his colours to the fence' – had been supplied by another priest. Bennett's life was probably sad enough before he was elected to his fellowship at New College. The bullying by the likes of Ayer certainly must have made it worse. It was a particularly grotesque touch that, before he went to meet his maker, this Christian clergyman killed his cat – or would seem to have done so. Anyway, Tiddles (or whatever he was called) was lying there too when Bennett was found. Though

Tiddles had probably caused less grief than Bennett's malice, the cat was not afforded the solemnity of a Pontifical Requiem. Of all the reversals of reputation to have happened to human beings I have known, the canonisation of the unfortunate Bennett is the strangest.

3

An evening with Eric

March 1974: dinner with JOB in New College. I always feel paralysed by shyness at High Table, and have no idea what to say to any of the dons, unless the genial, talkative Tony Quinton happens to be in. He wasn't there tonight. Instead, one got stuck next to Bennett, the sour-faced chaplain. He is ambitious – longs to be a bishop. He was rather nasty to me when I first arrived. William Hayter, the Warden, gave me the reason: my housemaster from school had begun his reference for me, 'This boy will one day become a bishop.' Perhaps Gary Bennett saw me as a rival for the coveted see of Durham! Although I am now at St Stephen's House studying for the priesthood, I don't think I shall be a rival for poor old Gary.

Anyway, JOB and I had a nice time, talking our usual nonsense of books and gossip, and everything broke up at about, oh, nine, I suppose.

'What about looking in on old Eric Christiansen?' asked JOB.

Christiansen, Fellow and tutor in medieval history, is, at thirty-five or so, a college 'character'. He is a bachelor don, but the reverse of homosexual. Most of the women I know have either been to bed with him or are in love with him. Some of them are extremely beautiful, which he isn't. Many, like the drippier lovelorn souls in IM's books, seem quite unable to shake off their feelings of love for him, and are prepared to humiliate themselves in front of their friends by displays of emotion, following him about like groupies. He keeps them in firmly separate compartments. They are only allowed to get in touch with him on his terms and in his time. I believe that he assigns a special 'day' to the favoured ones; woe betide the Thursday girl who tries to ring him up or see him on a Tuesday!

He also has his male followers too; not homosexual devotees, but pupils and colleagues who would like to imitate his style. Perhaps because Eric is not at all English (his grandparents ran a lucrative business, selling what exactly is never specified, in Copenhagen) his manner is that of the archetypal English gentleman. He is a regular attender at college chapel. He is a keen royalist. When one of his friends accused him of being 'churchy but not religious', he stopped speaking to them for over a year. He has already established a bit of a reputation for himself in the right-wing press as a jokey reviewer, writing about such figures as Dante, or the Emperor Henry II, or Guillaume de Loris in the facetious tones you might describe characters in P. G. Wodehouse. He always wears impeccable bespoke suits, made by Hall Bros the tailors in the High. He writes with an old-fashioned dip-pen, and his handwriting is a Victorian copperplate. His set of rooms, apart from the fact that they have electric lights, could be those of a mid-to-late Victorian clubman, heavy brown mahogany, a big leather daybed (on which many a seduction has taken place), darkened oil paintings in lumpy golden frames. It is quite an impressive act, and one says this objectively, since it has clearly impressed so many. JOB speaks playfully of Eric usually – particularly mocking some of his 'attitudes'; he is also a little in awe of him, as are most of the dons.

For a number of reasons, I find Eric heavy going, and suggest that if JOB wants to call in on him, I might head for home. I express gratitude for dinner, and make to turn away. But JOB says, 'Oh, p-p-please come with me, Andrew.'

It is quite clear that he wants a companion for the next stage of the evening, and that he does not want to call on Eric alone.

I do not know what to make of this. After all, JOB and Eric are colleagues. They eat many of their meals together. In the afternoons they quite often, together with some other dons, slope off to the cinema in Walton Street, though JOB usually leaves after about three-quarters of an hour, always able to predict, with uncanny accuracy, how the film will end. Why on earth should he need somebody with him when he enters Eric's rooms? The thought occurs, but I immediately dismiss it as ridiculous, that JOB has never been in these rooms before, and is somehow shy.

We ascend the staircase, and find the outer door open, the inner door closed. In Oxford, there is a whole arcane ritual attaching to doors. I've always found the slang for closing both doors – 'sporting your oak' – as baffling as it is embarrassing.

Are you meant to knock? There's some sign: if the door is in a certain position, it is a sign you are not to knock; if not, you should walk straight in . . . Anyway, like public-school slang, this is the sort of thing which I have never bothered to master.

JOB does lightly knock and pushes open the door. He stammers out, 'E-e-eric, my d-d-ear fellow' and it takes so long to add 'I've brought someone to see you' that it almost comes forth like a little song.

An extraordinary scene meets our eyes. Eric is lying on the large black leather daybed. Some bright turquoise arms are clutched about him, and a head of hair is tousled against his shoulder. The two figures are not undressed, but they are tightly entwined. Eric gets up very hastily from the daybed and blinkingly puts his spectacles back on his nose. The turquoise figure stands up. It is IM.

I have often thought of this scene, which took place when I had known JOB and IM about four years. In Richard Eyre's film *Iris* there is an episode when the young JOB comes to visit IM and finds her in bed with another man. He stands at the half-open doorway watching, and the character in the film clearly derives some enjoyment from the spectacle. On the evening with Eric, I was cringingly embarrassed. I was much younger than any of them, only in my early twenties. It never occurred to me at the time to wonder, as it has done since, whether JOB had actually planned for me to see IM and Eric together. Presumably JOB himself knew, or feared, that he would discover some such episode in progress? Was it something that he often had to endure? Did they talk about it afterwards on the way home in the car, or was it simply a taboo subject? None of us will ever know the answer to these questions. I would never have the face to ask JOB himself, and he has in all likelihood blotted it out of his consciousness.

IM fantasised in her inner life that she was a male homosexual, and in one of her journal entries she adds the adjective 'Sado-masochistic'. If, beneath the plump exterior of a slightly greedy nun, she was really a male homosexual sadist, had she found in JOB the ideal male slave whom she could torture?

We know that other people's relationships are impenetrable, which is presumably why we go on asking about them, and why gossip about our friends is the most absorbing of all conversations. Nor is it something to be despised. Out of such 'gossip' comes an idea of human nature, comes art, come plays, come novels, comes – which is more important than any, though necessary to them all – sympathy.

All their friends speculated endlessly about JOB and IM and, with the exception of Honor Tracy, already quoted, I seldom personally met anyone who did not see them as an ideal couple, superbly well matched. Friends such as David and Rachel Cecil or Reynolds and Janet Stone would speak of the experience of having JOB and IM to stay, and how they would hear the murmur of their constant talk, enlivened with bursts of laughter, whenever they were alone together in their room. Their suitedness to one another was absolutely obvious to anyone. It is against this background that I am indiscreet enough to mention the evening with Eric. It is now clear, thanks to the shockingly candid accounts already in print, just how promiscuous IM was. 'I have told lies to all those I loved most deeply, not once but continually,' she wrote in her journal.

*   *   *

IM's eyes met mine. I felt like a policeman whose torch had shone, not on a burglar, but on someone doing something shaming – a child peeing against a wall, a man flashing in the park. She looked positively surly, but also very red in the face. She got up from the sofa, tugged at her hair, said, 'Look here, I think we all need something to drink.'

She was very red and looked as if she had been drinking quite a lot already. Traces of their picnic meal lay upon the table and there was some red wine open, but Eric favoured Irish whiskey, and this was poured out for all of us. His manner, when dispensing it, was that of a courtly old man who found one's behaviour, manner, perhaps very existence, mildly ridiculous. He smirked and smiled as if at some private joke.

'H-h-how was the film, Eric?' asked John.

'What film was this?' IM asked, looking sternly first at JOB, then at Eric. She did not take much notice of me, but she watched with deep attention, like a spectator at Wimbledon, as each ball went over the net between her husband and her friend. Her eyes moved from left to right as she studied their features.

Eric went on to describe the film, which had been some kind of horror movie. It concerned a man who had lived his entire life in the London Underground. He is a sort of monster-man, and I forget why or how he came to be born, conceived and abandoned in the Tube, or how he managed to survive there. The only English sentence he knows is 'Mind the Gap! Mind the Gap!', which Eric imitates in sepulchral, creepy tones.

IM finds this very funny, and very exciting. She begins to

ask all sorts of questions about the 'monster' – what does he eat? Does he drink alcohol? Does he go to the bar on Sloane Square station? Does Eric know that there are two London Underground stations which have bars, the one in Sloane Square and another on Liverpool Street?

'I think I rather like the sound of this fellow!' she says of the monster, and we all laugh, grateful for the release from the horror of the earlier embarrassment.

May 1975: just finished reading A *Word Child*. Hard not to believe that about fourteen months ago I witnessed the conception of this strange and powerful story.

The narrator, Hilary Burde, says, 'I thought of calling this story *The Memoirs of an Underground Man* or just simply *The Inner Circle*.' It is about a morose 'monster' of a man who consoles himself by going round and round on the Circle Line of the London Underground.

Since the incident in Eric's room I have seen them all – Eric, JOB, IM – many times, and no allusion of any kind has been made to the 'incident'. It is as if it never was.

Hilary Burde and Eric are of differing social classes. Hilary has a sister who is completely uneducated, about whom he is very possessive and with whom he has a (disgusting-sounding) dinner once a week. Otherwise, however, he is noticeably like Eric. Though obviously heterosexual, he is an incurable bachelor. Women fall madly in love with him, and the woman who causes him most bother is more or less a portrait, a very malicious one too, of the ethereal and lovely B—— who loves Eric so much. Like B—— she is someone who commutes to a dull place where she earns a pittance 'teaching drama at a teachers' training college somewhere near King's Lynn'. Her long legs and her 'lucid Cairngorm misty eyes' are mentioned again and again. Perhaps IM is in love with, as well as jealous of, B——?

Hilary Burde is very like Eric physically. 'I am just over six feet tall, sturdy, dark, clean-shaven against a fierce beard with a head of thick greasy crinkly dark hair descending to my collar. A similar mat of thick hair furs my body to the navel . . . It is difficult to describe my face. It satisfies no canon of beauty, not even that of a gangster . . .'

There is much else which is clearly IM's vision of Eric, the fascinating solitary, perpetually 'bothered' by women falling in love with him.

But then again, Hilary Burde 'is' her. Hilary's lonely orphanage childhood, a period of delinquency followed by enlightenment from a wonderful teacher, this is a sort of fantasy about IM herself. 'I learnt from Mr Osmond how to write the best language in the world accurately and clearly and ultimately with a hard careful elegance. I discovered words and words were my salvation. I was not, except in some very broken-down sense of that ambiguous term, a love child. I was a word child.' Only, of course, IM was (literally) a love child, born as the result of a 'shot-gun' wedding, as JOB once told me, and in her own words living as an only child with her parents in 'a perfect Trinity of love'.

IM did not share Hilary Burde's childhood misery, or says she didn't. But maybe her father's childhood was a bit like it? I have just (1992) reread the book. In the light of what I found out when I was researching her life, I think that eighteen years ago I missed the figure of Hughes Murdoch, who also feeds into the character of Hilary Burde/Murdoch.

There is much more in this book of realistic humour, descriptions of office life and so on, than in any previous book. H. Burde, like H. Murdoch (IM's father), is employed at a fairly minor level in the Civil Service. She describes the office banter, and the excruciating ribbing which this shy man receives from the two with whom he shares a room.

One strange fact: there are allusions to 'Jenny Searle in Registry'. Jennifer Searle was the real name of one of JOB's research pupils. She was a lecturer at the University of East Anglia. JOB believed her innate conservatism (in her approach to the subject, not necessarily politically) suggested the figure of Miss Callender who resisted the evil machinations of the History Man in Malcolm Bradbury's novel of the same name. Bradbury, incidentally, was on IM's list of the Damned for his publication of a cruel, and not especially accurate, pastiche of her style. (The abstract from a novel, *The Sublime and the Ridiculous,* begins 'Flavia says that Hugo tells her that Augustina is in love with Fred'.)[*]

A Word Child contains all the usual Murdoch carelessness. One of the deep, deep mistakes of IM's artistic career was that she refused to be edited by a publisher, and would not alter a word of her typescripts once they had been submitted. In this book Burde says he feels like 'Natasha Rostov, just in from a brisk walk along the Nevsky Prospekt'. It must have been a very *long* brisk walk, since Natasha lives in Moscow and the Nevsky Prospekt is in St Petersburg. Burde sits on Paddington Station, which IM did at least every week of her life while writing this book, and hears

---

[*]Malcolm Bradbury, *Who Do You Think You Are?*, Secker & Warburg, 1976.

the announcer stating that the Swansea train passes through Cheltenham. This will have been surprising to any who regularly travel to Swansea. The tragedy of Burde's life happens some time in the 1950s when he and his mistress swerve off the motorway coming out of Oxford and he is killed. This is in fact ten years before any motorway in England was built and a good twenty years before the construction of the M40 from Oxford to London.

Cumulatively, these things matter. Much more disturbing is the fact that, as in so many of her books, something of immense power and intelligence and concentration in the first 150 pages descends in the second half to mere silliness.

In his life as an Oxford don, Hilary Burde has cuckolded another Fellow of the college. Twenty years pass, and this Fellow turns up as the Head of Department in Burde's branch of the Civil Service, where Burde works as a humble clerk.

Everything has prepared us for a situation of concentrated moral seriousness, of metaphysical interest. We have been prepared for a good novel, perhaps a great novel, about the possibility or impossibility of human beings forgiving great wrong. Can suffering ever redeem, can guilt ever be assuaged, if there isn't a God? All these themes are aired. There is much opportunity here, too, for the novelist to describe the sheer excruciating awkwardness of the situation, the embarrassment at work and the destruction of social life. (Hilary Burde and Gunnar, the man he has wronged, have friends in common.)

This is the novel, then, which the first half of the book leads up to, and which we expect we are about to read. It feels in these pages quite possible that we are about to read a writer who is in the very first rank, that another Dostoevsky has been born.

Instead, we have the usual Murdoch merry-go-round. First,

Hilary is pursued by the lady's maid of Gunnar's second wife, a beautiful Indian girl called Biscuit. He plays leapfrog with her in the snowy park. Her employer is called Lady Kitty, and it is no surprise to anyone who has read a Murdoch novel before that Hilary has soon fallen passionately in love with Lady Kitty, while trying to have an affair with Biscuit, and not before all the other women in the book, and one of the homosexual men, have fallen in love with him.

In what remains the most acute critical study of IM, a study of the early novels entitled *Degrees of Freedom*, A. S. Byatt in 1965 wrote that 'she has not yet measured up to the size of her purpose'. There is a sense in which IM never did measure up, although there are some books that contain chapters, or whole passages, which come as close to being great fiction as anything written in the United Kingdom during her own writing career. Then, mysteriously, she seems to lose whatever it was that she held. Byatt saw the trouble deriving from a conflict between IM's 'moral perceptiveness and her own ability too rapidly to make patterns of great complexity with it'. Another way of saying the same thing would be to notice that IM simply cannot stop herself being extremely silly.

This is a strange truth about a writer who is obviously, with one part of herself, tremendously serious.

Fascinatingly, IM was clearly very much aware of this paradox herself. Hilary hopes that Lady Kitty will be his redeemer. 'More strange still,' he adds, this hope 'coexisted, strangest of all, with my perfectly commonsense awareness that Kitty was not really a saint or a prophetess, but an ordinary and possibly rather silly woman who liked a mystery and the exercise of power.'

4

The Abbess of Imber

May 1977: deeply in love with Violet. Worse love-pain than ever. At first I thought our flirtation was a joke which, agonisingly, it still is. But last week-end when K and I went to stay with our friends the ——s, V was there too and we slipped out whenever we could to hold hands, kiss – nothing more . . . Yet . . . Raging love now distracts me, making all other thought impossible. I feel so miserable, guilty, confused, that I wonder if I am actually going mad.

Nearly cancelled my weekly lunch with JOB. But find myself wandering down to St Catz anyway. Lovely early summer day. Horse chestnuts bursting into candles of pink and cream. After lunch – at which I can't eat ('Ah! Your main-course nausea!' said J indulgently, when he saw me playing with my food) – we stroll slowly round Addison's Walk. Pause by the bridge to see the pike sunbathing beneath the stone.

I pour out my sorrows to J in an unstoppable flow – how I don't want to be in love with V at all, it just happened, how frightened I am by the situation getting out of control, how I feel myself almost going mad. J says why not just go to bed with her? This would surely take the heat out of the situation? Probably I'd find the whole affair blew over in a couple of weeks. I said what about poor K?

J hoped everything OK with her? I said, I thought probably the reverse. J said that I might not realise this, but she probably found it very difficult coming to terms with my novels – the persona who comes across from them not necessarily the Andrew she had married.

This thought had never occurred to me, and I say so.

J says that when he married IM, he had fallen in love with a woman he barely knew. Their early dates had been swimming expeditions in the river, or canoeing up to Wolvercote. When they were married they lived in Oxford before they moved out to Cedar Lodge. It was a *Swallows and Amazons* sort of relationship. Of course, he admired her mind, and her cleverness, but she did not speak to him about her philosophy and the fact that she wanted to be a novelist seemed curiously unimportant to him. He had admired her books when he had read them without necessarily considering them his kind of book.

Then they married, and she wrote another book. When it had been typed, she showed it to him: it was *The Bell*.

He read it and was appalled. He felt that the persona of the novelist who had created this book was completely uncongenial, not at all the person he thought he knew, thought he loved, thought he had married.

He hated the whole tone of the book. He felt it emanated from a mind which he could not like, let alone love. Moreover, IM had plainly used in this story things which JOB had told her in confidence. He felt betrayed, felt she had woven secret things, his secret things, into the texture of the story, as if absolutely anything was just *there* to be plundered by the Novelist.

I am completely stunned by this confession.

We continue to walk for a while in silence until we have circumambulated Addison's Walk.

Once more we are on the bridge looking for 'our' pike.

'What did Iris say when you told her?'

'T-t-told her, dear Andrew? T-t-told her what?'

'That you were so distressed by *The Bell*.'

'Oh, I didn't tell her, my dear. I said I th-th-thought it was a marvellous book. I even contributed a little paragraph or two of my own to it. I wrote the o-o-opening sentence, as a matter of fact. After that, whenever she'd finished a n-n-n-novel, she would have it typed and then show it to me for comment. I'd take it away for a day or two. Sometimes, I'd flick through a few pages to show w-w-willing, as it were, but sometimes I couldn't even bring myself to do that. Then I'd tell Iris how much I'd enjoyed it, and mention one or two things I'd spotted in the typescript as especially good.'

'But John! You mean you haven't . . . read anything Iris has written for the last . . . when was *The Bell* written? Nearly twenty years ago!'

'I think she probably knows and the little f-f-fiction suits her, so to say.'

Reading this a quarter of a century later, in 2002, I don't know what to make of this confession, since I can quite distinctly remember JOB urging me to read *Henry and Cato* when it came

173

out. Said it was an especially good one, and that, 'as a rule of thumb Iris writes one good one followed by one d-d-dud!'

The Bell is one of IM's most stylish and accomplished works. It *works* in a way that few of the later books wholly do. Few writers know who their friends are. I don't mean by this that they choose their companions unwisely, though it might seem as if some of them do so, but that it is hard for novelists to know their own strengths. Turgenev said that he could only write fiction when he was mildly in love. This was probably true of IM. But in order to fire on all cylinders, I think she needed to be in love with two objects at once; to be giving her heart to contradictory objects of desire.

Of the various father-figures, Prosperos, in her formative years (and her gestation-period as a writer was long, her formative years lasted well into her thirties), two stand out as being of supreme importance imaginatively speaking: her philosophy tutor Donald MacKinnon, agonised Anglican, tormented Kantian, the man who believed that Christianity was an essentially tragic vision of the world; and Canetti – who was an uncomplicated atheist. Religion and magic (often, it would seem from *Crowds and Power*, synonymous in Canetti's mind) were vehicles for human beings to exercise power over one another. IM had a big heart, and a tremendous desire to remain friends with ex-lovers, ex-mentors and even, a more taxing thing this, ex-friends. It is surely significant that the two with whom she failed to do this were MacKinnon and Canetti. Both men wanted disciples. Then she turned away from them, their interest in her transformed to revulsion. Canetti devoted some months of his old age to penning a denunciation of her vulgar talents, saying nothing which she had not said herself in her dissection of 'Arnold Baffin' in *The Black Prince*. MacKinnon had a religious compulsion which added zest to his denunciation. He would probably have agreed with her cousin Dr Chapman, who told me that IM's gifts have 'been wasted because of her lack of Christian belief'. MacKinnon chose an after-dinner speech, after he had been given an honorary degree at the University of London, to denounce IM. 'There was real evil there,' he decided.

No doubt this 'evil' was something which JOB had sensed when he read, and hated, *The Bell*. MacKinnon had been savagely anatomised in *The Red and the Green*. As 'Barney Drumm' kneels at the back of a Dublin church at Tenebrae – whose phrases and psalms were especially dear to MacKinnon – he stares at the figure of the crucified and can secretly make no sense of the notion of redemption through Christ's blood. He knew 'perfectly well that what utterly poisoned his life was the beastliness of his relations to his wife'. There is real cruelty in her burrowing down into MacKinnon's/Barney's soul and stating, 'He had thought of himself as a man haunted at least by goodness, but these hauntings were merely the bog fires of his own psyche. His "good resolutions" were not even play-acting, they were babbling.'

By the time MacKinnon has become Rozanov in *The Philosopher's Pupil* (1983), he has declared that 'philosophy is impossible' and he has become 'a magician'.

Barbara Pym used to speak of the process of writing novels as analogous – a typically homely image – to making chutney. You put in the various ingredients, fruit, onions, vinegar, which for some days retain their separateness. Then at some point they turn; they become something different. In her various portraits of Canetti-like mage-figures or MacKinnon-like religious sages or

175

dolts, there is no life at all. The novels that are successful are those which she has made interior to herself; in her meditations upon the persons in her life she has re-created, re-imagined them. She has also, in the best books, either taken leave of herself, or come to be a different self – and this was perhaps in part what JOB found so alarming when he read what is generally considered her best book, *The Bell*. In this book, about a group of eccentric lay-people living in a community on the edge of an enclosed Anglican convent, Imber Abbey, IM's imagination takes leave of any individual 'position' she might have adopted as a philosopher. She inhabits all the characters, and is perhaps equally sympathetic to them all. Some of the sagest and deepest lines are given to the Abbess of Imber. Yet who can doubt that the central intelligence, frivolous, worldly Dora Greenfield, married to a dry stick of a scholar, is also an aspect of IM's psyche? And her lover, the journalist Noel, speaks for a whole side of IM when he urges Dora, 'Don't forget, *what these people* [i.e. the nuns and the Christians at Imber] *believe isn't true.*' (My italics.)

IM herself used to go on retreat at West Malling, an enclosed Anglican nunnery; and she also had friends in the Catholic Stanbrook Abbey near Worcester. Nuns and the conventual life fascinated her. The only time I was ever pompous enough to ring up an interviewer, after I had given an interview, and ask her to remove a sentence was when Rosemary Harthill, then BBC Religious Affairs correspondent, asked me to describe my relationship with IM. I said, spontaneously and truthfully, that it felt like that between Julie Andrews and the Abbess in *The Sound of Music*. Partly I wanted to withdraw the remark because it seemed screamingly camp; partly I was afraid she would somehow sense mockery, and would almost certainly not have heard of the musical in question.

Her ignorance of popular culture in the last twenty years of her life was on a par with the great Darwell Stone, Principal of Pusey House in the 1930s, who, when told by an undergraduate that he had been to see a show with the Dolly Sisters in it, paused thoughtfully and replied, 'That is a religious order of which I have not heard.'

IM was a very believable Abbess of Imber; that is, of the Imber-tween world where unbelief is suspended and piety is allowed to flood the heart.

In his inaugural lecture at Cambridge, MacKinnon said:

In Germany, Dr Rudolf Bultmann, the distinguished New Testament scholar, has concerned himself for many years with the attempt to make Christian truth, purged of its supposedly mythological elements, capable of assimilation by men and women of the twentieth century. But in so far as he *sometimes* does this, mainly by carrying out ingenious translations of the creed into the characteristic idioms of Martin Heidegger, one is tempted to say that *on these occasions* if he makes what he is translating intelligible, he does so at the cost of making it repellent.

I did not take JOB's advice about Violet. The love passed away as these things do.

About ten days after my embarrassing confession to him in Addison's Walk, and his more startling confession about *The Bell*, the telephone rang. 'Look, Andrew? Old thing? It's' – that tone of amazement, the production of a rabbit from a hat – 'it's Iris! Is there any chance of you both coming to lunch this Saturday?'

There was excitement in her voice, and I immediately sensed

that JOB had told her about our walk together, and all that I had said on it. Had he at last told her about hating *The Bell*? Or did the pair of them now look back indulgently on the jealousies and troubles of their early married years and rather enjoy playing games with the emotional lives of their younger friends?

Saturday, May 1977: K and I motor to Steeple Aston. Cow parsley in hedges. The trees in their full beauty. IM flung open the front door as we sank into the drive (an operation which always feels slightly perilous). IM is beaming. JOB runs from behind her like a fluttery old lady. 'Aah! My dears!' Kisses, rather smelly, implanted on us both.

From the first there is the playful sense that they have something up their sleeves, an exhibit. Through the large dusty hall, with its large round table; the eye quickly takes in the fact that it is set for six. Into the smaller drawing-room on the left, hung with tapestry.

'Now, m-m-my dear Andrew – Katherine – m-m-may I introduce you to my old f-f-f-friend Katherine Watson and her friend . . .'

I have already forgotten the friend's name.

Two quiet mousy women are presented, Barbara Pym characters. Miss Watson, a pretty woman of about sixty (?), runs the bookshop in Burford and is a translator from the French. Intelligent, bright-eyed face. She sits nursing her drink.

'She's also a p-p-*poet*!' says JOB, as if this is his achievement as much as hers.

'Well, so are you, John,' says Miss Watson, and speaks with admiration of the poem with which JOB won the Newdigate.

178

I can't recollect much of the conversation. Miss Watson is quiet and shy, her friend even more so. One of them, at one point during lunch, asks, 'And weren't you thinking of being ordained? Was that right?'

I find this a subject which is v. difficult to talk about.

JOB rescues me with, 'Andrew's written rather an amusing n-n-novel about it all, haven't you, darling?'

He sounds like an excited macaw.

'Perhaps the moment wasn't right?' ventures Miss Watson, whom I sense immediately to be pious. The last thing I would want to discuss with her was my extremely smutty novel about theological college.

'The time wasn't quite . . .' I murmur.

'Right,' she repeats sympathetically. It is obvious that we are both as far as possible from IM's position of enjoying Doubt and Christology as subjects for table-talk.

When the two women had gone, IM announces, her eyes ablaze, 'You realise that John and Katherine Watson were once engaged?'

'The lady who has just left?' I ask, astonished. I had always understood from JOB's own accounts of his courtship of IM, and from Rachel Trickett's even more sentimental accounts of the matter, that IM had been only the second woman in his life (after, of course, his mother).

'S-s-sort of engaged,' says JOB, as if this makes the matter much clearer. 'It was a strange situation – so to say! I became totally infatuated by her p-p-poetry when it appeared in various little magazines I enjoyed reading, as you might say, in those days.'

'Which magazines?'

'The Cunt . . . the . . . C-c-countryman.'*

'My mother is a devotee of it. We take it at home.'

'I wrote her a f-f-fan letter and we s-started to meet and talk about poetry. And then I f-found I was getting in d-d-deeper than I'd meant to really – didn't I, darling?'

'You see,' said IM. And she paused. One felt she had choreographed the whole afternoon around the sentence she was about to utter. 'When John first knew Katherine, she was a nun.'

After the amazed silence, JOB added by way of illumination, 'Well, s-sort of.'

'Surely,' said KD-J with Aristotelian abrasiveness, 'she either was a nun or she wasn't?'

'You know much more about these things than I d-d-do, dear K-Katherine, but I think she was what's called a p-p-postulant. It was all very innocent. We were like Babes in the Wood and I'm sure she didn't really want to m-marry me any more than I wanted to marry her.'

'But did you ask her?' K persisted.

'Well, in a *way*. Luckily Iris intervened, as you might say – and then in that marvellous' – he laughed, and one realised that by 'marvellous', he actually meant 'infuriating' – 'way of yours, darling, you *took her over for a bit*.'

'Well, I wouldn't say that.' IM sounded at once very authoritative and very Irish. She had turned into a rather dykey novice-mistress. 'She was someone who, as it were,' IM

---

*I've read through (2002) *The Countryman* for the relevant years and can find none of Katherine Watson's poems. But *The Countryman* was produced in Burford, where she lived, which perhaps explains the confusion.

poured an umpteenth slug of wine, '*needed me* at that moment.'

IM then began to talk about nuns and nunneries. She spoke of her friend Lucy Someone (??), an old Somervillian contemporary who wanted to become a contemplative nun, but could not because she wasn't a virgin. She spoke of Honor Tracy, 'who has found peace of a kind, dear girl' living on the edge of the community at Stanbrook.

> There were many people . . . who can neither live in the world nor out of it. They are a kind of sick people, whose desire for God makes them unsatisfactory citizens of an ordinary life, but whose strength or temperament fails them to surrender the world completely; and present-day society, with its hurried pace and its mechanical and technical structure, offers no hope to these unhappy souls.

Miss Watson and her friend are Barbara Pym characters who had the misfortune to meet IM instead of Miss Pym, with whom they could have shared their love of Victorian poetry, church and village life. Instead, Katherine Watson, a neurotic woman who could not quite become a nun, becomes the barely altered Catherine Fawley, the poor aspirant sister in *The Bell* who is secretly in love with homosexual Michael Meade, and who is carted off to a clinic in London. One begins to see why JOB found the novel unwelcome reading in 1958.

If I was right in assuming that Miss Watson was one of the ingredients in the 'chutney' which became *The Bell*, then here was evidence of the distinctiveness of IM's imagination. Her 'take' on other people was powerfully idiosyncratic. Rachel Trickett used to smile about an exchange she had had with IM in the 1950s, when entering a party in progress. Who, asked Rachel, was the handsomest man in the room? There were a number of obvious candidates, including Stuart Hampshire. Dewy-eyed, IM replied, 'Wallace Robson' – a man of striking appearance, but by no normal criterion the sort women would call handsome.

I once asked her who was her favourite character in *The Archers*, the radio soap to which she was much addicted.

After the inevitable pause, she played for time – 'What do you mean by favourite?'

'Well – let us say, with whom would you most like to have an affair?' I thought the answer might be Chris, the married woman who ran the riding stables; or Nelson Gabriel, the *antiquaire* with a risqué past, who owned a wine bar in Borchester and seemed like a figure from Chelsea in the 1950s.

'Jack Woolley,' she said firmly. Woolley is one of the most boring characters in *The Archers* – the proprietor of the big 'country club' hotel, a former Birmingham tycoon. Goodness knows what he seemed in IM's imagination, perhaps a figure of pure goodness? Or a frightening Demon, in the Canetti-mould, driven by the Will to dominate others?

It would be an amusing exercise to imagine how others would appear, had they passed through the mincing-machine of IM's imagination. *Pride and Prejudice* as rewritten by IM would probably make Mr Collins into an agonised atheist priest, perhaps having an affair with Lady Catherine de Bourgh. Lizzie Bennet would surely discover that Mr Darcy was homosexual and in love with Wickham, which is why he intervened in the elopement of that young man with Lydia . . .

* * *

Twenty-five years after I met Miss Watson, I ordered up her book of poems, *The Source*, in the British Library. It is a handsomely produced book, published by the Oxford University Press. It reveals a deep piety, much influenced by Gerard Manley Hopkins.

> Shall there never rest?

she asks

> The price of having hunger unfulfilled?
> Beauty more loved, the more unutterable?
>
> Oh that I were a bird, all being, being praise
> Christe, Christe, Christe calling . . .

In the poem about Mary Magdalene:

> Her not-to-be-appeasèd pain, of love,

is seen as

> The everlasting Easter of the heart.

I take the book back to the reserve desk, guiltily aware that I have not been reading, but prying.

Miss Watson is not Catherine Fawley in *The Bell*. I was wrong there, twenty-five years ago when I wrote up the experience of meeting her. That is not the way novelists work. They do not simply 'put' people into books. They do use them, though; and use them ruthlessly. Without Miss Watson, Catherine Fawley is unimaginable. Without what must once have been the private pain of a young postulant, the melodrama of *The Bell* would not have caught fire. That scene – Catherine going mad – is one of the best things in IM's novel.

5

A country wedding

It was perhaps the summer we saw the most of them, that of 1977.
A little later after our lunch with Miss Watson, we agreed to drive
down to Wiltshire for a wedding. A day out in their battered white
Volkswagen – christened from its number plate, OWL – promised to be as uncomfortable as an expedition in my decayed, half-
timbered Morris Traveller, but they were insistent. JOB would
drive, in their car. Kind granny would take the children for the
day.

11th June 1977: JOB and IM arrive in a Volkswagen to take
us to the wedding of Mark My Words and Lucy Neville-Rolfe.
It is a dark-green Volkswagen, much posher than OWL.
    'Have you sold OWL?' I enquire.
    'In a way,' says JOB.
    'We keep this one for longer journeys,' says IM.
    'It is a bit more comfortable,' JOB concedes.
    [Many years after this, Anthony Powell told me that when
he and his wife visited Steeple Aston, they noted the number

of clapped-out old Volkswagens, some half buried by creeper, which littered the drive. Violet Powell asked JOB about them and he said they were 'A hedge against inflation'.]

Mark My Words (Peter Quennell's nickname for him) was my contemporary and friend at New College, where we were both pupils of JOB. We both attended KD-J's Victorian poetry class, and in February 1970 I sent her a Valentine card. K told Rachel Toynbee, a pupil of hers, that she hoped it was Mark who had sent the card, since 'the other one looks a bit wet'. She also suspected the other one – me – of being RC. Mark has 'done well' in the few years since we went down. Already he has a successful career at the Chancery Bar and is established as a northern landowner, where he likes shooting, etc. Cf. IM/Bradley Pearson in *The Black Prince:*

They were shooting pigeons. What an image of our condition, loud report, the poor flopping bundle upon the ground, trying desperately, vainly to rise again. Through tears . . . I saw and heard their sudden weight, their pitiful surrender to gravity. How hardening to the heart it must be to do this thing: to change an innocent soaring being into a bundle of struggling rags and pain.

The bridal pair are being married at Lucy's home in Dorset – the parish church, in spite of L being RC.

The Bayleys have decided we should make a day of it, which is why we are leaving early, after breakfast. We are going to explore Fonthill, then have lunch with the young Stones, who are also coming to the wedding.

JOB used to drive army trucks in Germany when in the Guards at the end of the war. He likes cars but, as is the case with Cedar Lodge, he needs to stamp his mark, to foul his own nest. The large VW is marginally less filled with crumbs, old examination papers, books, etc. than OWL. Nevertheless it has that lived-in feel – lived in by what or whom, Sherlock Holmes would hesitate to say, were he to come upon it parked beside the road. J has pasted strips of paper over part of the windscreen and side windows.

'My version of Venetian blinds!'

JOB and IM mess everything they touch. The car smells as if rodents lived in it, and perhaps they do. I have seen field mice in OWL. The guinea-piggish odours in this car, mingled not unpleasingly with J's Dutch aromatic pipe-tobacco, are surely those of the owners?

I have fairly often been driven by JOB, back from college dinners, etc., and sometimes back to Steeple Aston. He leans forward gingerly when at the wheel and has a number of strange tricks, such as slowing to about eight miles per hour when approaching a traffic light in anticipation of it turning to red. Then, if it does not do so, he suddenly spurts forward.

I'd never travelled with IM in the car, however. She and I sit in the back. She is a very nervous passenger, and an impenitent back-seat driver.

'I say, old thing . . . not so fast! Slow down!' Or – dangerously touching his shoulder – 'There's a bend coming up!'

These observations and injunctions are studiedly ignored by the driver, who hunches over the wheel like a cross schoolboy.

In the front of the car, JOB and K indulge in a stream of chatter about their colleagues in the English faculty.

'John Carey's like Hitler! The masses adore him!'

'Anne Barton is just John Wilders without a blazer.'

One of them has but to say one of these colleague's names, and it is as if the clowns have come somersaulting into the ring at the circus. There are whoops of merriment – not really unkindly meant.

In the back, when not directing the traffic, IM asks me how my work is going, by which she means my novels.

Boringly, I tell her about my agent, Mark Hamilton, and ask her if she has ever had an agent. She says, No, she has never bothered with one. They would only embarrass her by talking about money. She has a perfect relationship with Norah Smallwood at Chatto.

'I suppose an agent would get one a large advance . . .'

'Advance? *Advance?* I have never been paid a *penny* in advance.'

Both these statements were untrue. About a year later, at Steeple Aston, we met Diana Avebury, who introduced herself as 'Iris's agent'. It is true that she did not negotiate the contracts of IM's novels with Chatto & Windus, but she did act for IM in other areas, such as theatrical work. As for advances, Chatto always paid them to IM, as the archives at Reading University made clear. When, several years after this conversation, IM engaged Ed Victor as her agent, he got Chatto to pay her advances of £100,000 for the British and Commonwealth publication of her novels.

She goes on to advise me to keep my manuscripts and type-scripts for sale to an American library. As soon as she has finished one of these, it is posted off to Iowa University.

K, overhearing, recalls the story which for her encapsulates the insularity and self-confidence of Oxford life.

A don at High Table in All Souls enquires of a guest where he comes from.

'Iowa.'

'Ah,' says the Oxford don, smugly correcting him, '*we* call that Ohio.'

Boswelling away, I drag IM back to the subject.

'Do you make notes before writing a book?'

'Yes. I make punctilious notes – well, you must do this yourself? I plan the whole book in advance.'

I say that isn't how I've written my first two novels. I just started to write. The first one seemed to write itself, and I made almost no notes or corrections at all; the second got stuck and I rewrote it.

IM looks shocked, but says, 'Everyone must write in their own way. I plan everything in advance, the plot, the characters' names, and so on. I fill many notebooks with this material. I would never, ever sell these notebooks, it is only the finished manuscripts and typescripts which go to Iowa.'

'Do you alter much between the first draft and the fair copy?'

On the front seat, JOB and K are on to the one about Mrs Sumner asking Lindemann, 'The Prof', what it was he did.

'I'm a scientist.'

'My husband,' chirrup K and JOB in unison, 'says that with a first in Greats, a man can get up science in a fortnight.'

Before long they are reciting Bowra-isms, such as his remark at Warden Sumner's funeral, as the coffin was carried into the chapel ('Sumner is a-comin' in!').

IM gives me another piece of advice.

'This is apostolic succession, as it were. William Plomer gave it to Ian Fleming, and Ian Fleming gave it to me – and that is: *Keep at it!* When you've finished a book, just sit down and write another. The public won't want just one book from you – they want the new Ian Fleming, the new . . .'

'They might want the new Iris Murdoch, but will they want the new A. N. Wilson?'

'Of course.'

'What happens if you get stuck?'

'I just carry on writing. I don't honestly hold with novelists who write only a little. Take E. M. Forster. *Passage to India* is all very well, but dash it, Forster old chap, you wrote that in 1924, and what have you done since?'

JOB and K discuss the merits, or, as they on the whole think, faults of EMF. K says how embarrassingly feeble she considers *Maurice*.

JOB recalls an occasion when he was in the middle of giving a tutorial at New College. That week he had written an article in *The Listener* saying what a pity it was that Forster had fallen silent as a novelist. He wondered whether the reason for this was that, given the current climate (it was pre-Wolfenden), he was unable to come clean about his homosexuality.

Anyway, there was JOB, puffing his pipe and giving his tutorial in NC, when he heard this shuffling on the uncarpeted stairs outside his room. A knock at the door. He went to open it, and found the bespectacled, mustachioed figure of the celebrated Cambridge novelist brandishing that week's *The Listener*.

'Do you realise,' Forster asked furiously, 'I could be sent to PRISON for what you have written in this paper?'

Our expedition before lunch is to Fonthill Gifford to see what remains of the eccentric William Beckford's faux-Gothic abbey. We burble about *Vathek*, which I have been teaching to my Stamford pupils at Cliveden, and about Beckford in general, about high camp and the homosexual imagination.

IM asks if I've read Brigid [Brophy]'s book on Firbank. I haven't, and say I don't like Firbank.

What a difference between then and now! I have read *Prancing Novelist* – surely one of the best bits of biographical criticism of a writer, and I am a devotee of Firbank, indeed, I think him one of the best English writers. I wonder, especially in the light of the conversation that follows, whether my 'distaste' for Firbank was based on some fear of the residual homosexuality in my own make-up? As this faded, and I became boringly 'hetero', as Rowse used to call it, I developed a much stronger taste for such writers as Firbank, Corvo and E. F. Benson.

Incidentally, my friend Alan Hollinghurst wrote a thesis on the subject that the Bayleys and Wilsons were discussing in the car that day: the title was something like 'The Uses of Suppression, the Creative Use of Homosexuality in Literature'. One of the writers he discussed was Forster, another was Firbank. The advertisement for his viva voce from the *University Gazette* appeared in *Private Eye*: 'Alan Hollinghurst, having submitted a thesis, etc., etc., will be orally examined in the English Faculty Building on such and such a date . . .'

When this oral examination – ho, ho – took place, one of the examiners was an ex-fiancé of IM's, Wallace Robson, an inspiring lecturer and scholar, by now a married man with children. He leaned forward his great Johnsonian frame and said in his plaintive tones, 'Mr Hollinghurst, you've called your thesis' – etc., etc., whatever it was called. 'What reason do you have for supposing that Firbank was a homosexual?'

This silenced Hol – for of course there is no 'reason' at all in Firbank's asexual, church-obsessed life to link the high camp of his imagination with being queer. Now that homosexual fashions are so butch, and all one's younger gay male friends have haircuts like lavatory-brushes and wear bovver boots, one can see the force of what Wallace Robson was saying to Hol.

Back to the car, in June 1977, as we drove into Beckford's Wiltshire!

> IM: All great artists have been bisexual.
>
> The two in front protest, humorously at first.
>
> IM: I don't necessarily mean practising bisexuals, though who cares about that. I mean that, in their imaginations, they inhabit either sex or both. Shakespeare, of course, was bisexual in both senses of the word.
>
> JOB: I always think old Rowse has got Shakespeare about right, don't you, K-Katherine, dear?
>
> K: Not really, no.
>
> JOB: I mean, it's obvious when you read the Sonnets that he doesn't have any sexual feelings at ALL for the young man, only for the Dark Lady, and Rowse was one of the first people to point that out.
>
> K: You mean, 'Since she pricked thee out for woman's pleasure', and so on. But isn't making jokes about a man's

penis just the sort of thing a homosexual man would do?

JOB: Ah! Well, I don't really think you're right, actually.

This was extraordinary, since it was the first time I had ever heard JOB express a disagreement with anyone. Normally if you said, 'Shakespeare was a Dutchman', he'd have been happy to say, 'Quite so', and then agree with the next person who said he was a Hottentot.

IM: Oh, come ON, John! Damn it, the Sonnets are about falling passionately in love with a BOY.

K: I'm rather inclined to agree.

IM has certain 'pets' in her life, creatures or categories whom she especially cherishes. They include badgers, foxes, Buddhists, Jews and male homosexuals. When she speaks of them a smile that is all but beatific lights up her face. She obviously sees Shakespeare and Plato and Sherlock Holmes (three especially favourite homosexuals) as being exactly like her queer friends in London.

'And not just in the Sonnets, John. It is obvious, for example, that Antonio is in love with Bassanio in *The Merchant of Venice*; and in *Twelfth Night*, Orsino's love for the boy-girl Viola . . .'

The car has screeched to a halt on the grass verge somewhere between Berkshire and Wiltshire. When JOB comes back from peeing into the hedge, he seems really furious. He peers into the back window of the car, and when his Pickwickian face approaches the glass it suddenly seems threatening.

'Shakespeare WASN'T a queer!' he says furiously.

K makes a joke. The atmosphere lightens.

'I don't know about anyone else, but I think we need a drink,' says IM brightly.

JOB produces a plastic bottle from the supermarket Budgens. Though it is labelled Budgens Own Brand Lemonade, it appears to contain a copious medical specimen, and it is with some alarm that I watch JOB pour some into a glass, produced from somewhere, and offer it to K.

'We f-f-f- – don't we, d-d-darling – find that a glass of gin and f-f—'

'French,' I butt in.

'Does the trick.'

'I need a drink very badly indeed,' says IM.

When we had all swigged the potent mixture, the row about bisexuality had evaporated. Standing on the greensward beneath the splendour of the great arch of Beckford's Fonthill, we drank some more gin and a great calm descended; and then we went to lunch with Humphrey Stone and his beautiful wife. Lovely simple food – pasta – cream – chives. A pair of very camp men our fellow-lunchers, one of whom sings Sunday School hymns in falsetto:

> Dropping, dropping, dropping,
> hear those pennies fall,
> Every-one for JESUS! [top C]
> He shall have them all.

JOB laughs uproariously, tears darting down his cheeks, and clutches the singer's arm, calls him Darling.

The wedding was the classic English wedding, public-school hymns, even the RC priest, Father Tranmar, SJ, seemed like a public-school housemaster. Large old church – St John the Baptist,

Tisbury. Medieval, but with eighteenth-century obelisk pinnacles. Inside lovely carved vaulting. Jacobean pews and pulpit. A cobwebby old helmet hanging over a tomb in a side aisle, Kipling's parents buried in the churchyard.

At the party, Mark My Words made a crashingly tactless speech, saying that if he'd known the Neville-Rolfes could afford a wedding breakfast on this scale, he would have proposed to Lucy long before. No laughter. Ouch! But a nice, boozy party. My memory of its close, when the music had begun, was of IM, bright purple tights beneath her dress, dreamily and affectionately dancing with Caroline Dawnay in the garden. CD's outfit made JOB and IM christen her 'The Queen of the Upper Volta'. We discussed her earnestly over a pub supper at Wilton. K had hoped to get into the park where the Countess of Pembroke entertained her brother Sir Philip Sidney, but instead it was Scampi in a Basket at The Pembroke Arms. IM asked obsessively about Caroline – who loved her, with whom was she in love, etc. In the car on the way home, IM held my hand and sang soulfully with tears on her cheeks:

> The mission bells told me,
> That I shouldn't stay
> South of the border,
> Down Mexico way.

If the drive to Wiltshire had shown anything, it was that the subject of Shakespeare's sexual preferences was potentially explosive. IM's suggestion, endorsed by me in the back of the car, that Shakespeare was a bisexual *imagination* had been enough to make JOB into a spluttering old colonel, indignant, wild.

The drive took place in the very year when IM and JOB paid

their first visit to Israel. They were part of a delegation which included Beryl Bainbridge, Bernice Rubens, Michael Holroyd, William Trevor and Melvyn Bragg. English writers were invited to meet Israeli writers for a cultural exchange. JOB acted up the role of being lovesick for the young Israeli reservist soldiers, expressing – to the general amusement of his fellow-delegates – an adoration of the sight of them in uniform. IM, throughout the trip, called him 'Princess'.

At a dinner after she had died, held in Hertford College, JOB put on a comparable show of enchantment with the black waiter, pursuing him into his pantry with the merry greeting, 'Hurl-hurl-hurl-hello, Othello!'

While Shakespeare's heterosexuality was not to be discussed, JOB's attitude to these things keeps everyone guessing. Over one of our lunches in the old days he quoted Yeats's 'Lapis Lazuli' – 'They know that Hamlet and Lear are gay'. 'It's obviously not true of Hamlet,' quipped JOB, 'but it would explain a hell of a lot about King Lear.'

6

How's God, old thing?

When I read *Henry and Cato* on its publication in 1976, I was twenty-five years old and, like all egomaniacs who read a novel by someone they know, I felt that it must in part have been inspired by conversations about my own life I had had with the author. Like Cato, I had longed to be a priest, though I had not, like Cato, gone the whole hog and been ordained. Indeed, after the age of twenty-three I had seen that I would be a somewhat unlikely priest.

I have reread *Henry and Cato* lately. It's one of the best, I think. It has a particularly good plot device. Henry inherits a big country house and estate upon the unexpected death of his brother. He finds out, when he returns to England from America to take up his inheritance, that there is also a London flat of which no one knew. The first time he goes there, he opens the fridge and finds a jug of milk . . . which is fresh. Thus he meets Stephanie Whitehouse, his brother's mistress, a former stripper and prostitute. Stephanie is a particularly successful example of the vulnerable, randy woman who is in part a self-projection. The novel also contains the figure of Cato Forbes, the tormented priest. It is hard to think of any English-speaking novelist who could describe so well the experiences through which Cato passes – a love affair with Christ, a desire to give himself to God, followed by darkness, despair, loss of faith.

As a young man:

He entered quite quietly into a sort of white joy, as if he had not only emerged from the cave, but was looking at the Sun and finding that it was easy to look at, and that all was white and pure and not dazzling, not extreme, but gentle and complete, and that everything was there, kept safe and pulsating silently inside the circle of the Sun . . . Cato, never, at that time or later, dignified these happenings with any grand name, such as 'mystical experiences'. What he had learnt was that all was mystical. He did not need any spectacular vision of Christ. He was with Christ, he was Christ.

Yet, after a number of years in the priesthood, all this has vanished. After a period of 'dryness':

Cato woke up one morning with the absolute conviction that he had been mistaken and that there was no God. The conviction faded; but from that moment Cato began to treat himself carefully, almost tenderly, like someone who has discovered in himself the symptoms of a serious disease, and for whom the world in consequence is totally altered.

There are comparably excellent passages in *Nuns and Soldiers*

(1980), the finest book of her later period. Anne Cavidge, a clever graduate who decides to enter a religious order, goes through a journey that is comparable to Cato's. She spends a few years as a nun. There is then a particularly astute description of her 'halfway phase' when she has not completely acknowledged to herself that her faith has left her:

> That the concept of a personal God began to seem to her more and more problematic did not too much dismay her. She lived as a member of a small mutually tacit 'intelligentsia' among those of simpler faith, a faith which she and her like refrained from disturbing. 'The clever ones' looked into each other's eyes and said, on the whole, little, certainly less than all, about the changes they perceived in themselves, and which, isolated as they were, they could not help connecting with the deep spiritually guided movement of a certain Time Ghost.

It is fascinating that (as in *The Time of the Angels*, a phrase which tells us that a personal God has fled, leaving the human race in a halfway state in which the angels still hover) IM should use such an uncomplicatedly Hegelian terminology. The loss of God was a Victorian phenomenon. Thomas Hardy was the only great English novelist to make it an overt theme, and he was not really able to explore the theme in his fiction, partly because of his domestic circumstances (his wife was a believer), partly because his publishers believed, surely falsely, that the public was unready for frankness in this area.

Most of the best novelists in the English language since Hardy have been tacit in their allusions to God's removal from the scene, or they have, like Evelyn Waugh and Agatha Christie, been religious believers. The extraordinary phenomenon of loss of faith, a dominant fact in the personal lives of millions in the last century, is not much treated in English fiction. To those for whom all this stuff is mere fantasy, simply creepy, it is perhaps of small or no interest. It remains to many others, however, one of the most interesting areas of life. When I look back at my own experience, I should find it difficult to explain or describe what was going on in my life, from about the age of fourteen to about the age of thirty, when I was wholly absorbed and obsessed by such experiences and such questions.

Of course Cato is not me. After 1976, when I first read the book, it began to dawn on me that there were dozens of Catos in IM's life, and indeed in the Western world. As the institutional Church gradually began to unscramble, hundreds, thousands, of men and women who had given their lives to Christ – as priests, nuns, religious sisters, or simply as committed lay-people – found themselves staring into the abyss and deciding that they had made a fundamental mistake, that there was 'nothing there'. IM's books spoke to us with a peculiar eloquence.

It is possible for faith to ebb and flow. Some people go on gaining and losing religious faith all their lives. The first time I lost my religious faith completely, as a schoolboy, two figures haunted my fantasy life. One was Dr Albert Schweitzer, who in those more innocent times was still regarded as a hero, and the other was Iris Murdoch. My housemaster was trying to persuade me, in the months after I left school and went on to the next stage – whether art school or university was not yet decided – to go out to Africa and work with the Community of the Resurrection (the Mirfield fathers) in what is now Zimbabwe. It is the one major regret of my life that I never did this, and I cannot even now remember why I did not.

We had all read Father Huddleston's book *Naught for your Comfort*, and in my fantasy life I imagined myself as a skinny monk, African children in some shanty-town pulling at the skirts of my threadbare cassock. When God vanished in a big way, and I had one of those periods of believing there was nothing there – just pointlessness, darkness, emptiness, and death in a suffering, point-less universe – the thought of such figures as Father Huddleston, or Dr Schweitzer, made Christianity seem more, and not less, appealing.

Surely, to live a life of unselfishness, such as that of Huddleston and Schweitzer, a life moreover focused on Christ was the best possible gesture one could make against the darkness. It was a highly 'existentialist' faith, challenged by forces which seemed too obviously unworthy – the overpowering force of Eros, and the chic of such writers as Sartre, whom I'd read a lot while doing *Les Mouches* for A level.

IM's *The Sovereignty of Good* was something which, aged seven-teen to nineteen, I read so often that my copy fell to pieces. Here seemed on offer a way of being religious, and even of worshipping something, or almost worshipping it, and yet not having to believe the impossible – i.e. a personal loving God whose existence was clearly incompatible with the innocent and pointless suffering of the universe. I had read the *Phaedo* with Mr Buckney at Rugby. How lucky I was to have such teachers! In one year, I read *King Lear*, *Antony and Cleopatra*, much of Corneille, the *Phaedo*, Thucydides Book VII, *The Odyssey* and *Crime and Punishment*. Our headmaster, Walter Hamilton, was a Platonist, and his translation of *The Symposium* for Penguin Classics is written in an English prose as limpid and perfect as any written in my lifetime. There is no substitute for reading the truly great books in late adolescence when they become etched on your mind. No reading experience later can match it.

IM, in *The Sovereignty of Good*, seemed to be offering the possibility of being 'religious' while not having to believe. The stuff about Kant and Hegel passed me by. I latched on to the Platonism. I was comforted to find that even an atheist could see that 'of course prayer and sacraments may be "misused" by the believer as mere instruments of consolation. But whatever one thinks in its theological context, it does seem that prayer can actually induce a better quality of consciousness and provide an energy for good action which would not otherwise be available.'

IM was an important person in my life before I met her. It is symptomatic of the position she occupied for tens of thousands of readers in the 1960s and 1970s. Doubt and faith came and went in my life like the seasons.

Like IM, I am a religious person for whom the practice of Christianity is all but impossible – temperamentally because the life-change demanded by the Gospel is impossible to fulfil, and intellectually – well, because there are too many difficulties to list. Did she choose an intellectually too easy form of atheism, while continuing to assert that she was a Platonist – even on occasion a Christian? It is not for me to judge, but a bit more worryingly, she spoke sometimes as if she thought she had begun to tread the path of righteousness or enlightenment. She made no complaints when a book was published in 1986, long before her dementia set in, entitled *Iris Murdoch, The Saint and the Artist*, by Peter J. Conradi.

There is a nobility in the 'tragic Christians' like Schweitzer, who doubted the objective truth of Christianity, but still chose to deny himself, take up his cross and follow Christ by giving his whole life to running an African hospital. Merely talking about Jesus as another Buddha at dinner parties, and exalting 'The Good' to anyone prepared to listen, is not comparably impressive.

Anyway, my ambition to be a priest, albeit as a Doubting Thomas, was from the first of interest to IM, and in the summer of 1971 it became an obsession.

When I told JOB that I wanted to be a priest, his reaction caused me some surprise. He was extremely enthusiastic. 'Dear old C of E,' he liked to say, and though obviously a non-believer, he had no objection to putting on a surplice when duty required this of a Fellow at college Evensong. My surprise at his enthusiasm for the notion of me as a priest had nothing to do with JOB's religious views. As disappointment coursed through my being, I realised that I had *hoped* he'd say, 'My dear, don't become a parson. Become a don! Put in for the All Souls fellowship!' The immediate disappointment was the first true indication that the idea of my 'priestly vocation' was in fact a personal fantasy which would never be realised. Naturally, I kept my feelings secret, considering them to be deeply unworthy.

In fact, I was never going to get a good enough degree to become a proper don. Had I done so, I still think I would not have qualified for the part. JOB always used to say that no one should become a don who could possibly survive in the world in any other capacity. He saw the Oxford colleges as refuges for freaks who could not manage 'ordinary life'. He could see that I was, in spite of an effete manner, fundamentally robust. JOB was not always the most conscientious teacher, but he was a good tutor in the sense of doing the right thing by his pupils. Like a good mother bird, he wanted them to flee the nest when the time came, and he was assiduous in finding them jobs, positions and areas of life that would suit them. One blushes to think of the number of hours a university tutor must spend writing references for scores of old pupils, and how airily, in one's youth, one applies for jobs giving a tutor's name.

I think he partly liked the idea of my being a priest because it would amuse IM. When K and I were married, both the Bayleys, who in some senses made the match, took a powerful sight of notice, frequently inviting us to Cedar Lodge, and even 'stalking' us at one point. We lived down a remote lane on Boar's Hill, which was a no-through road. It ended with a stile, and a field sloping down to Sunningwell. Neither of the Bayleys knew anyone in our road, yet the white Volkswagen with its OWL number plate was often seen in the lane. We even found them one day bent over outside the garden and peering through our high hedge. Quite what they were expecting to see I don't know. It always amuses me, in the many tributes to IM – including some of them in the TV programme I helped to make with and about her – that her friends piously repeat how little she liked to gossip. It is true that she did not often pass on gossip, but she absorbed it, via her carrier pigeon JOB, with alacrity.

My ambition to take holy orders was followed with eagerness by IM. When JOB wrote me a reference for the Selection Conference, she suggested emendations to his script, and they both waited with eagerness to learn how I had got on. In those days, in order to be accepted for training as a clergyman in the Church of England, you had to attend a conference organised by the Advisory Council for the Church's Ministry (ACCM).

Whether it still exists, I don't know. I went to a conference at a retreat house in Ealing.

I imagine that the selection procedure was modelled on officer training in the armed forces, and on similar procedures for the Civil Service. Twenty or so candidates gathered, to be assessed by two or three of the officer class. Our conference was presided over by a retired bishop, and a couple of other clerics.

When we had all consumed our first cup of coffee with a ginger-nut biscuit, we were seated in a circle and asked to introduce ourselves in a few sentences. The extraordinary variety of the Church of England was thereby revealed: Bunyanesque visionaries who had seen the Lord with their own eyes rubbing shoulders with those, such as myself, who found it next to impossible to talk of religious experiences, and indeed were not sure we had had them. There were grown-ups who had felt the call while working in offices or factories. There was a monk, who nevertheless had to go through the selection procedure before being ordained as a priest. A high proportion of those present seemed to be barmy. No doubt this was how I appeared to them.

I only blurted out a few sentences about myself before retreating into blushes and silence. Had I been gifted with an autobiographical fluency, the evidence I should have presented would not have made me an obvious candidate for Holy Orders. I was still only twenty. I had married a woman ten years older than myself and she was now several months pregnant. I had blown hot and cold about religion ever since my confirmation, being now a Tolstoyan simple-lifer, then an unbeliever, then for a very brief period a Roman Catholic, then back to unbelief, then Anglican. Of course I spelt none of this out when introducing myself, merely managing to say that I went to St Mary Magdalen's church at Oxford.

This detail – the church being conspicuously 'High' – made me seem like an obvious soulmate for Barry, a young man from Brighton who had long blond hair in what seemed like a perm.

His first remark to me when the circle broke up was, 'Horribly low, some of the young ladies they've sent us along with – as you SAW, dear.'

He made no attempt to lower his voice when he said this, and I immediately felt myself labelled, in the eyes of all the others, as one of Barry's kindred spirits. After supper, and Compline, it was suggested that we all turn in for the night. We were to treat the conference as a sort of retreat. Barry, however, had – as he put it – charmed one of the nuns who ran the place and obtained a front-door key, so as to be able to return to the house after lock-up. I had no great desire to go out with him, but – a besetting sin of mine – I did not want to appear stuffy, and so allowed myself to be led out of the hall to the accompaniment of 'Now, sweet-heart! Let's see what Ealing has to offer in terms of gay bars.'

This remark caused many of our fellow-conferands to look askance.

'Don't worry,' Barry assured them, with a winsome movement of his blond head in my direction, 'she's married – she'll come to no harm with me.'

Both parts of the sentence were true, and I quite enjoyed my evenings out with him each night. He told me that he had been to two conferences before and had been turned down as a result of a police record. It was the first time I had heard the word 'cottaging' and, as we sipped our gin in some Ealing pub which was in no senses of the word gay, I could not at first imagine what it could entail. The word 'cottage', suggestive of Miss Marple, trailing lobelias and a trug with secateurs beside the brick step and the back door, gave no hint of the activities for which Barry had been up before the magistrates.

During the next three days I was interviewed by each of the assessors. I was quizzed about my experiences of the world. I was required to 'chair' a discussion about some issue of the day. It was no great surprise to me when, a week or so later, I received a letter saying that while they did not wish to turn me down for Orders, they thought I needed a little more experience of life before committing myself. They suggested that I took some form of secular employment and applied again in two or three years.

This was clearly a sensible piece of advice, but when the Bayleys heard of it, they were both indignant. IM took it as a personal insult to JOB that his reference, and her added paragraphs, should not have carried more weight. They immediately decided that matters should be taken into their own hands.

Their great friend Janet Stone, the daughter of a bishop, and the sister of two other bishops, was consulted. She took JOB and IM to lunch with her brother, the Bishop of Worcester. When they arrived, he was wearing a purple cassock. He came breezing into the hall of his palace and said, 'You go in and help yourself to drinks. I'm just going to change.'

JOB said afterwards that he had privately hoped that this meant 'change into something more elaborate', and that the bishop might, for example, reappear wearing a cope and mitre. But he came back wearing a grey suit. When he heard of my letter from ACCM, Bishop Stone apparently exclaimed, 'This is monstrous! Send him to me and I will ordain him on the spot – he does not even have to go through any training!'

The Bayleys were probably exaggerating. The bishop could not have done this even if he had wished to, since the canonical age for ordaining priests in the Church of England is twenty-three and I had still not reached my twenty-first birthday. It was clearly a semi-serious possibility, however, since I have a letter from Helen Gardner at this date, begging me not to take up the bishop's offer.

> A reading of Iris's novels will show you that she is not really very *au fait* with today's church, and her grasp of reality is not her strong point! If you wish to be ordained, it is essential that you should submit yourself to the authority of the church. Being a priest is not something you do on your own. You are ordained by the whole church of God and it is obviously right that you should wait on the mind of that church. If you need financial assistance at this time, you know that you only have to ask me. Meanwhile, I have written to Dan Davin suggesting that he might employ you at the University Press in some capacity when you come down from New College next year . . .

Dear Helen. She had the reputation of being a monster. When a timid scholarship candidate poked her head around Helen's door at St Hilda's, the great Donne scholar and friend of T. S. Eliot put down her cigarette and said, 'Do you know who I am?'

'Aye,' said this Scottish lassie, 'you're the one who makes the gurrls cry.'

Helen Gardner had a withering tongue and a hot temper, but she was one of those dons (A. L. Rowse was another) who from the first was kind to me, and with practical kindness. The Bayleys took the common view of Helen as a bossy, overbearing person, and she was one of those I heard IM describe, quite unjustly, as 'a bad person'. Rowse was another. How very wrong she was.

I have often wondered since what would have happened, though, if I had taken up the bishop's offer and just become a priest: jumped in at the deep end with no further consideration. Would I have had the strength, and the imagination and boldness, to stick to it? Or would there have been the inevitable backslidings, and possible scandals? I will always be a 'spoiled priest', haunted – like some of the figures in IM's books – by a God in whom he can only intermittently believe.

The question of 'what I should do' was left in the air. JOB and I used to enjoy singing to one another the Lord Chancellor's song from *Ruddigore*: 'When I went to the bar, as a very young man . . .'

> In other professions in which men engage,
> Said I to myself said I –
> The Army, the Navy, the Church and the Stage . . .

Unlike the Chancellor, I did not pursue a career at the Bar. I drifted. A bit of this and a bit of that. Schoolmastering for two happy years at Merchant Taylors'. Then back to Oxford to teach very inadequately, since I am no scholar, medieval languages and literature at St Hugh's College and New College. JOB moved on to become a Professor at St Catherine's.

Because I married in my second year, I did not have much experience of undergraduate life. My impression, though, is that compared with some of those who came before and after, mine was a rather dull generation at Oxford. I arrived when some great exotics, such as Tina Brown, Martin Amis and Craig Raine, were on the point of leaving, to make their mark on the great world. Then came us – the Oxford of Gyles Brandreth and Ann Widdecombe. After that, when I'd begun to be a teacher at Oxford, came some real dazzlers: Andrew Motion, Amanda Greave, Hugh Grant, Stephen Pickles, Alan Hollinghurst. The Piers Gaveston Society was formed – a self-consciously decadent club in which mascara and togas were worn by the men, and both sexes absorbed copious quantities of alcohol and other stimulants.

Stephen Pickles was much the most brilliant man of his generation. He came to New College about five years after me. He was small – about five foot five in height – with slight features, and elfin beauty. Many of both sexes were in love with him. He made a sort of pair with Amanda Greave, the 'toast' of her generation, who with her short-cropped hair and bright stars for eyes seemed like one of the more animated androgynes of Shakespearean comedy.

As an undergraduate, Pickles – ubiquitous, and universally revered – seemed capable of anything. He was musical, knew all about opera, acted with brilliance, his First Class degree was a foregone conclusion. In the time I got to know him best, he was hanging about in Oxford not doing very much, except produce the odd play (the best *Three Sisters* I ever saw and a brilliant *Twelfth Night* with himself as Feste) and nurse a painfully un-requited passion for Hugh Grant.

Hugh was a pupil of mine. He was a young man of consummate charm and good manners from the very first, though I used sometimes – when observing the agonies through which poor Pickles went on Hugh's behalf – to think of the young man in Shakespeare's sonnets who 'moving others are themselves as stone/unmoved cold and to temptation slow'. Obviously he did not respond to male advances because he was straight; but one sensed that in all his romances and friendships he was unable entirely to lower the drawbridge and allow others into his secret.

Pickles – the first to alert me to Hugh's star quality – was a good friend in those days, and his house in Cobden Crescent, always called for some reason 'The Cobden', was a place where I and my little family were welcome. He and his two house-mates, Andrew Motion and Alan Hollinghurst, were kind to my young daughters. There was a memorable day, for the girls at least, when Motion and Hol (as everyone called him then) took them upriver for a picnic on their 'camping punt'. No pun intended; it was a floating tent, a punt with a canvas roof.

The household was on the whole a harmonious one, though they were all great diarists and made the mistake of leaving these volumes lying about where they could be read by the others. It was a painful few weeks after Pickles read the entries by Hol about his inability to do anything silently – an eloquent evocation of his exhalations as he read a book, the melodramatic way in which he closed or opened doors. Motion became Poet Laureate. Hol is a famous novelist. At the time, though, Pickles was always the one of the three who was most strikingly brilliant.

16th October 1978: party at the Cobden. Poor Pickles is in agony wondering whether H[ugh] will turn up at the party being thrown by him, Hol and Motion. It is a nice little party. I got there early but not so early as IM, who thinks that when he puts 6.30 on an invitation card, the host will be even more pleased if guests turn up at 6.20. She is wearing a rich royal-blue 'top', ski-pants and lace-up shoes, slightly misshapen, from Marks & Sparks. As I approach her, she raises her glass with a radiant smile, and says, 'You've heard the news?' 'No . . . What?' 'A Polish Pope – they've elected a Polish Pope!'

'How exciting – who is he?'

'He's the Archbishop of Cracow, he's an intellectual, oh, this is simply the best news for years in the Roman Church.'

John Fuller standing by suggests that Poles are even more conservative than Italians when it comes to religious matters.

John, together with James Fenton, wrote an hilarious piece of anti-Catholic invective which was even more extreme than anything IM could dream of in her most Paisleyite ravings. Its refrain was 'I hate the Catholics and their Catholic God . . .'

'But no, no – this is marvellous news. I love Poland, I love Poles . . .'

'But it doesn't mean that the Roman Church will change . . .'

'Of course it won't, in one sense . . . but I don't know! It HAS to. It is bound eventually to accept women priests, for instance.'

'You think a Polish Pope will ordain women?'

'I don't see why not. The Roman Church has changed much more radically in many ways than the Anglican Church, than my Church, if I can call it that . . .'

'Do you think that the Polish Pope will ordain women before they ordain women in the Church of England?' I ask.

IM is swigging the white wine very fast and has already put away about half a litre of the stuff when she asserts, 'Certainly!' (Sortunlah!)

'Like to bet?'

'I'll bet on it, yes!' She shakes my hand. 'No, no, I see the whole of Christianity making great changes. It's vital, vitally important that we should all have access to this – stuff!'

John Fuller asks, 'What stuff?'

'To religion,' she answers shortly.

Most people edge away, but she continues to talk to me. Colin Haycraft, a London publisher I met at a dinner recently (brother of John, whom we know from Walberswick), tried to be clever by asking – 'How do you define a religious maniac? Answer – someone who believes in God!' But IM shows that it is possible to be a religious maniac who doesn't believe in God. She is in no orthodox sense a believer in any of it, but she enjoys nothing more than apparently serious discussions about the Trinity. She speaks constantly of her desire to find – perhaps to found, for there is more than a little in her character of some pioneering nun like Teresa of Avila – a new Christianity which has discarded the fiction of God and focuses on the spiritual Christ. She can stand around at a party and ask brightly, 'I wonder who invented the notion of the Trinity?'

She is slightly deaf, and becoming more so. But this is more than a physical condition. She asks, asks, asks questions about other people's religious persuasions, but never seems to hear their disquiet or embarrassment that such matters should be aired in the first place.

I would calculate that there have been well over fifty occasions when she has asked me who invented the Trinity. Though it is fashioned as a question, it does not stay for an answer. It is really just an observation. This famous Platonist never wants to discuss the hints of a Trinitarian

213

myth in the *Timaeus*, or the way this was developed by Plotinus, nor the use of it by Christian Platonists such as Clement of Alexandria or Origen. She gives off the paradoxical air of someone who thinks these things are the deep things of life, but that she can't be bothered to study them, only to talk about them.

She says she is a fellow-traveller with Christianity, but she is actually its enemy.

JOB has now arrived at the party and has come to join us. She is repeating herself about the Trinity. JOB joins in with, 'I believe in the holy Catholic Church, the Communion of Saints, the Forgiveness of sins, the Resurrection of the body, and the life everlasting! – rather marvellous in a way. I wonder who wrote that – Cranmer, I suppose?'

I recollect before she introduced me to John Ashton, a Jesuit pupil of hers who subsequently abandoned his priesthood, she said how she had been delighted, during her period at St Anne's of giving philosophy tutorials, in persuading believers to abandon their faith. It is rather strange, given her hypnotic spiritual ability to bewitch religious men, that the Jesuits entrusted so many scholastics to her tutelage. The fact is that since the days of Father d'Arcy, the English Province of the Society of Jesus is star-struck and makes a cult of celebrities or aristocrats.

'Old Iris sees off those Js!' JOB remarked approvingly at the time. 'Had quite a good b-b-bag of them, so to say, didn't you, darling?'

At the other end of the room I find a lovelorn Pickles. Hugh Grant has turned up, but is talking animatedly to a pretty woman at the other side of the room.

Pickles says that IM engages in these 'philosophical' discussions while in Oxford, but that you can tell from her face that she isn't interested in them at all. Says she's really happiest when in London among artists, actors, art students, London queens. Probably a lot of truth in this.

7

We authors

Writing to Larkin in 1977, JOB remarked, 'A former pupil of mine called Andrew Wilson has just written quite a good sort of novel called *The Sweets of Pimlico* (bad title) out in a few weeks. It faintly reminds me of my nonce-offering *In Another Country*, 1954, which at the time achieved a modest reprint before vanishing for good.'

Larkin was that year the chairman of the Booker judges. He evidently picked up on my pushingness since on 27th June 1977 he wrote to Barbara Pym, 'I'm just reading a first novel by a protégé of [JOB]'s, A. N. Wilson, *The Sweets of Pimlico* ('For John Bayley and Iris Murdoch'), for Booker. Oh, the wicked world.'* IM herself had announced, in her youth, that she was determined to 'make her mark' and I fully understand this urge.

Writers might pretend to be without it, but the truth is that all of them are possessed to a lesser or greater degree by this desire not merely to succeed, but to win in some competition whose

---

*Barbara Pym Papers, Bodleian Library, Oxford.

rules and prizes are invisible to the rest of the world, but which are clear enough to the 'young enthusiast', as Samuel Johnson called such a pusher.

My competitiveness, to the point of aggression, was manifested to me, not unshockingly, when, a few weeks after Mark My Word's wedding, IM asked us to lunch at Cedar Lodge. It was a glorious summer day. The windows of the house were all open, and the garden at that date, still kept in some kind of order by JOB, was meadowy and floreate, heavy with butterflies and insects.

They'd asked a handful of the usual neighbours, a couple of members of the English faculty and, standing in the large room, which served as a hall, the rotund and unmistakable figure of J. B. Priestley and his wife Jacquetta Hawkes.

I never met IM with Canetti, or with Professor Fraenkel, so I never saw her in the presence of those whom JOB has called the *Dichter*. (The word simply means poet in German, but he seems to use it as if it connoted a dictator or a guru, one who wished to exercise power over disciples.) The body language between IM and Priestley gave me a little glimpse of what her demeanour might have been like in the presence of such emotional bullies. Although plump always, IM was never as tubby as the author of *The Good Companions*. She appeared, beside him, like a tree, bending over to suck nourishment from water, or like a geisha obeisant to her master.

J. B. Priestley was distinguished in at least three areas of literary or quasi-literary life. For younger readers, to whom he is little more than a name, it is conceivably worth rehearsing what these were. Born in Bradford and retaining the distinctive accent of his native town, Priestley first became famous with the publication of

The Good Companions in 1929, a robust realist tale of provincial life which was an immediate bestseller. (At its peak by Christmas 1929, Heinemann were despatching 5,000 per day from their warehouse.[*])

Priestley was to know a different order of fame during the Second World War when his gravelly tones became familiar to wireless audiences. IM wrote that 'his frequent broadcasts, uttered in his rich Yorkshire voice, were a constant inspiration'. These broadcasts, entitled *Postscripts*, were aired after the nine o'clock news on the BBC's Home Service. Twenty-nine per cent of the adult population tuned in. They *are* superb broadcasts, their sentimentality held in check, with their evocation of English life, and the scenes, history, characters and values which they were fighting to preserve against Hitler.

The third great area of Priestley's success was the theatre, and it was here that IM came into his orbit. She first met him when they appeared on television together in the 1950s. When she wrote a play based on *A Severed Head* she showed it to Priestley, who said, 'This won't do, Duckie.'[**] Rewritten by Priestley, the play ran for two and a half years at the Criterion Theatre. After its preliminary run, IM wrote, 'Darling Jack, after my experiences on Tuesday night in Bristol I feel fairly certain about one thing. I think WE HAVE WRITTEN A TERRIFIC PLAY . . . Hooray for us! I embrace you.'[***]

She told Priestley's fellow-Yorkshireman, John Braine, 'I adored him – at once. What a man, what a character, what an appetite

---

[*]Vincent Brome, *J. B. Priestley*, Hamish Hamilton, 1988, p.94. Diana Collins, *Time and the Priestleys. The Story of a Friendship*, 1994, p.vii.
[**]Collins, op.cit., p.viii.
[***]Brome, op.cit., p.426.

for life!'* She saw him as a Falstaff, and as a king; also as 'in a deep sense spiritual'.

Since she was being kind enough to take me up, act as a patroness, it was clear that she would want me to meet this hero.

From early childhood I have been aware of a facial expression, a certain 'look' passing over the countenances of a small proportion of the people I meet. One of Cyril Connolly's wives asked, 'What's that on your face?' to receive the reply, 'Hate.' The 'look' I am describing, when I encounter it, is not just instant dislike – though it is this. It is dislike, combined with considerable irritation. They would appear to believe not merely that I am annoying them, but that I have set out to do so.

'And you can wipe that expression off your face, Wilson.'

'What expression, sir?'

'See me afterwards, Wilson.'

Schoolmasters, scoutmasters, the clergy . . . One has seen this 'look' appear and been powerless to do anything about it.

'I don't like that one,' remarked Mrs Gordon, Helen Gardner's housekeeper, the first time she met me. ''E tosses iz 'ead.'

Much to my embarrassment, I saw that I was having this instantaneous effect upon J. B. Priestley. IM, so deferential to him, so kindly disposed towards me, so sweetly anxious that her house should be aglow with human love, looked anxious almost at once, her antennae immediately alerted to her old hero's bristling hostility. She had obviously lent, or given, a copy of my book to Priestley, perhaps put it beside his bed if he had been staying the night. While she reminded him that I had just written a novel, which had received golden opinions, Priestley sucked upon a

---

*Ibid.

noisome tobacco-pipe and surveyed me. His facial expression was less suggestive of an eminent writer meeting one younger and in every way more minor than of a ham actor in a film comedy, angry that some buffoon had just broken his window, or inadvertently hurled a custard pie at his face.

'Andrew's written an absolutely splendid . . .' IM's voice died away.

'Ah, I suppose he thinks,' said Priestley, 'that he's done something clever, does he? Sophisticated? Let me tell you the sort of story someone nowadays would consider sophisticated. A young woman, thinking herself a bit of a highbrow, gets involved with a man in Chelsea, starts to meet his friends, doesn't realise that he and his chums are a pack of homosexuals? Don't get me wrong – I helped change the law of the land to make it more tolerant of homosexuality, but I do *not*' – his tone suggested an indignant belief that I'd been asserting the opposite – 'consider that it *and it alone* will make a novel *sophisticated.*'

He lit his pipe, which had gone out, and for the first time he looked me straight in the face.

'Do you know,' he asked me, 'that when *The Good Companions* was published in 1929, it was advertised on hoardings on the London Underground!'

I expressed myself suitably overawed by this information, aware, as I did so, that I was making matters worse by something that was beyond my control, an inability to 'wipe that expression off my face'.

'People responded to *The Good Companions* because it was about *real life!*' he barked.

I tried to pacify him. A non-fictional work, *English Journey*, published in 1934, is subtitled by Priestley 'a rambling but truthful account of what one man saw and heard and felt and thought during a journey through England during the autumn of the year 1933'. When he visited the Wedgwood works, still in their old factory at Etruria in Stoke-on-Trent, my father, a director of the firm, gave him lunch, and I told Priestley how, at home, *English Journey* was a favourite book. The passage is proudly marked where he writes, 'I joined three very pleasant and intelligent young men who appeared to be in complete charge of the big complicated works. This in itself was a happy change, for as a rule one sees nothing but middle-aged or elderly faces round these directors' dining tables.'

My recollection of the passage gave the author no pleasure whatever, even though I could quote it word for word. He looked at me as if to suggest that, while fondness for his work was to be expected in the vast majority of cheerful, hard-working English folk (a very J. B. Priestley word), in myself it could only be affectation or, worse, downright impertinence.

A few weeks later I found myself approaching the M40, driving out of London in the Morris Traveller towards Oxford. At a set of traffic lights in Acton, I drew level with a small turquoise car, with a tubby figure clad in a fedora seated in the driving seat. The furious old turnip-head turned a little to the right and gazed idly, waiting for the lights to change, and the eyes of the great novelist once again met mine. He did not recognise me at first. Then the 'look' came into his face and I knew he had 'clicked'. I waved. He stared impassively. The lights changed, and I drove off.

Neither my Traveller nor his little turquoise car was built for speeding. Yet as I pulled away, and watched the needle on my speedometer rise through 40 to 50 mph, I became aware of something turquoise in my nearside mirror. The old man was trying to overtake me on the inside lane; trying, and succeeding. I trod on the gas and rose to 60 – he was juddering towards 65, 70.

We had now begun to exchange looks of undisguised hostility as, clutching our wheels, we drove like maniacs. As we came down the hill towards West Wycombe, roaring like lawn mowers that had gone berserk, we touched 80: my engine began to overheat; the wooden frames of the shooting brake and the very chassis felt as if they might at any moment disintegrate. The noisome pipe had disappeared from my rival's mouth. Perhaps he'd eaten it, or perhaps it had fallen in his lap and was burning a hole in his trousers. Somewhere beyond High Wycombe, Jacquetta Hawkes, his wife in the passenger seat, must have screamed at him to slow down, for the Traveller pulled ahead and we roared back to Oxford in record time. It felt like the supreme achievement of my literary career.

IM would no doubt have been distressed by such childish behaviour had she ever heard about it, but she was not without the irrational sense of other authors as her natural enemy. It used to be said that Virginia Woolf was less distressed by ill-natured reviews of her own books than she was by reading adulation of the novels of I. Compton-Burnett. IM found praise of Muriel Spark hard to stomach, and if JOB wished to cheer her up he would ask the company to agree that *The Ballad of Peckham Rye* was 'not any good'. Graham Greene, who had once been unkind about IM's books, 'wasn't any good *at all*' and both – it went without saying – were Catholics.

I shared with JOB, and with Katherine Duncan-Jones, a fondness for the novels of Barbara Pym. A fellow-novelist, Paul Binding, was always trying to arrange a meeting, but it was not in the will of the Fates. He did, however, invite JOB (who had taught him at New College) and IM to his cottage near Banbury to meet the author of *Some Tame Gazelle*.

In a letter to Larkin about the occasion, Pym records:[*]

> We met John Bayley and Iris at drinks with a young friend some weeks ago. I thought they were extremely nice and we had some agreeable conversation, enlivened by John suddenly dropping his glass which seemed to go off with a loud explosion and there we were all scrabbling on the floor picking up bits of glass! Iris was much smaller than I had imagined – I'd always thought of her as tall, but I seemed to tower above her (though only in height, of course).

When Barbara Pym was being interviewed as a schoolgirl for her place at St Hilda's College, Oxford, she craned forward to see if she could decipher, upside down, what the tutor was writing about her. Rather than 'percipient thoughts on John Donne', the phrase 'tall girl, big teeth' had been scribbled on the jotter. She was notably tall, and IM of average height for a woman, certainly not noticeably small.

Where they would stand in a League Table of Twentieth-Century English Novelists is a matter of taste. Most readers, surely, would recognise that IM was attempting toweringly more ambitious work than Pym. What JOB 'really thought' about anything was probably not worth asking, but he certainly used to read and reread Pym. When we supped together, he and I would go on and on and *on* about how much we liked Pym's novels. I think IM found this worse than boring. It sometimes

---

[*]19th November 1977, *A Very Private Eye*, Macmillan, 1984, p.309.

made her angry. Eventually I realised that to praise another writer at a novelist's table is never safe, even when the novelist is as lofty and 'important' in the scheme of things as IM. Even if you have won every literary prize, and been made a Dame Commander of the British Empire, you can still be made uneasy if your husband and your biographer spend the evening braying about the brilliance of *Excellent Women*. It was as tactful, on our part, as sitting at a woman's table and talking all evening about another woman's sexual attractions.

Such crossness as there was, however, was more usually disguised as deafness. And she never *read* a Barbara Pym novel; or, as far as her conversation threw light on the question, many of her female contemporaries. Anthony Powell's *A Dance to the Music of Time* she read, saying that it was the product of an only child. Not only is the great sequence an account of an only child acquiring, through marriage, innumerable relations; more than that, an only child naturally peoples the world with imagined friends and siblings. IM used to say that she and Powell were agreed on this, that their lives as novelists had begun in their solitary childhoods.

The Lord of the Rings she read and reread, enjoying detailed conversations about it with its author, or with Christopher Tolkien, the author's son. She loved the Hornblower stories and the Patrick O'Brian sea stories, though she deplored the love interest and felt that Stephen Lefanu's infatuation with Diana Villiers was soppy stuff which spoilt the excitement of the adventures. At mention of the works of Olivia Manning, Elizabeth Taylor or Jean Rhys, let alone Penelope Lively or Margaret Drabble, she would merely smile and shake her head. She spoke, always, with love and respect of Elizabeth Bowen, her mentor, and A. S. Byatt, her disciple and interpreter, but she spoke of them as 'beloved beings'. Bowen herself dissected the novels of contemporaries, read them closely, remembered what she admired about them. IM never spoke in this way about the work of female contemporaries.

When JOB himself wrote a novel, after a gap of a quarter of a century, it was a different matter. *Alice* was the overtly lesbian novel IM had never quite been able to write. She appeared genuinely thrilled. Yet it was on the evening to celebrate the publication of this charming book that one first heard the dread chords playing in the orchestra. In retrospect, one saw that evening in 1994 as the beginning of the End.

IM was in Chicago on the day that *Alice* was published. She was to return at the very end of the party, held in the Museum of Modern Art in Oxford, and sup with us afterwards in Charlbury Road.

I went to Oxford that afternoon. Ruth, my second wife, was to drive Alice Thomas Ellis and Beryl Bainbridge to the party from London. The novelist Alice Thomas Ellis is Anna Haycraft; her husband Colin, proprietor and managing director of Duckworth, was JOB's publisher. By the time I arrived at the party in the Museum of Modern Art, IM had also arrived, very red in the face, from the airport. She had been attending a conference on her own philosophical works organised by the philosophical faculty at the University of Chicago. I asked her how it had gone.

'I'm very tired.'

'I bet – it's always worse, flying the Atlantic eastwards than westwards for some reason. Anyway, here's to John's book.' I raised my glass of red.

She downed hers and repeated, 'I'm very tired.'

'What form did the conference take?' I persisted. 'Did someone read a paper on *The Sovereignty of Good* and then ask you to comment?'

'O God!' she said, tugging at her hair.

In the gents twenty minutes later I came upon JOB. He'd been standing at the urinals for some minutes.

'N-n-nope – no good, I fear. I'm going to have the op. D-d-dear old prostate.'

'Oh, John.'

'Look, my dear Andrew, Iris is in rather a bad way. She wants you and Ruth and Fram and Candia to come back for supper, but she can't quite f-f-*face* B-b-beryl and A-a-nna, so to say.'

'The trouble is, we've promised to drive Anna and Beryl back to London.'

I should have read all the signals, and said that of course IM was too tired to hold a large supper party in her kitchen. It would have been perfectly possible to take the chain-smoking London crowd to a restaurant before ferrying them back to Camden Town. But in my moment of dither, JOB said, 'It'll be okay – no, *do* bring them all.'

'We won't stay long.'

In the kitchen JOB had laid out one of his picnics.

'I remembered you liked pies, my dear Andrew.'

It is true that I liked pies. On this occasion this was just as well, since not very much else was on offer – lattice pies, pork pies, veal, ham and egg pies, bought in some profusion from Budgens. Some had been cut in half, others were being served in their cellophane wrappers. There were some tomatoes, and plentiful quantities of booze. It was fine. No one minded remotely. It was an agony for me because I knew that IM actually wanted none of us there. As the others roared and smoked and repeated themselves, she looked wretched. She tried to answer my earlier questions about the conference and to talk about philosophy.

'I don't feel I was especially helpful to them,' she said sadly. 'They seemed . . . Well, these matters were all of great interest.' Sigh. Clutch of hair with fist.

IM always had the disconcerting habit of suddenly leaving a conversation and drifting into vacancy. I have spoken to those who knew her as a young woman and they have said it was a feature of her behaviour even then. She would stop speaking. A glazed, often almost joyful, expression would pass over her face and she would be gone, communing with one knew not what or whom.

Sitting beside her on that evening of 1994, knowing she was tired and jet-lagged and slightly drunk, it did not surprise me that she was failing to finish sentences. Later that year, on 15th September, IM and JOB had lunch with Hardy Amies (her Cornwall Gardens neighbour in London) at Langford. The diarist James Lees-Milne was present and he wrote, with prophetic percipience, 'Party included John Bayley and his wife Iris Murdoch. IM not easy and rather deaf (I suspect) but amiable. I was amazed when she kissed me. Looks like a sad full moon longing to wane. Almost piteous, on verge of declension. He most attentive and adoring.'

8

Die Kehre

A great change had come upon IM when she had passed her sixtieth birthday. I have said that she was of a sunny disposition, and this was true. I have suggested that, in common with other novelists – perhaps with most novelists – she had a capacity to bank, or to use, experience that enabled her to weather griefs which in others would have induced depression or despair. Certainly she always spoke disparagingly of Freud and distrustfully of psychoanalysis, psychotherapy or 'talk cures'. It was better for an unhappy (on-hoppy) person to write a novel, she would aver, than to 'waste time on that "stuff"'.

This was to suggest a connection between a writer's inner life, her unresolved fears and fantasies, and her work which, if applied in IM's own case, she would always deny or avoid.

When she was asked to give the 1982 Gifford Lectures in Edinburgh, she was given the chance to articulate in a formal manner what, in conversation, and stray lectures or essays, she had been discussing for years, namely her views on the philosophy of religion. Perhaps the most celebrated Gifford Lectures were

William James's *The Varieties of Religious Experience*, but there were many others which became landmarks in the literature of religious philosophy. The roll-call of previous Gifford Lecturers is awe-inspiring. Rudolf Bultmann, Edward Caird, Austin Farrer and Donald MacKinnon, J. G. Frazer of *Golden Bough* fame, Étienne Gilson, expert in Dante and medieval philosophy, Arthur Balfour and Lord Haldane, Dean Inge, Reinhold Niebuhr, Josiah Royce and William Temple had all given Gifford Lectures.

Perhaps the invitation came at the wrong time in IM's life. In the first two decades of her married life, the relationship with JOB actually depended on distance. Socially, and indeed on the podium giving their joint lectures for the British Council, they were a glorious Double Act. But their fondness did not appear to require seeing one another all the time. They both liked a word used, perhaps coined, by their friends the Geaches (Elizabeth Anscombe and Peter Geach, who were devotedly married but had jobs in different towns). They were *telegamous*. IM went to London at the beginning of most weeks, and would return towards the end. JOB pottered about in Steeple Aston, or in college, reading his books and having his thoughts.

The time came, however, when they needed to be together much more than this. Presumably this coincided with a general quietening down of the erotic impulse in them both. At a lunch party given by Jo and Rosalind Pennybacker in 1981, JOB, sitting on a garden bench with a glass of wine in his hand and speaking of sex, remarked airily, 'I seem to have completely given up in that department – no one appears to mind or notice!' He laughed at his own remark. IM, seated at another end of the garden table, looked up sharply but smiled, looked down and continued with what she was saying about the radio drama, *The Archers*.

When IM went to Edinburgh in 1982 to give the Gifford Lectures, one became conscious of a change coming upon them both. In the first instance, she had considered going to Edinburgh for a whole term, but when she had been away for a few days, they both found the absence of the other intolerable. JOB decided to get on a train and go to Edinburgh.

The experience demonstrated to him just how far their shared oddity had been allowed to go. He was no longer really at home in the world. Travel, even quite short distances, had for years been undertaken only under duress, and with IM as his chaperone. Time was, in the 1950s, when he had been seen going up to London. (He amused and surprised his colleagues by thinking you should wear a bowler hat to do this, and he wore his father's old bowler until the 1960s, when it was replaced by Oxfam tweed caps.)

But it was now 1982, years since he had travelled by train, preferring the womb-like securities of his various rodent-infested VWs. Only desperation, to see his Miss Trotwood, made this Mr Dick venture out into the hostile world of 'British Rail', 'Supersavers', 'Awaydays' and 'Travellers' Fare'.

He telephoned IM in Edinburgh and told her that he would be on a certain train. She anxiously awaited it at the other end, and was intensely worried when he did not appear at the barrier in Waverley Station. Enquiries at the stationmaster's did not shed any light on the matter.

JOB had caught the direct train to Edinburgh at Oxford station. Much to his chagrin, he had found himself opposite someone who had wanted to talk.

'What do you do, then?' the man had chattily enquired.

JOB replied as non-committally as possible.

'Something clever, I expect,' insisted the man. 'My bet is, a lawyer. Yes, that'd be it. Are you a lawyer?'

JOB replied, 'S-s-sort of,' and desperately tried to bury himself in a book.

His companion was not to be put down so easily.

'Where are you going, then?'

JOB then wildly replied, 'Birmingham,' knowing as he did so that this was a mistake. What he meant by the lie, if he meant anything at all, was that he hoped their conversation would not have to last beyond Birmingham, a journey of a little over an hour from Oxford. When they reached Birmingham New Street, the man leaned over and said, not unmenacingly as JOB saw it, 'This is where you get off.'

Unable to admit that he had lied to the man, and fearful of going to sit in a different part of the train, JOB had gathered his holdall and scampered obediently off the train. I have forgotten whether he sheepishly returned to Oxford or went on up to Edinburgh for a few days to join IM.

When their friend Wallace Robson (who was once engaged to IM) became the Masson Professor of Rhetoric at the University of Edinburgh, he had been terribly homesick for Oxford and used to tell his old friends that he 'did not want his old bones to lie north of the Border'. IM was miserable too.

Although she spent so much time in London and abroad, she was one of the many who see Oxford as home, Oxford as the womb; life away from it now felt like hell. Had I known IM in her younger, London incarnations, I probably would have seen a more playful person, more Dora Greenfield than the Abbess of Imber.

IM found the task of giving the Gifford Lectures onerous. For weeks before she went to Scotland she conveyed to all her friends how nervous she was about the task, and there is no doubt in my mind as I look back on it all that this period marked the beginning of an emotional breakdown in her. I am not suggesting that she had moved a step in the direction of the dementia which would one day engulf her mind – very far from it. But something got lost. It was not the chilly world of Edinburgh, however, but an incident at Cedar Lodge which heralded the beginning of the trouble.

Cedar Lodge was being neglected. For extended periods the previous summer and autumn, the Bayleys were abroad on their joint lecture-tours. There was a spell at Berkeley, lasting a whole semester. Whenever possible, they stayed with friends at weekends and during vacations – with the Stones, with the Cecils, with the Spenders in France and with Boris and Audi Villers in their various foreign residences. Cedar Lodge, which had been scruffily lived-in, began to acquire a cold, damp, neglected 'feel'. JOB complained of the cold, and they spent more and more time huddled in the kitchen, behind cunningly devised blanket-curtains in an atmosphere of fought-for, food-spattered snug.

One day, while they were away in Edinburgh, vandals came into the garden and smashed up some of IM's favourite statues. She was bitterly upset, the more so when it became obvious that most of her friends regarded the attack good-humouredly.

'How can she *tell* that someone has vandalised her garden?' was the predictable response from the unsympathetic dons.

It is true that by now the house had a Sleeping Beauty air of neglect. The creeper which used to rampage over garage and house now festooned both so thickly that you could not see through it. JOB once airily remarked that they had lost one of their cars somewhere in the undergrowth.

But the attack on the garden – 'our lovely garden,' as she described it to me when, with quivering lips and red eyes, she related the incident – was taken personally.

Relations with 'the village' in Steeple Aston had always – as far as one could tell, as an occasional visitor to the house – been cordial enough. At one stage, IM, as one would expect, had a row with the vicar, on a point of theology. But they entertained neighbours. JOB's boyhood in Gerrards Cross and Romney Marsh made him perfectly accustomed to the sort of Betjeman-characters who belong to tennis clubs and golf clubs. At their many charming lunch or supper parties you were far more likely to meet village neighbours than famous figures from the literary world; and these would be mingled with their academic colleagues in a perfectly amiable mix. One got the impression that both JOB and IM, though regarded as somewhat eccentric, were liked by 'the village', and were part of the inevitable circuit of little drinks parties which are the norm in such middle-class enclaves.

The little vandals who destroyed the garden statuary and messed the place up a bit were no doubt boys of about twelve. The careless and wanton destructiveness, however, touched the nerve of paranoia which was always there in IM. Presumably she had imbibed it from her Irish parents who arrived, friendless, in Acton in 1919.

'They don't like us, they don't want us here. Someone did this out of hate.'

That is what she kept saying.

This was one of the main reasons, I always supposed, that JOB, on impulse one day, screeched OWL to a halt outside an estate agent in the north Oxford suburb of Summertown and went inside.

He bought 68 Hamilton Road, a hideous little house in a mean street, while IM was away.

When the first American edition of her Sartre book was published, in 1987, IM wistfully wrote of the time when 'Existentialism was the new religion, the new salvation'. She recalled that when she had seen him in 1945, Sartre had been treated like a pop star. Chico Marx, who was in the city at the same time, was less rapturously received. She added that the only comparable scene, of a philosopher being hailed as a prophet and mobbed, was in 1984 when she attended a lecture by Jacques Derrida in California.

IM would not have been human if she had not hoped that her own 'Message to the Planet' would not be received with comparable rapture. The Romanes Lecture in 1976, which she wrote up and expanded as *The Fire and the Sun: Why Plato Banished the Artists*, had been delivered to a packed Sheldonian Theatre in Oxford, and it was very well received. There was, on that occasion, a strong sense that we had, if not a prophet among us, then something very like it.

The trashing of the garden at Steeple Aston, and the cold reception given to her Gifford Lectures, were major blows to her confidence, and instead of publishing the text of these lectures immediately, she took them upstairs in Hamilton Road and began to rewrite feverishly. At the same time – or during the intervals, perhaps – she was also engaged in writing a book about Heidegger.

It was a very uncomfortable house indeed – instantly depressing, as one squeezed into the narrow hall. What a contrast with the large hall at Cedar Lodge, where the round table had seen so many happy meals with friends! Nearly all IM's beautiful things, acquired over many years in junk shops and at sales, were themselves despatched to salerooms. She even sold her father's first editions of Jane Austen: precious, almost totemic items in her personal mythology.

The novels which she wrote at this period had fantasies about renunciation and giving up the world for mystic or Christ-like reasons.

The truth is, the purchase of Hamilton Road was presented to her by JOB almost as a *fait accompli*. There she sat, in a miserable little house. Her study, a poky back bedroom, overlooked a noisy crèche for under-fives. Here she read, or attempted to read, and reread Wittgenstein and Heidegger.

The Time of the Angels, published in 1966, was an existentialist fable, about a vicarage isolated among the bombsites near St Paul's Cathedral, perpetually surrounded by thick fog. In this symbolic setting, Father Carel Fisher, atheist priest, has his creepy household, committing incest with his daughter and keeping the half-Irish, half-black maid Pattie as his mistress. There is the predictable cast-list of earnest old refugee (this time a Russian), beautiful amoral boy (who pretends to steal the refugee's most treasured possession, an icon) and 'good' brother of the priest, who is engaged upon a work of philosophy.

In one of the less convincing scenes, Pattie is cleaning Father Carel's study and comes across an open copy of Martin Heidegger's *Sein und Zeit*. A paragraph is quoted in full ('The ending which we have in view when we speak of death does not signify Dasein's Being-at-an-end, but a Being-towards-the-end of this entity', etc., etc.).

[Pattie] read these words in the book which lay open upon his desk. She read them, or rather it was not reading since

235

they meant absolutely nothing to her. The words sounded senseless and awful, like the distant boom of some big catastrophe. Was this what the world was like when people were intellectual and clever enough to see it in its reality?

Pedants might have asked Pattie, if the words of Heidegger meant nothing to her (and she would not have been alone in this), how they could represent to her a world view, whether of intellectuals or of anyone else?

The strange novelistic moment seems like a symbol, or indeed a prophecy, of IM's own writing life. In the end, she came to be imprisoned in fog, staring at Heidegger's pages and unable to know what to make of them.

The sinister priest has a much more benign brother called Marcus. He is engaged in writing a book entitled *Morality in a World without God*. 'He would speak simply, with the sole authority of his own voice, and his crystalline densely textured argument need not be flawed by references to others, though at the close he might modestly admit to being, after all, a Platonist.'

In trying to explain his book to a bishop at a later stage of the story, Marcus admits that he is going to devote a chapter to the ontological proof. And, in another place, it is clear that Marcus's 'philosophy' is identical to the positions IM herself adopted from the publication of *The Sovereignty of Good* onwards:

If the idea of Good is severed from the idea of perfection it is emasculated and any theory which tolerates this severance, however high-minded it professes to be, is in the end a vulgar relativism. If the idea of Good is not severed from the idea of perfection it is impossible to avoid the problem of 'the transcendent'. Thus the authority of goodness returns, and must return, to the picture in an even more puzzling form.

The book that Marcus struggles to write would eventually be the subject of IM's Gifford Lectures in 1982, and she would still be haunted, like Pattie, by the figure of Heidegger, a haunting that would delay the actual publication of the Gifford Lectures for years. When *Metaphysics as a Guide to Morals* eventually appeared (and it could just as well have been called *Morality in a World without God*) there must have been many who read it with some dismay and wondered what had happened.

A friendly but devastating analysis of IM's religio-philosophical thinking was undertaken by Fergus Kerr, of the Order of Preachers, in his book *Immortal Longings: Versions of Transcending Humanity.** Kerr begins by stating that 'She offers the most sustained and eloquent attempt by any philosopher, in the Anglo-American analytical tradition at least, to open up a way of conceiving ourselves as finite beings, who are nevertheless capable of a certain self-transcendence which fulfils and does not negate our humanity.'** He notes her agreement with G. E. Moore 'that good was a supersensible reality'.

It is when he comes to consider her love of 'Demythologised Christianity' that this kindly Roman Catholic friar begins to discover incoherence. In her *Metaphysics as a Guide to Morals* IM refers to Don Cupitt, the atheist Anglican theologian, as 'a very great and valuable pioneer and a learned and accessible thinker . . . We need a theology which can continue without God.' But,

---

*SPCK, 1997.
**Ibid., p.68.

as Kerr patiently points out, Cupitt's version of Christianity depends on a dichotomy which she firmly rejects, the dichotomy between fact and value. 'It is surprising to find Murdoch treating his remarks so sympathetically.' Cupitt believes that the descriptive element in religious myth is *factually* untrue, but contains a core of *value* to which we can respond. This is to repeat the equation of Morality with the Will which IM found most repellent.

On a number of occasions I spoke to IM about Don Cupitt, expecting in my ham-fisted and ill-considered way that she would respect a theologian who did not believe in God. She dismissed the 'tired old determinism' of his thought, and even, after one vinous lunch in Arlington Road, corrected an earlier assertion that Cupitt's ideas were 'devilish'.

'I don't want to say he comes from the Devil. He *is* the Devil. He is' – pause for refill of the wine glass – 'Satan himself.'

Fergus Kerr is understandably baffled by the misplaced *politesse* towards Cupitt in *Metaphysics as a Guide to Morals*, misplaced because a philosophical lecture is not the place to praise ideas with which you fundamentally disagree. IM's heaping of complimentary epithets on Cupitt's head while not sharing his views shows her, until this point most uncharacteristically, adopting a JOB-ish attitude to her task.

Her sentence (or is it a quotation from Cupitt?) – 'That there is no God is also God' – is treated calmly by the Aberdeen Doctor of Divinity, Kerr: 'It is worth noting that, as a philosopher in the analytical school, she regards a remark such as the one last quoted as making sense.'

Kerr goes on to draw many moments of interest from IM's philosophical writings, but by the time he has pointed out her ignorance of medieval theology, her muddle about whether God is '*a* person', it is hard to believe that he rates her very highly as a thinker. MacKinnon often quotes A. N. Whitehead – speaking of Christianity as 'a religion perennially in search of a metaphysic, but never able to rest in one'. The same would appear to be true of IM's distinctive blend of Christian Platonism.

The myth which is central to the Platonic theory of Being is that of a soul trapped in a body. The world, for the Platonist, is not where we are at home. The earthy, the sensual, the natural, the contingent, all that makes for the comic, are so many clods to be cast off until we take wing to return to our pure, our spiritual selves.

Heidegger's *Dasein* (his word for our being here at all, our being capable of reflection upon existence, our *awareness* of existence) is, unlike Plato's *psyche* or *soul*, a contingent being, or if not a contingent being precisely, then a being who only makes sense – as something to discuss, as an entity – in this function of reflection. His undermining of Platonism, and of the Western philosophical tradition since Plato, is very deep and very strong. After he had finished writing *Sein und Zeit* in 1927, Heidegger experienced a sharp turn, a U-bend – eine Kehre – in his thinking. He slowly moved from the out-and-out subjectivism of *Sein und Zeit* to attempt the nature of something he termed authenticity (*Eigentlichkeit*). The waiting for the *eigentlich*, the stripping away of illusion, required an inner turning. It was like, if it was not actually, religious change. In 1949, when he was aged sixty, Heidegger wrote an essay entitled *Der Feldweg*. It is not an overtly philosophical work. It seems like a piece of autobiography, in which he recalls following a path from the town of Messkirch, where he grew up. The path skirts the woods. He had a vivid sense as he walked of the independent existence of the oakwood, the tree which was open to the sky, but rooted in the earth. 'Everything real and true only prospers if mankind fulfils at the same time the two conditions of being ready for the demands of highest heaven and of being safe in the shelter of the fruitful earth: the oak continually repeats this to the country lane, whose track runs past it.'*

For IM, in *Metaphysics as a Guide to Morals*, Heidegger is 'one of the nastiest', 'sinister', 'dull', 'devoid of moral judgement' etc. If this was her view of him, why did she spend the better part of her last active decade reading him and trying to write about him?

I have spent rather longer than that asking myself the question and I am still none the wiser. Clearly Heidegger dominates the later novels, especially *The Green Knight* and *The Message to the Planet*, books that deal with the weird borderlands where gods became demons and metaphysics became magic.

In an interview with the magazine *Der Spiegel* in 1966, Heidegger said, '*Nur ein Gott kann uns retten.*' IM quoted this in her Gifford Lectures, but in her conclusions to that book she insists, 'No existing thing could be what we have meant by God. Any existing God would be less than God. An existent God would be an idol or a demon . . . God does not and cannot exist. But what led us to conceive of him does exist and is *constantly* experienced and pictured.'

Metaphysics as a Guide to Morals is an imperfect work, rambling and occasionally incoherent. Yet its patient, Kantian insistence on the reality of goodness lies at the heart of IM's work and life. 'What led us to conceive of him does exist.' It is hard to imagine

---

*See John Macquarrie, *Heidegger and Christianity*, SCM, 1994; Michael Gelven, *A Commentary on Heidegger's Being and Time*, Harper & Row, New York, 1970; Michael E. Zimmerman, *Eclipse of the Self. The Development of Heidegger's Concept of Authenticity*, Ohio University Press, Athens, 1981.

a paragraph which more persuasively argues for her version of religious atheism. In this too-long, troubled book there are occasional passages of greater insight and precision than anything else she ever wrote.

9

Questioning

11 June. In the evening to the Savile Club with Mary Kay for the Hawthornden Prizegiving. I sit between Anthony Quinton and Iris Murdoch and am grateful for the worldliness of the one and the unworldliness of the other. Quinton chatting easily and with seeming gusto and also being very funny, despite having flown back from Boston that day, while Dame Iris keeps up a constant flow of questions. 'Where do you live? Do you drive a car? What colour is it? Where have you parked?' A nice purling stream as she tucks into the Savile's duck followed by apple sorbet.

1989, Alan Bennett Diaries: 1980–90

IM's habit of persistent questioning disconcerted many a friend and acquaintance. Some found the habit intrusive. One of JOB's colleagues who had painfully lost his religious faith expressed deep dismay when, after an interval abroad of some five years, he met IM again and she subjected him to a catechism. 'How's your prayer life since you stopped believing in God? You *have* stopped believing in God? Though now an unbeliever, what would you teach a child about God? Do you pray with your children? Would you if they asked you to do so?' On and on she had questioned him.

This man felt bruised, angered, by the experience. He felt it was an inquisition which was quite unsuited to a dinner table. 'How *dare* she speak like that?' was what he said at the time. Most of IM's acquaintances had a slightly different view of the unrelenting interrogatory manner.

'She asks because she is not interested, not because she is,' said one don's wife to me. 'She asks but doesn't really listen to the answers.'

Sometimes, perhaps, this was true. Much of the time she asked because she found life puzzling. The 'ordinary experiences' of the humdrum, to which most of us are subjected by circumstance, were not hers. The only child never had to learn how to cook, or to go shopping. She was childless. She was in many respects detached from the mundane. Small wonder that such matters as where Alan Bennett parked his car could have seemed puzzling.

Moreover, like many clever people, she was capable of failing to understand what is perfectly obvious to lesser beings. There is a popular radio programme called *I'm Sorry I Haven't a Clue*. Its *raison d'être* is absurdity. One of the games played by the panellists is to mix up two popular airs, and to sing, for example, the National Anthem to the tune of 'I Do Like to be Beside the Seaside'. Other games include puns. A feature of each episode is the round of an invented game called 'Mornington Crescent' in which the contestants, in the manner of chess or cricket bores, dispute or debate the finer points of the rules. In fact, as they call out – *Edgware Road!* or *Hyde Park Corner!*, or other stations on the London Underground – they do so completely arbitrarily, though the impression given is that, with great skill, they are moving to a position where their opponents are checkmated with the cry of *Mornington Crescent!*

'Do you listen much to the radio?' IM asked me one day.

'From time to time, a lot – then not much for long gaps.'

'I remembered you like *The Archers?*'

'Yes, I like *The Archers.*'

'And how about the quiz shows?'

'Yes – some of them.'

'Do you listen to *I'm Sorry I Haven't a Clue?*'

'Yes – I think it's my favourite radio programme.'

'Ah! My dear, you can help me with a difficulty. Even John can't help with this.'

'I'll oblige if I can.'

'Can you explain the rules of "Mornington Crescent"?'

I peered at her smiling, intent face, for signs that she was indulging, in the manner of Willie Rushton and the other comedians on the show, in some arcane humour. No flicker of a sign was given.

'But Iris – the point of the game is that there *isn't* a point.'

She shook her head and laughed. 'No, no. They quite often stop the game and discuss the rules.'

'But that's the joke.'

'But they never explain what the rules ARE.'

It was strange to think of this intellectually alert woman, week after week, laying down her pen, ceasing from the invention of some elaborate plot and listening to these clownish men. She would smile no doubt, at the roar of audience laughter in the recording theatre; but it would be the smile of a highly intelligent only child who found the world a puzzle, and therefore needed to explain it to herself by means of fantasy.

Alan Bennett's diary entry captures the quality of IM's questioning when, as it were, she was 'on automatic' – 'a nice purling stream'. The truth is that, unlike JOB, who could talk to and charm anyone, IM was diffident, and when in clam-mode did not know what to say. Sentimentalists believe that children, with their never-ending questions, have more enquiring minds than adults. Some do, some don't, presumably. But the 'nice purling stream' of a child's questioning is to fill a void which real adults fill with conversation.

8th April 1992: Ruth and I supped with the Bayleys at IM's flat in Cornwall Gardens. It is on the top floor of one of those enormous creamy stucco houses off the Gloucester Road. Hardy Amies lives in the grandest of the flats, several floors beneath them. The person who has the misfortune to live immediately below is a German lady who has made complaints to the landlords and to the local council about the moths – probably other pests too – who have colonised IM's flat and now infest the whole building. JOB tells some story – it is incoherent because he is laughing about it so much – about shaking a mat out of the window and it merely evaporating into dust, but a cloud of moths flying from it, and down to the German lady's flat through her bathroom window. The small kitchen, and above all the bathroom in the flat, are dirty on a scale which it would require a new vocabulary to describe. The loo is not merely stained, but encrusted, a bas-relief of limescale, ancient excrement and some not so ancient. Sink and shower grimy. The soap filthy, hair-matted, grey. In the kitchen, a thick mud of blackened grease coats sink, stove and the heaps of unwashed crockery. In each of the living-rooms is an unmade single bed, socks, underwear, jumpers scattered on its rumpled candlewick bedspread. Books spill from shelves on to carpets. The armchairs are the sort which get left to the end of a sale and are usually unsold, even to the cheapest furniture trader, the auction house paying for their removal by scrap-merchants.

Ruth's informed eyes pick out the very good paintings which hang on the walls of this pigsty. She notes a Gerald Wilde and IM seems impressed that she makes out from its bright smudge of colours that it represents Europa and the Bull. There is a tiny Samuel Palmer, and various other 'good' modern artists. IM and R talk a bit about Wilde, whom IM knew, and of the circle, which included Dylan Thomas, who liked drinking in pubs with Joyce Cary, and Dan Davin. R an enthusiast for Joyce Cary and so is IM. R says that it was a mistake, wasn't it, to suppose Wilde was Gulley Jimson, the artist in Cary's novel *The Horse's Mouth*? We all talk about that book.

But once the 'meal' gets under way, IM reverts to her persistent interrogatory mode. It is curious, given the subjects in which R had previously shown an interest, that IM chose to ask her, fixing her with a very intent stare –

'Do you own a vacuum cleaner?'

A catechism followed about our domestic arrangements, whether we employed a cleaner, how often, etc., etc. It was, to put it mildly, bizarre to be hearing such a dialogue in such a setting.

I placed the word 'meal' in inverted commas since there is very little offered. A small pie has been cut into pieces and served on a dish with some salami which has known better days and some whiskery olives. A bit of salad in garlicky oil. After a while, JOB rises to his feet and brings considerable cheer by saying – 'Next course!' He adds, 'I remembered your "Main-Course Nausea", dear Andrew, so I thought it was better to serve, as it were, t-t-t-tapas.'

The 'main-course nausea' was a phrase I first heard on JOB's lips in the early seventies, but he always quotes it as my coinage. Luckily it is not something which afflicts me these days, and after a one-inch cube of pork pie and two slithers of salami I am ravenous.

After about five minutes he comes back with a doll-sized saucepan.

'Only one egg unfortunately.'

He has scrambled it quite skilfully and we eat the result with some cheese and biscuits, followed by a couple of packets of Mr Kipling cakes.

There has been no shortage of alcohol, and by the cake stage of the meal, one has drunk gin and vermouth, two sorts of white wine and a *mélange* of reds. JOB talks engagingly to R, and IM, turning to me, reverts to 'our book'. For a year or two now I have been having the idea that rather than writing a formal biography, we should write an extended Platonic dialogue based on *The Republic*. IM likes this idea. It would let me off the hook as far as dealing with the love affairs was concerned. Obviously one would hope for not *too much* about vacuum cleaners – though her preoccupation with the domestic arrangements of friends is revealing, and what it reveals is less a novelistic interest in other people than something like despondency about the mess in which she and JOB live.

ANW   Clearly, part of our Dialogue would concern politics.

IM   Certainly.

ANW   We would talk about your early belief in Socialism, in Marxism . . .

IM   Well, I hope we would talk about why these beliefs were *wrong*, why a belief in the *individual*, in freedom . . . This is vital. We were all drawn to Marxism, as it were, as a way of fighting Hitler, Fascism, but . . . What has always interested me is the idea of *freedom*, of individual freedom. Simone Weil reminds us in *L'Enracinement* that human societies have always been totalitarian. Louis Quatorze was totalitarian. We thought – poor children that we were – that Communism would bring freedom.

ANW   Whereas I suppose that now you would agree with Johnson that 'most schemes of political improvement are very laughable things'.

IM   Who is that?

ANW   Johnson – Dr Johnson.

IM   (Laughing): Oh, Johnson. No, no, I wouldn't agree with that at all. It is possible to *think* and as a result of thought we can devise political schemes which are better than others. Of course we can.

ANW   We are surely a long way off from an ideal Republic.

IM   I'm not sure! We have a constitutional monarchy – that's ideal by many standards. We have freedom of thought, freedom of speech – these things were *fought for*. Of course the values of the Conservative Party are better than those of the Socialists.

ANW   So you would think that Mr Major represented your political *beau idéal*.

IM   Well, why bring it down to Mr Major?

ANW   Because there is a General Election tomorrow morning and he is the Prime Minister and . . .

JOB   (Intervening): God, we've all got to *vote*, don't you think?

IM   Certainly. You must promise me – both of you – dear people – that you will vote tomorrow.

ANW   Vote Conservative?

IM   Yes!

ANW   I'm a small 'c' conservative, of course—

IM   What does that mean? If you are a conservative, you should vote Conservative. Do you want Kinnock to be the Prime Minister?

ANW   No – I just feel it's a bit bizarre that we began this conversation with Plato's *Republic* and we were going to try to find out the ideal political system which the human mind could devise and now you are asking me to promise to . . .

IM   (Seemingly deaf): You must vote Conservative.

ANW   It wouldn't do any good. The country has had

enough of the Tories. They don't stand a chance.

JOB   My guess is that Major'll win by twenty seats.

The Annual Register* records, 'Even the exit-polls left the TV election programmes floundering and unprepared for the Tory victory. The government was returned with an overall majority of 21 seats.'

---

*Longman, 1993, p.12.

10

Colonel Petticate at Sea

The figure of J. I. M. Stewart was often to be observed out and about in Oxford during my undergraduate days. In memory, I associate him especially with the winter months, a trim figure in a smart suit, an immaculate MA gown and, as often as not, wearing his academic square, or mortar-board, on his head. His perambulations called to mind the phrase in P. G. Wodehouse, applied, is it to Jeeves, of somebody making 'a stately procession of one'. The route for the procession was normally between Christ Church, the grandest of the colleges, where he taught English literature, and the newly built English faculty building in Manor Road, a construction by the architects Sir Leslie Martin and Colin St John Wilson, which seemed to allude to the ziggurats of ancient Mesopotamia.

J. I. M. Stewart, whose appearance by the late Sixties had something very distinctly old-fashioned about it, was a popular lecturer on such stalwarts as Henry James, Thomas Hardy and Joseph Conrad. I twice attended his lectures on Hardy. Their perfectly modulated paragraphs were delivered in a clipped Edinburgh voice, with short 'a's for Casterbridge and Master. With Helen Gardner and Christopher Tolkien, he was one of the best lecturers in the English faculty in those days.

Added to the satisfaction of his performance from the podium, and the always insightful commentary on the author whom he had chosen to elucidate, was the knowledge that he was himself an author. It now strikes me as strange, since he was one of my favourite authors, that I never once met him, or dared approach him, even though he was on Christian-name terms with my wife – a fellow-member of the English faculty. I once asked one of the more worldly dons, a friend of JOB and IM, what Stewart was like, and received the reply, 'Oh, he wasn't worth *knowing*, just a boring little Scotsman.' He lived some little way out of Oxford, and had a large family. Evidently, the stately manners shown in the lecture hall were maintained in a domestic setting, since he once remarked to Philip Larkin that he would not be pleased if such-and-such a thing had happened 'in my wife's drawing-room', which Larkin, an ardent fan, had felt to be an affectation too far.

There were three strings to Stewart's bow as a writer. First, he was a literary scholar and critic, being the author of the *Eight Modern Writers* volume in the *Oxford History of English Literature*, and of a stylish book entitled *Character and Motive in Shakespeare*. Second, under his own name, he was a prolific novelist and, after retirement as a don, he penned the quintet of novels entitled *A Staircase in Surrey*. In his last few months on earth, Larkin reread these books. The last conversation which I had with the poet, when I visited him in Hull, concerned Stewart's qualities as a writer. Larkin said he admired Stewart more and more, and thought the *Staircase in Surrey* sequence in every way superior to *A Dance to the Music of Time*. Whereas Powell had simply used himself as the narrator Nick Jenkins and never strayed significantly from areas of his own experience, Stewart had boldly chosen a persona different from himself, a playwright with a comparably Scottish background, but who comes to Oxford as a comparative stranger. Stewart was the greater inventor, Larkin averred; he was funnier than Powell, more interesting. I disagreed with this view at the time, and disagree with it even more strongly now, even though my affection and admiration for all J. I. M. Stewart's books are undiminished. Even the later ones have something enjoyable in them, and if I had to calculate the pleasure given to me by English writers whose lifespan overlapped with my own, I could not think there was any writer whose work had given me more delight.

But, like most of his admirers, it is in his third persona, as the mystery-writer Michael Innes, that I have enjoyed Stewart the most. *The Secret Vanguard, Hamlet, Revenge!, The Journeying Boy, Operation Pax, The Daffodil Affair, Appleby's End* . . . When I think of the hours of fun these books have brought me, by their ingenious plots, their strokes of fantasy, their brilliant depictions of place, how intensely I wish I had the chance, just once, to tell that man of my gratitude.

The fashionable don who told me that Stewart was 'just a boring little Scotsman' enjoyed the Michael Innes novels as much as I did, though he preferred dining with JOB and IM. Sir Oswald Mosley, Bt, was said to have remarked to a political colleague at one juncture in his career that one should vote Labour and f*** Tory. A comparable social position was adopted by many of IM's Oxford friends, one suspects, in that they preferred to dine Bayley but read Innes.

What J. I. M. Stewart, or Michael Innes, made of the Bayleys

I do not know. His ingenious novels had been making an appear-ance a good decade before the publication of *Under the Net*, and he would not have been human if he had not cast a slightly wistful eye on the very, very high praise which IM attracted, not perhaps from her academic friends in Oxford, but from the committees who dole out literary prizes, from the foreign academies, from the mysterious 'literary world' in London . . . Stewart was a colleague for many years of JOB's in the English faculty and shared with JOB a passion for Kipling. (Stewart's Kipling book could not be improved.) No doubt this quietly affected, humorous Scotsman, who enjoyed puffing his pipe and talking of books, drew out of JOB the most traditionalist side of his character, the side which IM saw, in *The Sea, The Sea*, as the peppery little figure of Ben Fitch, the domestic tyrant of Nibletts. The Christ Church don, intensely aware of the rank and status of his aristocratic pupils, would have cottoned on to the army side of JOB.

Michael Innes's novel *The New Sonia Wayward* (1960) tells the story of a clever, literary-minded retired army doctor called Colonel Ffolliot Petticate, married to a popular novelist called Sonia Wayward:

> The name Sonia Wayward was a household word. If the households of which this held true scarcely included those of the most intellectual bent or ripest literary cultivation, it was at least a fact that Sonia's romances had earned the regard of gratifyingly large sections of the public alike in England and America. This meant that she earned a lot of money. And these were circumstances which Petticate found entirely agreeable. Sonia's wasn't a sort of reputation that

need make an intelligent and sophisticated husband feel himself cast into the shade; and when he did grow a little tired of it he had the resource of a small society of cronies with whom he could share an attitude of civilised irony towards the whole affair.

Stewart / Innes titles often carry double-, even triple-meaning. Sonia dies while having a yachting holiday with her husband, the colonel, in the very first chapter, entitled 'Colonel Petticate at Sea'. In a drunken moment, Petticate throws his wife's corpse off the boat and decides to continue his lucrative source of income by impersonating his wife, and writing the next, the 'new Sonia Wayward', himself. In a plot which bristles with wild improbabilities, he even finds himself shacked up at the end of the story with another stout old lady, a Sonia look-alike whom he can parade at parties, prize-givings and the like.

It would be an absurdity, and an offensive absurdity at that, to suggest that Colonel Petticate and Sonia Wayward were meant by 'Michael Innes' as a portrait of JOB and IM.

Some of their friends, however, might have had flickering memories of the tale, and smiled a little wistfully to themselves, when they witnessed the blossoming of JOB's literary career, just as IM's light was growing dimmer and her books had dried up.

Professor John Sutherland, writing in the *Guardian* in March 2001, observed:

John Bayley's obituary file must be, since it first began being stocked in the 1960s, the most rewritten in Fleet Street. Up to his retirement in 1990 from the Warton Chair in Oxford, he was superdon – one of the most respected academic critics in the country, but little known outside his profession. In retirement – so miscalled – professor emeritus Bayley established himself as one of the country's leading journalists and reviewers. When in the late 1990s his wife's descent into terminal illness began, he was elevated to near sanctity. Best of husbands, on his wife's death he amazed his friends with two memoirs whose candour Blake Morrison might have envied. Jilly Cooper could have envied his sales and the film adaptation inspired by *Iris*. He remarried. And now, John Bayley sexual athlete. What next? Superdon on Mars?

Perhaps there is a small element of donnish malice in Professor Sutherland's analysis, but the transformation process of JOB from man in the shadows to man in the limelight was a palpable fact. Sutherland's joke about sexual athleticism is a reference to JOB's book *Widower's House*, a description of life without IM and his tentative decision to marry their old friend Audi Villers. It is an account of being pursued by two women, one of whom he names Margot, an old friend who wants to cook him casseroles and have him to stay in her house in the country; and the other, Mella, a research student of his, who wants to mop and clean up his house. Both women force their way into his bed, and there are some staggeringly ungallant descriptions of their attempts to arouse him sexually. When the book was published, it was these passages that were serialised in the *Daily Telegraph*. When challenged by a journalist from the *Sunday Times* about the incidents, 'John Bayley sexual athlete' said that the episodes were fiction, pure inventions. This dismayed the *Telegraph*, which had bought the serialisation rights on the specific understanding that the incidents were factual. Even here, however, there was a Bayleyesque blurring of fact and fiction, since the paper illustrated his articles with pictures of actresses depicting the unfortunate 'Margot' and 'Mella'. The book ends with JOB running away from his predatory admirers to Lanzarote, where he finds comfort with Audi. It omits to mention that for the last couple of years of IM's life, Audi and JOB would walk about clasping one another like lovers while a bedraggled old IM tagged behind.

No one wanted to deny JOB a bit of happiness in his old age, but the public was beginning to taste that confusion of borders between truth and falsehood which had characterised JOB all his life. 'I've never set much store by the t-t-truth,' he beguilingly told Anthony Clare on a radio programme called *In the Psychiatrist's Chair*, on 10th October 1999.

Friends were distressed by *Widower's House*, less by its fibs than by what they considered the nastiness of its tone. Women who had faithfully cooked for the Bayleys during the terrible years of IM's illness, or who had tried to offer help, felt themselves lampooned.

More disturbing was the sense conveyed by all three of the memoirs – *Widower's House*, *Iris: A Memoir of Iris Murdoch* and *Iris and the Friends* – that JOB had perhaps released demons from his inner psyche which he did not quite know were there. *Iris*, the book on which the successful film was chiefly based, was published a year before IM had so much as died. It chronicled their love for one another; of course it did. And when I read it for the first time, I was deeply moved by its depictions of their early love, his tentative coming-to-terms with her earlier promiscuities, their enviable partnership of forty years, and his solicitude towards her when she began to sail into the dark.

Other friends felt less sure. They were, in particular, uncon-
vinced by JOB's statement that this book was 'what Iris would
have wanted', as he persistently repeated in interviews to publi-
cise it. She was an intensely private woman, and it is more or less
inconceivable to me that she would have wanted the details of
her first kiss with JOB, their first fumbling attempts at lovemaking
or the thinly disguised lovers to be paraded in a book: for here,
quite unmistakably, are Fraenkel (named), Canetti, Momigliano
and others.

> 'Perhaps it is time we made love', and she had shown me
> how, although as I had no condom with me . . . she did not
> permit me to get very far. We had done better once or twice
> after that, but in a genial and wholly unserious way that did
> not in the least mar for me the unfamiliar magic of the
> proceedings . . .

Others took exception to the candour, as it seemed to them,
the near-mercilessness, with which JOB described IM after she
had succumbed completely to Alzheimer's disease. In Book One,
we read of her pathetic love of a TV programme for infants called
Teletubbies, of her abject dependency on JOB, of her mouse-like
grunts and snores, and of his rages with her – 'You bad animal!
Can't you leave me alone for just one minute.' The first book is
completely compelling, precisely because we feel the narrator to
be revealing much more of himself and his own mixture of motives
and emotions than he can have appreciated when he sent the
typescript to the publisher. He tells us that he feels more physical
affection for IM demented than he had done for IM when sane.
One has uncomfortable memories, when reading *Iris: A Memoir*,

of Hartley being kept a prisoner in *The Sea, The Sea*. Or, again, one remembers *The Queer Captain*, JOB's own Michael Innes-ish thriller, in which a woman is imprisoned in a remote house, rather like Mrs Crean-Smith in *The Unicorn*. The borderlines between love-object and victim, or lover and prison guard, form part of both the Bayleys' published fantasy life. It was deeply disconcerting to watch these confusions of role now, it seemed, being enacted in real life.

By the time he had come to write the second of his memoirs, *Iris and the Friends*, JOB was able to share with us such thoughts as these:

> I don't know how it is with three-year-olds, but Iris's toilet habits, if you can call them that, have become unpredictable. Sometimes she will go to the right place, even though she makes a mess of it. More often, she will do it on the carpet outside, or in another room. Then she lays the results, as if with care, on a neighbouring chair or bookshelf.

The following sentence can only be disingenuous:

> I don't mind a bit cleaning up, an operation which seems mildly to amuse her . . . a small domestic challenge I can easily meet, and Iris seems to enjoy seeing me do it.

JOB has stated, over and over again, that he wrote these best-sellers in order to 'help' others whose spouses or relations are suffering from Alzheimer's. If such help has been found, by anyone, one can only be grateful. It is not difficult, however, to imagine how IM herself, when in possession of her health and her wits, would have regarded the publication of such details, had the indiscretion been perpetrated by one of her friends concerning their husband or wife.

Now, thanks to these volumes, and the film which has been made on the basis of them, the name 'Iris Murdoch' has been inextricably associated with Alzheimer's disease. The actress playing the young IM in the film, Kate Winslet, stated that she 'hugely admired' IM, but alas, with her busy schedule, Miss Winslet 'had not had time' to read *any* of IM's writings.

In the twilight years, when IM was still alive but out of things, JOB would sometimes murmur to me that he felt he had to keep on writing books, 'as it were *for* Iris'.

I had always thought of him as dear, sweet, bumbling, smiling JOB, who 'didn't mind a bit' when IM received all the plaudits, achieved international fame and acclaim as a writer of genius, took many lovers and had many friends, and then declined into being a demanding, incontinent old wreck. I changed my view and began to wonder whether, inside this uncomplaining little leprechaun, there was a screaming, hate-filled child who minded very much indeed. Colonel Petticate had once overheard Sonia Wayward referring to him as 'the quaintest little creature in the world'. JOB's preservation of his version of IM's memory could now be viewed as a kind of revenge. He had now displaced his wife as the one in the partnership who was the writer.

Comforting IM after one of her screaming fits: 'I think of my dislike of babies and children, more than dislike – hatred – when I see them in the supermarket, showing off and screaming.'

Poor man. He who 'hated kids', and who persuaded himself that IM had never wanted them, ended up with a companion who had come to resemble the category of being whom he most loathed.

A young colleague at St Catherine's who had a two- or three-year-old child which always struggled and screamed as it was being dressed, was asked by JOB how he could stand it. 'Because I love M****' was the reply. JOB repeated this story to me with the bafflement of an explorer who had come across some tribal custom, deep in an impenetrable part of the world, which to his outlook was incomprehensible.

In the book that made JOB's name, *The Characters of Love*, published four years after he married IM, he muses not only on the nature of literature but of love. It is perhaps significant that the three love stories which he chose to study – Chaucer's *Troilus and Criseyde*, Shakespeare's *Othello* and Henry James's *The Golden Bowl* – are all stories of betrayal and jealousy. Troilus thinks he has found 'true love' but Criseyde leaves him. Othello, the jealous husband, destroys his wife. Maggie Verver thinks she has found love with the Prince, and only learns too late of his previous, and continuing, love for Charlotte.

These dark themes are explored in the sunniest of moods, however, perhaps not least because the author, together with Chaucer, has seen that 'what destroys poor Troilus, that most vulnerable and Boethian of heroes, is a source of deep satisfaction to the Wife of Bath':

> It tickleth me about myn herte roote.
> Unto this day it doth my herte boote
> That I have had the world as in my tyme.

When I look at the pictures of IM at a wedding of 1971 – my own – I see a figure in a broad-brimmed medieval-looking hat, not unlike Chaucer's Wife of Bath, who, it will be remembered, after a wide range of partners, ended up with a younger man, a 'clerk of Oxenford'. I was a child when I first knew her: a clever one and in a quiet way a pushing one, but certainly one whose attitudes to life and whose behaviour makes the fifty-something-year-old who recalls them blush. Proust wrote that there is hardly a single action we perform in that early phase of manhood 'which we would not give anything, in later life, to be able to annul'.

I should annul much of my early behaviour and attitudes, but not my knowing IM and JOB. I suppose, looking back, that I first met them when they were at the peak of their happiness together. IM was tapping a rich, happy, sexy phase of her writing life. JOB was a college Fellow, poised to become a professor. The emotional troubles of the past could be looked back upon with the indulgence of the Wife of Bath – 'Alaas, alaas, that evere love was sinne!'

If you had asked me then, in 1971, what I wanted to be or do with my life, I should have answered that I wanted to be a clerical don at Oxford, smoking my pipe in the medieval cloisters which had been built about the time Chaucer began to write. I suppose I was ambitious, but quite how I intended to 'make my mark' was ill-defined. The actual experiences of human life, about which Chaucer and IM in their writings are so wise, had only just begun to happen. Thirty years help to place early experiences into perspective. The chaos of the human heart in its quest for sacred and profane love – this was IM's great theme. She did not merely speak for a whole generation, as she fashioned her novels and struggled with her metaphysical essays and books. She was also, to those who knew her personally, a Wise Woman, a person quite out of the ordinary.

The privilege of having known her was incalculable. Only the Oxford equivalent of laddishness can ever have blinded me to this. It shocks me to read my first reactions when she asked me to write her biography – my jokey reaction to her novels and her philosophy. Perhaps this jokiness of mine, so misplaced, was the sort of embarrassment boys feel when their mothers kiss them in the playground in front of the other children. I did not wish to own, even to my private diary, how much I owed her. Her novels, more than any other, inspired me to want to be a novelist. Her conversations and reflections on religion made me know that I could never adhere to what she called the Christian mythology, however much I revered the Christian spiritual tradition. Her patient, humble example of a working life was an example to any writer. *Nulla dies sine linea*, as Erasmus decreed – not a day should pass without writing something. She was entirely without fuss in her approach to work. When JOB broke his ankle with Pott's fracture, she sat at the end of his hospital bed with a large pad, writing her novel. If she had an hour to kill waiting for a train, out would come the pad once more. There was no nonsense about needing to write in a special place or with special nibs. She was humbly the servant of her craft, and she visibly loved it – loved her pens, loved the activity of moving an ink-stained hand over a page and forming letters.

Humility is not the same as false modesty. She knew she was a good writer and there was no nonsense about this knowledge. I once suggested to her that 'recognition' was unimportant for a writer.

'I'm sure it wouldn't worry you, Iris, if you had never won the Booker, for example.'

'On the contrary,' she said, 'I deserved to win the Booker. It was right for me to win it. I should have minded very much not to win it.'

This sounds like arrogance, but it was, I should contend, not merely honest, but a humble recognition of her gift.

Her humility showed itself too in her reaction to the great writers whom she loved. She spoke of them, as she did of her school and Oxford teachers, as revered friends.

'No! No! Please! I will not hear this said against my friend Colette!' she protested once in my hearing when some foolish person was mocking that writer.

'How well did you know her?' someone asked.

'I met her – she was kind to me – but she was my friend because I love the *Chéri* books. These are very good books, they are not to be dismissed!'

When I first met IM, a vulgar excitement at her fame stopped me asking any of the interesting questions about what was going on behind that inscrutable, soft face, and those bright eyes, which were at once so sad and so humorous. Later, when she and I began work on our project, to write her life, a no less vulgar barrier was created – namely my over-awareness of her love affairs, hence my inability to ask about either them or any other aspect of her inner life.

Little did we know then what would happen next, of the dark that would engulf her last days, or of the distortion of her image in the public mind by various books, and by the film. She was doomed to become the Alzheimer's Lady. Her face is used now by the picture editors of newspapers to illustrate the medical pages, when doctors believe they have some clue about possible cures or alleviations for that wretched condition. She appears more often in such pages than in the part of the paper concerned with literature. Clumsy Oxford seeks to perpetuate her memory, not by a Chair of Literature or Philosophy but of Alzheimers. The great are now to be remembered by the diseases which killed them rather than by their gifts, as though the Tolkien Chair should be, not of Old English Philology, but of Bronchitis.

Her mystery – what was going on behind that face – remains a mystery to me. If in this book I had hoped to come up with some simple 'explanation' – how this woman came to write those books – then I have failed. For me, however, the exercise has brought her into focus once again. Her? The Iris Murdoch I knew. At last, as far as I am concerned, she has come back to life, the very delightful social companion whose arrival on my doorstep always caused an uplift to the heart. Here was a woman who meant business, who was intelligently focused on the interesting things in life, even when drunk.

Contemplating her, it occurs to me that it does not really matter that I have not prised out her secret. Perhaps, like the sphinx, she did not have one. Perhaps the Iris Murdoch I knew, primarily, remains the one known not to cinema-goers but to readers. Millions of individuals throughout the world are in her debt. They see her as a compellingly readable novelist who describes almost better than any other the strange things which happen when people fall in love; also as a spiritual seeker, who, finding what she looked for neither in church nor in the works of modern philosophy, gazed longingly upon The Good, just as those in Plato's cave turned from the Fire to the Sun.

Index

Works by Iris Murdoch appear directly under title; works by others under authors' names.

The initials IM stand for Iris Murdoch; JOB for John Bayley; ANW for A.N. Wilson

Index